Praise for Belle de Jour

Belle de Jour is the nom de plume of a London call girl. *The Intimate Adventures of a London Call Girl*, based on her web log that won the *Guardian* Best Blog Award in 2003, is a bestseller. Belle is a regular contributor to a number of newspapers and magazines. She lives and works in London.

The Further Adventures of a London Call Girl

BELLE DE JOUR

PHOENIX

A PHOENIX PAPERBACK

First published in Great Britain in 2006
by Weidenfeld & Nicolson
This paperback edition published in 2008
by Phoenix,
an imprint of Orion Books Ltd,
Orion House, 5 Upper St Martin's Lane,
London WC2H 9EA

An Hachette Livre UK Company

3 5 7 9 10 8 6 4 2

A CIP catalogue record for this book
is available from the British Library.

ISBN 978-0-7538-2549-5

Printed and bound in Great Britain by
Clays Ltd, St Ives plc

The Orion Publishing Group's policy is to use papers
that are natural, renewable and recyclable products and
made from wood grown in sustainable forests. The logging
and manufacturing processes are expected to conform to
the environmental regulations of the country of origin.

www.orionbooks.co.uk

*Dedicated to everyone who
wonders if I'm writing about them.
I am.*

This book would not have been possible without the boundless enthusiasm of Patrick Walsh and Helen Garnons-Williams. Thanks also to Ross Jones, Erica Wagner and Joy Lo Dico for putting their reputations on the line to keep me in pennies and cake. Finally, grateful appreciation goes to Michael Burton, who is discreet enough not to recognise me in public.

Cast of Characters

A1

Ex-boyfriend of long standing. The man who introduced little old me to the world of kinky sex, for which I think we were both eternally grateful. Homeboy, raconteur and all-round living legend. Married. You'll notice his wife does not appear in this list. Introduced me to A2 and A4. Doesn't know what I do for a living.

A2

Ex of medium standing. Often mistaken for my sibling; in fact, the bank allowed him access to my accounts for some time before realising we are not in fact related. Luckily he never took advantage. I would have. Introduced me to A3. Does know about my choice of career; never mentions it.

A3

Not so much an ex as a never was. Dour Northerner and ginger to boot; great taste in music which along with a science degree makes him the most desirable man on Earth. Keeps long-term girlfriend well hidden. Colleague of A2. Not aware that I take money for sex.

A4

Ex of fairly recent vintage. Smart, generous and not bad-looking. Can I pick them or what? Unfortunately he un-picked me but we still behave like a couple of old marrieds. Simpatico and all-round brilliant person. Makes a cracking cup of tea. Works for A2. Knows everything and is, if not completely cool with it, awfully supportive.

Angel

Another working girl and friend of N. Party girl rapidly approaching age at which it is no longer acceptable to ride a Ducati round the streets of London in a miniskirt. In state of constant crisis. Always knows more than she lets on.

Belle

That would be yours truly, kids.

Boy, the

Ex of most recent vintage. Ambivalent on my choice of career as result of too-high regard for what his poncey friends think. Can jump off a cliff, for all I care. Unfortunately, knows everything there is to know about me – hopefully, is too embarrassed he dated a whore to tell anyone.

Dr C

Friend of A2 and recent conquest. Built like the proverbial outhouse and no slouch in the bedroom department. He doesn't know about my . . . unusual . . . means of staying solvent yet. Unfortunately, lives overseas but comes back to visit often. At least, I hope so.

Manager, the

Lady proprietor of the escort agency. Legs like a West End dancer, face like a Dartmoor pony. Was previously a call girl herself. Unidentifiable accent; she could be from anywhere: Germany, Iran and Mexico are my current top guesses.

N

Co-conspirator and wing man. Has been in on my secrets from the beginning. Lovable wide boy who works as a bouncer and looks after his aged mum. Always seems to have a string of women on the go, claiming no technique more complex than 'I just talk to women.' Peerless source of local info, such as best driving routes, good local cafés and where to buy lube at 2 a.m.

Parents, the

Still living Oop North in the family home. Mum small and dark, Dad slim and fair. Strong Northern accents. Been together since the January of for ever. Either blissfully unaware or blessedly quiet on the subject of what their eldest does for a living.

Septembre

dimanche, le 5 septembre

'What I want, what I really want . . . this probably sounds silly . . . is to please you.'

The client was fiftyish, dressed office-casual. Oh great, I thought, another half-hour of earnest licking from a man whose wife no doubt thinks her body stops at the waist. 'That's a gorgeous idea,' I purred.

'Tell me your fantasies,' he said, tracing the cup of my bra with his finger. 'What do you desire right now more than anything?'

I thought. 'Well, it's a good long time since I had a titwank,' I said.

'Pardon?'

'You know,' I said, and sat on his lap. 'All those lovely things you do when you're a teenager, because they're very exciting, but never do again when you get to having real sex. Tossing someone off in the back of the cinema. Kissing until your jaw hurts. A titwank.'

'That doesn't sound like you'd get much pleasure, though,' he said.

'I do actually. There's something so . . . satisfying . . . about the feel of someone using your breasts to wank himself. Or when the come hits your face, just . . .'

'Um, that's nice. How about if I go down on you instead?' he asked, turfing me off his lap.

'Oh, okay, whatever you want,' I said.

'Oh no,' he said, slipping his face down to my inner thighs. 'It's all about what you want.'

lundi, le 6 septembre

The first thing I do is shower, wash hair, dry with clean fluffy towel. Check all shaving is shaven, all plucking plucked. Moisturise and ample deodorant: even after going through the routine so many times, I still get nervous.

I imagine there are hundreds – if not thousands – of women like me in London, doing precisely what I'm doing right now.

Hair carefully styled. Glossy but not girlish, professional but not stiff. Nice suit, just back from the cleaners. A blouse unbuttoned to the base of the neck – mustn't go flashing cleavage or people will look at you strangely. Underwear and stockings. The good shoes. Jewellery – just enough, not too much. First impressions are everything. The goal is to be asked back a second time.

Check everything in my bag. Address, phone number, toiletries. Must turn up on time, never early, never late.

I leave the flat, lock the door, and walk to the corner. Hold my hand out to attract the driver's attention. The hulking vehicle slows as it approaches. I finger the wallet in my purse anxiously. 'Morning, love,' the driver says as I flash him my bus pass. I find a seat upstairs. It's daytime and not night. No taxi waiting for me, not today.

It's a job interview I'm going to, you see, not an appointment.

mardi, le 7 septembre

I come in from an appointment with a client, strip and shower. Hanging on the back of the bathroom door is the jacket of my interview suit. It went well, I think; so well that going back to trawling the hotel circuit today was a bit of a comedown.

The man who interviewed me was round, fortyish, Chinese; very successful, very chatty. I'd had clients like him.

His eyebrows shot up as he looked over my application again; as the half-hour went on, his voice grew more and more excited. One of his colleagues dropped by – a dour Israeli with a mouth like liver sausages – and commented, 'Well, it looks like you have this under control. Let me know when you've made your mind up, though it looks like you already have.' I was surprised. Either my luck was in or I was setting myself up for yet another disappointment. I had come home, shed my clothes, and steeled myself for the follow-up. There was a call within the hour. They wanted me to come back.

Phone rings. No name and no number. Either the manager ringing to tell me about a client, I think, or a call from overseas. I pick it up, anticipating the latter.

'So how did it go in the end?' Dr C asks.

I smile involuntarily. Even the sound of his voice is enough to make me melt, and I feel my knickers going slightly sticky. 'Really well, as it happens. I have a second interview.'

'Oh, that's great news. I can help you get ready on the morning.'

'It's after you've gone, unfortunately,' I say. Couldn't he possibly have asked for more than a week off work? I bite my tongue: that would sound aggressive. Besides, no matter how little time we have together I am sure the sex will be worth it – I don't usually send out to California for a takeaway, but in his case I can make an exception. 'But you can help me prepare.'

'What was the interview like?' he asks. 'Did you bowl them over with your talent and wit?'

'Actually, they seemed a little more bowled over by my referees.'

'How do you mean?'

I tell him that most of the interview was spent on questions about A2, how well I knew him, whether I could set up a meeting between him and the company's directors, and so on.

'He's on your CV?'

'Why shouldn't he be?'

'He's your ex-boyfriend.'

And the man who introduced me to Dr C, for which I should really send a thank-you note at the least. 'He's a *character reference*.' Yikes, I shouldn't have mentioned it. Maybe it was improper business practice or something. I must admit my ethics radar has been somewhat recalibrated since I started having sex for money.

'And the fact that he's one of the most respected business-men in his field has nothing to do with it?'

'I knew him when he was living off Pot Noodle and beans on toast. You can't say I hitched my trailer to a star know-ingly.'

Dr C laughs. 'Don't worry, if I'd thought it would improve my job prospects, I'd have done it, too. Most people end up exaggerating in their interviews. You do, of course, have explicit permission to use me as a reference if need be.'

'Ta, love, I'll keep it in mind.'

'That's a no, then?'

'I'd rather have explicit permission just to use you in general.' We laugh.

jeudi, le 9 septembre

Sometimes I feel I've been doing this job for ever, then I remember it's only been about two years. Funny how steep the learning curve is with sex work. Also how quickly you can tire of it – I can't help feeling I've seen all these men, had all these requests, before.

'Where do you want it . . . here or here?'

'You know where I want it,' I said in my sauciest voice.

'I want to hear you tell me.' The end of his cock was twitch-ing, and with one of his hands on the shaft and one on his balls I could tell he was holding back until the right moment.

'I want you to come all over my face.' You know what would be nice about landing a legitimate job? Not having to wash come and makeup off my face more than once a day.

'Beg me.'

Well, whatever works for him. 'Please,' I said. Please let him give me a big tip. 'Please, I need you to come all over my face.' At that moment, he released his hands and sprayed.

Of course, it rarely ends up where you want it to. You can hardly blame the client – the moment of ejaculation is not the right time to say, 'Er, actually you're mostly just getting my hair there.' But it's a fact of life, if you want some on the face, be prepared for any result. And for your own sake keep your eyes shut – that stuff's like battery acid.

Other tips for a successful facial:

- Eyelashes. Waterproof mascara at a minimum; those long-lasting three-day formulations aren't bad; personally I go for the eyelash tinting option. It wouldn't do for people to think you've been crying, or, worse, guess what you've been up to.
- Pillow. Adjust your head height and angle accordingly. If you studied physics, you'll be able to calculate from the angle of his penis and expected pressure the distance the ejaculation will travel. But save yourself the time and simply prop your head up in front of the cock, not below.
- Smile! It's the mental photograph he's after, and we all want to look good in a photo, don't we?

vendredi, le 10 septembre

'Looking forward to seeing your man, am I right?' N asked. We were watching telly and eating crisps. He'd brought round a bottle of wine; I put it in the cupboard and opened

7

a bottle of Bailey's instead. He smiled; it's terribly unfashionable but we love it. A little of what you fancy always does you good.

'Can't wait,' I said. I was a bit nervous, though: Dr C had been to visit twice since we first met, and it was rapidly passing the point at which I should have told him how I pay the rent in between looking for other work.

'Damn sight better than the last one,' N said. 'You ever hear from that arsehole again?'

'Um, no,' I said and sat down, turning the television volume higher.

I felt bad about lying, but it had to be done. The Boy kept sending texts – all of which I ignored – for ages after we split. Then one night a month ago he rang. I was feeling soft and a bit lonely, and Dr C and I never asked many questions about what each other's lives were like outside seeing each other. The Boy and I hooked up. I swore it would be only the once.

Plus there are a number of reasons not to go there again:

1 His friends hate me. Well, to be fair, most of them never even *met* me. But the ones who do know me definitely do not approve.
2 He's a snob. Not that this is a deal breaker in and of itself. But to him and his friends, girls like me are on the bottom rung of middle class and always looking for an opportunity to marry up. Never mind that I couldn't possibly be on the make because a) I don't want to marry anyone and b) I make more than he does; it's a class thing.
3 He's not the sharpest knife in the drawer. Yes, I'm a snob too. I see enough arses in a day; I don't need to be dating someone who constantly talks out of his.

Anyway it turned out to be only the once, as planned.

samedi, le 11 septembre

Note to self: if in future really really need hair cut, but usual stylist is away, WAIT UNTIL SHE RETURNS. No one else will understand what is meant by 'shorter but not too much shorter'. And pulling the hair won't make it grow back any faster.

The colour's rubbish, too. No excuses there – same person as always. You know the dingy look from too many hours in the swimming pool? It's like that. Why? Why???

dimanche, le 12 septembre

Wake up. Panic. Straight to mirror; yes, hair is still rubbish. Shower, rubbing scalp vigorously. Circulation helps hair grow, right?

Run out door. Just catch bus; thank heavens for whatever genius invented Routemaster. Must learn to schedule time better before this route is phased out.

Tube. Which change to make? Slower train with fewer stops, or faster with more? Compromise and go for alternative slower with infinite stops route; only just make train.

Arrive panting at airport to learn flight is delayed by two hours. Spend six pounds on hot chocolate and try to make it last.

Lose track of time. Feel tap on shoulder and look up and he's standing, bags in hand, by my table. Dr C smiles and I can't help but grin.

Worth the wait.

We sat on the sofa reading, my legs round Dr C's hips, his head in the hollow of my shoulder. From here it's like reading to a child, I thought, all softness and nuzzle and warmth. Though I did have to hold the book out at a strange angle in order to not block his view. After a few minutes, the raised hand started to tingle, and I put the book face-down on the table. I have always had the most appalling habit of breaking book bindings, but it's something to read, not a collector's item, right?

I love it that Dr C doesn't ask many questions. What goes on in my life is seldom up for examination, and that seems fine with him. Though it is beginning to bother me: when is a good time to tell someone you have sex with other men for money? I suspect he knows there are other people and chooses not to mention it. But I'm not sure most men can make the jump from thinking their girl has an active social life to thinking she's a whore.

The big problem is that I've been making an effort to be as nonconfrontational as possible with this relationship. When I think back on my most recent boyfriend, the shouting, the slammed doors, it doesn't bear much examination. We were both passionate people, yes, but at the heart of it was that he couldn't bear what I did for a living. I never want things to go like that again.

I've been imagining how the conversation with Dr C might go:

'You remember when I went back to your hotel with you the first time we met? I do that professionally, you know.'

'I'm glad you enjoyed the blowjob. I've had a lot of feedback on that particular move, and eighty per cent of my clients agree.'

'How about a little role play in the bedroom? I'll pretend to be a call girl, and you'll pretend not to be freaked out about it.'

Er, probably not.

He sighed and shifted in the sofa cushions. 'This is like heaven.'

'I was just thinking the same.' Actually, I was really thinking how I'd forgotten to use any deodorant that morning and with his nose practically in my armpit, I hoped he didn't notice.

mercredi, le 15 septembre

Dr C dashed off after quick breakfast and sex to see parents in Bournemouth. He didn't invite me; I didn't ask. Don't want to impose when things are still relatively new. Every month in a long-distance affair is like a week in a normal one, so by that reckoning we're not even at asking about each other's careers yet.

Also, I think I've learned my lesson from the Boy. Be the calm one, the collected one; be the cool girl. Don't be the freaky oddball. When he says he'll call, he'll call. You have to trust a man sometimes.

vendredi, le 17 septembre

Dr C called late, to say he'd be back even later. I said fine, did he want someone to meet him at the train? That's sweet, he said, but no, you keep the bed warm.

I kept the bed warm reading, feeling very virtuous for not throwing a scene. We had so little time together, but what was more important was that we didn't argue.

Switched the light off some two hours after deciding that probably he couldn't get to a phone to let me know he'd caught an even later train.

Fell asleep certain he'd be home any minute.

Just before dawn, heard someone try the door. I'd left it on the latch. Heard his soft steps on the stairs and rolled over in what I hoped was a sleepy yet sexy way.

'I'm wiped,' he said, throwing a black bag on the floor. 'Absolute madness at my parents'. No wonder I left the country. You don't mind if I crash for the next twelve hours, do you?'

'Of course not, love,' I said. Because it's all about compromise.

samedi, le 18 septembre

A quiet day in. I asked Dr C if there was anywhere he wanted to go, maybe see some of the sights that have been built since he moved to America, like the London Eye?

'Eugh, no thank you,' he said. 'Not really my sort of thing. I left the city for a reason, you know.'

I didn't know, not particularly. Sometimes he says things – nothing specific, just a way with a phrase – that make me think he's been married once, maybe in London. But if so it probably wasn't a good idea to ask. If he wanted to, he'd bring it up.

Met N later for a meal. Chinese. Dr C made a flourish of picking up chopsticks instead of the fork. 'No Chinese restaurant in California would even think of putting those on the table,' he smirked. Unfortunately, it was a little lost on us, as N and I are both adepts. Particularly impressive in N, who had never even been to a Chinese before we met. You'd be surprised how motivated you can be to learn the correct method when you're hungry.

N and I chattered away about people we knew. Dr C turned to me and started a conversation about our mutual friend A2. Oh, yes, N knew him, too, and soon we were talking nineteen to the dozen. I noticed Dr C going quiet and pushing noodles round his plate.

'Everything okay, darling?' I asked when N went to the toilet.

He squeezed my thigh under the table. 'Just longing to get you home,' he said. 'I'm leaving tomorrow night.'

He growled in my ear, a move that sent a shiver up my back. 'We'll make it quick,' I said, squeezing his thigh, higher, harder.

dimanche, le 19 septembre

The morning was not spent, as I'd have preferred, nibbling on smoked salmon and enjoying the weekend papers. It was spent on an alarm set for stupid o'clock in the morning and an emergency shop for things he couldn't get back in California (Marmite, and lime shower gel). But I was determined to enjoy every minute, smiling bravely as we negotiated the bus, Tube and then train to the airport. When he suggested – repeatedly – that maybe we should have arranged a car, I didn't disagree. I waved him off (sexy embrace in front of security, check; goofy kissy faces from other side of barrier, check) and made my way home. It had been a good visit if a little brief.

N came round, and as it was so late, I made supper for two. Nothing special – pasta, cream, mushrooms, asparagus. Wildly out of season but I find it so hard to resist, and try to make up for it by only eating British apples. N wolfed his down, declared it the best effort yet, and for a moment it looked as if he was going to dive for mine. That or he was looking down my top. Either way it was flattering.

The phone rang. Unknown number – could be a client, but more likely Dr C. I answered; it was the latter. N could tell by my smile what was up and he discreetly removed himself upstairs.

'I take it you made it home safely?' I did the maths. 'It's, what, lunchtime there?'

'Yeah,' he said. He sounded tired, and no wonder. Very thoughtful to ring me first thing, though.

'How was the flight? Any good films on?'

'Um, mostly I spent the time thinking.' My heart dropped, and I knew. He wasn't calling because it was the sweet, romantic thing to do. He was calling to end it. He said he thought the distance was too far and that he was too busy to be in a relationship, anyway – man code for 'I'd like it if you were more convenient, but don't worry, I'll find someone who is.' He said he'd been thinking this since before the visit, but he didn't want to ruin my good time.

Ruin my good time? We'd barely spent three evenings together, I wasn't the one who'd made a 12,000-mile round trip. I said nothing, just let him spool out the list of reasons. No sense trying to argue about it; I'd parted ways with so many men it was practically a lifestyle choice as well as a career. As soon as he said 'I don't want to hurt you . . .' I felt a door shut in my heart.

He paused, possibly waiting for the vitriol. Still I said nothing. 'Well,' he said, clearing his throat, 'I hope we can still be friends.'

Oh, cringe. Friends? I'll say who gets to be my friend, thanks. I can play at being civilised but there is a line. There is a fucking line and he crossed it, right then, and I was not going to be Cool Girl any more. 'No, thank you. I have enough friends as it is.' I hung up and turned the phone off. When I looked up N was in the doorway.

'I'm sorry,' he said.

'You're not the one who has to apologise.'

'Someone should,' he said. 'Want a hug?' And even though I thought I didn't, I really did.

mardi, le 21 septembre

Positive aspects of breakup:

- Money saved on travel expenses
- Never having to have awkward conversation about being a call girl
- Noticed some hairs growing out of his nose when we were on the sofa. Will not have to deal with that

Negative aspects of breakup:

- Phone bill for calls to California not coming for another three weeks
- Having to announce yet another failed relationship to family
- Looking at phone so hard likely to cause blindness, if not insanity

jeudi 23

'It's an impressive CV, all right,' the young man said, flipping through my application. 'And your references are impeccable. My colleague was very impressed when he met you. But I'd like to ask, where do you see yourself in five years' time?'

I smiled weakly. I hadn't had breakfast or lunch, and was constantly checking my phone. But Dr C took me at my word and hadn't rung. I'd turned it off before coming into the room for the interview but was starting to regret that; surely the man sitting across from me could tell how distracted I was?

Possibly not. 'Because in this company, we're interested not only in our bottom line, but also in our people. Developing your skills to the best they can be. Investing in you. Yes, we think we're just the right size to be able to deliver excellent service to our clients, while still maintaining a family atmosphere among the associates.' I had the distinct feeling he was eyeing the line of my cleavage through my shirt, which, given that it was a very conservative, high-buttoned stripey number too starchy for call-girl work, was an impressive feat.

I crossed my legs at the knee. Excellent service to the clients, eh? I noticed his eyes following my leg from conservative, mid-heeled shoe to conservative, mid-knee skirt.

So that's the way it's going to be, I thought. Fine, if that's what gets me through this, he can check me out. Then I can go home and cry myself to sleep. I leaned closer to the desk, pulling my arms in to emphasise my bust. Let him do the talking. And he did, for almost an hour.

'The fact is, we'd like to offer you a job,' he said eventually.

'The fact is, I'd like to take it,' I said. Fucking Dr C. When was he going to realise what a mistake he'd made and ring me? I'd better get out of here and fast.

The young man seemed taken aback with my answer. 'Ah, uh, okay. Well, when can you start?'

'When will you have me?' I raised an eyebrow. If he'd been a client this would have been the part where he pushed me back on the bed. In real life this is where he stood up and offered me his hand.

'Immediately. Please call me Giles, I'll be your supervisor.'

'Splendid, Giles.' I stood and shook the offered hand. 'I'll see you tomorrow.'

vendredi, le 24 septembre

Turned up early to be shown around the offices and meet my co-workers. Everyone seems keen to ask questions, most of which I don't know how to answer. Smile and glide, I think. Stay cool. Smile and glide.

The mobile rang repeatedly in my handbag; I peeked at the

number. Cripes. It was the manager. How was I going to talk to her without anyone in the office noticing?

'Just off to the loo,' I announced. Giles nodded. I scampered off to the toilet to ring the manager back.

It wasn't my lucky day. There was a queue for the toilet. The woman in front of me smiled and half shrugged, as if to say, My, isn't this terrible? She had no bloody idea. All she was doing was trying to keep from wetting herself. I was a prostitute trying to manage her appointments.

I waited until the last cubicle was free and phoned the manager back. 'Darling, hello,' she said. 'There is a lovely man who wishes to meet you Sunday—'

'Um, wait,' I cut her off. The woman in the cubicle next to me was wrestling with the toilet roll dispenser; how much could she hear? 'I've been thinking that, well, you know, perhaps it's time that I, I mean we . . . What I want to say is, er . . . I'd like to consider, you know, quitting.'

'Pardon?'

The rustling on the other side of the toilet wall stopped abruptly.

'Well, yes. My schedule outside work has been very busy lately, and I'd like to . . . consider . . . other options.'

'Haven't we had this conversation before, sweetie?' she cooed reassuringly. 'I'm sending only the most carefully selected men to you now.'

'Yes, but maybe it's time for me to stop for good.'

'Oh, darling,' the manager sighed. 'If it's a matter of more money . . .'

I turned in to the corner of the cubicle. I swear my voice was echoing. 'It's not about the money. I have enough. It's more, well, it's taking a lot out of my personal life,' I whispered hotly. And what if someone here stumbled across the website? It had been hard enough to land a job; that would kill any career for certain.

'Sweetheart, darling,' the manager laughed. 'That happens to everyone.'

I froze. The woman in the next cubicle hadn't gone yet. She

must be eavesdropping. 'Yes, well, I'm worried about my' – I lowered my voice to almost subaudible level – 'privacy.'

'Your what?' the manager asked sweetly.

'My privacy,' I whispered, only a touch louder.

'Darling, I'm sorry, you must be losing signal, I can't hear a word you're saying.'

'My privacy!' I shouted. 'I'm concerned about my privacy!'

A snort from the next cubicle. 'You might consider not taking phone calls in the toilet,' a voice said.

'Oh, darling, if only you'd said,' the manager cooed. 'It is a very simple matter. I can anonymise your photos on the website, so that no one recognises you. Okay? Okay. Good. Now I'll text you the details for the weekend and we'll speak tomorrow.' She hung up.

'Great. Talk tomorrow,' I said to the dead line.

dimanche, le 26 septembre

The client was younger than me. We met at a private address. He said it was his house, but I wasn't sure. How many twenty-somethings have homes over four floors of a building in central London? Apart from someone you'd recognise in films, I mean. Exactly. Probably his parents' house.

I was rushed up to the top bedroom. 'You'd better undress,' he said. I untied the wrap dress but left on the suspenders and stockings – he'd requested them specially. He looked at me a few minutes.

'All the way,' he said, indicating the lingerie. I did.

He wanted oral; I gave it. He sat back in the half-dark and I sensed he was bored. 'Okay, enough,' he said, pulling me off his member. 'Tell me something dirty.'

I started a story about me and a girl at a club, in the toilets.

'Would you ever do a threesome?' he interrupted.

'I've done plenty,' I said. 'How about you?'

'Yeah, of course.'

'Were they friends or strangers?'

'Two girls,' he said. 'Strippers. I made them both come.'

It seems to me that there is no need for a man to try to impress a woman he is paying for sex, but then the male of the species is an odd creature. Maybe they look on it as practice for the women they meet in real life. Maybe they can't help themselves.

I rolled a condom on him and we went at it, me sitting on him facing away – the classic Reverse Cowgirl position. An absolute lifesaver when you have to make like you're enjoying the experience, but aren't up to looking the part. It appalled me to think that I was counting down the minutes until it would be over.

Maybe I got a little carried away with the counting, because even with ball-tickling and toe-licking he was still going soft. Without any clues to go on, I didn't know what would help. Talking dirty? Squealing girlishly? Struggling a little?

No luck there. He asked me to suck him again. Oral sex after a condom is always distasteful: the shaft tastes strongly of latex, and before long my lips start to swell and will be painful for the rest of the night. But the hour was winding up, and I didn't think he'd take the suggestion to have a wash first very well.

The effect was minimal. 'You can stop now,' he sighed. I smiled and tried to hide my relief; my lips were aching already. So what if he didn't come? What a world-weary little worm. We sat in silence for a few minutes. 'I'm sorry,' he said. 'I was a bit nervous, and took a Xanax before you came over. Do you think that would have an effect on . . . ?' and he indicated his penis.

I felt guilty about judging him harshly. 'You poor thing,' I said, stroking his chest. 'I suppose it would. I hope you didn't find me too frightening.'

'No, I think you're a nice girl. I'll call again next month – it's my birthday.' In spite of feeling sorry for him I sincerely hoped he wouldn't. 'I think you should take the full fee anyway.'

Well, duh. If I'm going to turn up at work tomorrow on three hours' sleep it had damn well better have been for pay.

lundi, le 27 septembre

Meeting people for the first time is something I'm used to.

The stilted conversations, the awkward questions as I negotiate my way round a new set of rules, the polite introductions and biting of the tongue. I'm well practised in the art of nodding and smiling; it's served me well thus far.

Reserving my judgments of people encountered at work for a late phone call with N, tick. Remembering not to wear too short a skirt in a professional setting, handled. Repressing the urge to imitate the flat accent of the Canadian sitting behind me, this I can do.

Having to come back every day and do it all over again is a bit harder.

mardi, le 28 septembre

Home from yet another half-hearted assignment on the call-girl front. I can't blame the man, he was unobjectionable; I blame myself and an inability to say no. Sometimes I think the manager is trying to punish me. Maybe I'm simply at a low ebb but it all feels terribly tedious sometimes. On the other hand, any job probably feels this way. It's simply that there are a number of conversations I never want to have with a client again, such as:

1 What's a Nice Girl like you doing in a place like this?
  Do you ask the woman at the Superdrug till why she's not frolicking in the stacks at the library? Do you question a

building-site manager's choice of career when you walk past? No.

2 My wife doesn't understand me.

Honey, it goes without saying. That you've decided to call a professional in on the job pre-empts further explanation.

3 Tell me about your manager/the other girls/your other clients.

They're all shining examples of humanity, impeccably behaved and jewels among the dross; every man a gentleman. Oh, and they're all Nobel laureates, too. Please, please don't ask if I've slept with anyone famous. I have, it was unremarkable, and no, I will not name names.

4 How did you vote in the elections?

Are you kidding? You selected your evening's companion based on a picture of me bending over in hot pants. Unless this is a research project seeking to connect labial size with political leanings, it is about as relevant as asking Jordan what she thinks of joining the euro. And the odds are I will just tell you what you want to hear, anyway.

mercredi, le 29 septembre

The Canadian came round and introduced herself today. 'Hi, I'm Erin,' she chirruped. 'How're you finding it so far?'

'Fine, thank you,' I said. By now everyone in the company has made a reason to stroll by my desk at least once. I don't know if there's something on my blouse or if they're simply curious. And I've learned more names than I can possibly remember.

Worse still, she probably wants to be friends. And if there's one thing I can't take it's *making friends* with women.

Don't get me wrong; I have female friends, though they are admittedly outnumbered by men. But '*making friends*', that pink-covered, sugar-coated state heavily promoted by women's magazines (Is she your Bessie Mate 4-evah? Find out on page 42!) in which two people audition each other over the course of months, years, or possibly the rest of their lives, applying criteria higher than you'd use for selecting a gynaecologist or partner, I have no patience with it.

As a result, I have few female friends and the exceptions are people of some character. Such as Angel, another working girl, who is about as batty as they come but rarely sticks around long enough to be too annoying, and L.

When L and I meet – sometimes after a gap of months or even years, but that's okay, because we're friends, not completing some creepy tick list of 'friendship' – it's as if we never left off. The two girls who used to pass filthy notes about their teachers written in schoolgirl French are much the same, but with wider hips and better shoes. I'm really not counting on *making friends* at work.

'Well, if you need anything, just gimme a shout,' Erin said. Given her general volume I suspect that was meant literally.

'Cheers, I will do.' I leaned over and ran a finger inside my aching instep. When you've been used to either stilettos or flats, court shoes are murder. 'Bye.'

'Byeeeeee.'

jeudi, le 30 septembre

Great Pub Games #1 – Obscure claims to fame.

- A2's lady friend: Was at school with Richard E. Grant in Swaziland.
  'Not bad.'
  'I propose having been to Swaziland is obscure enough.'
  ObScore: 6/10
- A2: Sent threatening letters to Cliff Richard when Sir Cliff was dating Olivia Newton-John.
  'I was young. It was a confusing time.'
  'How young?'

'Around twelve.'

'That's no excuse.'

ObScore: 2/10

- A1: Was in Berlin when the wall came down.

  'Eh, you and everyone else.'

  'But it was historically important!'

  'That's a different game.'

  ObScore: 1/10

- A4: Is named for an ancestor of his who was hanged for being a Luddite.

  'Oooooh.'

  ObScore: 8/10

- Me: Was kissed by the singer from Franz Ferdinand.

  'It was only a peck. His girlfriend was right there.'

  'Not that you would usually find that a problem . . .'

  'I was on a date with his brother's friend, you see.'

  'Did the friend get to kiss you?'

  'He didn't even try.'

  ObScore: 4/10

- N: Lives round the corner from Cynthia Payne.

  'Britain's première prostitute. She ever invite you in?'

  'Hey, I resent that!'

  ObScore: 6/10

- A3: Had a ticket for one of what turned out to be one of Joy Division's last ever gigs; it was cancelled when the singer had an epileptic fit; everyone rushed the stage.

  'I don't think any of us can top that.'

- ObScore: 9/10 (and the winner)

Dear Belle

Dear Belle,
I recently arranged a blind date on a gay hook-up website – and the man who came to meet me was my closeted father. Family dinner conversation is now somewhat stilted. Do I tell Mum?

Dear Twisted Sister,
Only if you two are now an item.

———◆———

Dear Belle,
My boyfriend fantasises about covering me in strawberry jam. Maybe I am a bit of a stereotypical gayer, but I like my body to be clean and sweet-smelling, and can't bear the idea of properly sticky sex and then hours in a bath scrubbing syrup off my whatsits. Can you suggest how I gently turn down his suggestion, or another substance we could substitute for the jam? To his credit, he is a Bonne Maman man.

Dear Squeaky Clean,
Few things taste better than cream tea on a human plate, but I do understand your reservations. Whole fruits, organic and in season, are far cleaner than messy jam. Failing that, supply him with yummy fruity-smelling soaps and similar in a picnic hamper or resign yourself to the fact that getting sticky is one of those things we have to do for love.

———◆———

Dear Belle,
I'm quite capable of coming up with a chat-up line. My problem is what to say next. Any suggestions?

Dear Tongue-Tied,
Your name and a suggestion to buy the object of your affection a drink are usually a good place to start. But I have a question for you: what's a nice lad like you doing in a column like this?

———◆———

Dear Belle,
I've fallen for a gorgeous Catholic girl. She's pledged to stay a

virgin until she's married. I've pledged to shag her before the summer. How can I tempt her into the sins of the flesh?

Dear Mortal Sin,

Pop the question. It doesn't mean you have to go through with it, and if my understanding is correct Catholic girls will normally let you have one sample before buying.

Octobre

vendredi, le 1 octobre

N reinstated as a fuck buddy for the time being. Is good because: he's good in bed, has a car, and can take a hint when he's not welcome. Is bad because: wait, can't think why it would be bad. Will come back to that later if there is time.

'Hey, pretty lady. Been trying to ring you all day,' N said.

'Sorry. Dropped in and saw A1 after work. He's in a mobile black spot.'

'Fair enough. How is the big guy?'

'He's fine, said to say hi to you. Ended up waiting for him ages, though, got cornered by his boss. If that man sucked up more air from the room you'd have to call him Dyson.'

'Yikes. That bad?'

'Worse. He went to the opera with his wife last week – poor thing, I bet she doesn't get a moment's peace. Anyway, they went to see *Les Mamelles de Tirésias*, which the boss took a lot of pleasure in telling me meant Theresa's Tits.'

'Patronising twat.'

'No kidding. Then he was off on some lecture about breasts and how some academic boffin or other proposed that men like breasts because Neanderthals preferred their coitus from behind and the mammary glands remind one of buttocks. Or something.'

'Rubbish,' N said. 'How many arses have you ever seen with nipples on?'

How to fuck someone and still be friends. Or, your cut-and-keep guide to being a good fuck buddy (or as N calls it, Friends with Privileges).

1 The Sex. Must be good. Otherwise, why bother? This person is not going to raise children with you.
2 The Companionship. It helps if this is someone you get on with and see around socially. Puts a nice ending on all those group nights out when it looks like you aren't going to pull (or pull anything decent). You've pulled before you even arrived. What if he's pulled and you haven't? Even better: take them both home.
3 The Gossip. People will assume you're a couple. Get your stories straight and nip this in the bud.
4 The Jealousy. There shouldn't be any. If you suspect this is someone whose dalliances with others you might be even remotely miffed about, move on. It's not going to work.
5 The Talk. Must be open and frequent. Nothing sucks quite like finding your fuck buddy has secretly fallen for you.
6 The Protection. Never forget he has carte blanche to fool around, and so have you. Regular does not equal clean.
7 The Foreplay. Don't play the whole 'I'm drunk, club's shut, didn't pull, I know you're home alone' booty call shtick. Not more than half the time, anyway.
8 The Threesomes. With luck, there should be plenty. N is kind enough – even when we're not fucking – to ask women he's with if they would like to sleep with me, too. Say it together: awww!
9 The Others. If a potential amour asks if you're sleeping with your fuck buddy, don't deny it. Disclosure might send a third party running, but you were going to have to lie to someone like that to keep the peace, anyway. You don't have to be explicit – 'Yes, and just this morning I woke to him wanking on my face.' Just be honest.

10 The Goodbyes. You must behave like adults. Don't ring him three weeks later from Africa and say you'd marry him if he'd have you back. It's a lay, not a life.

lundi le 4 octobre

Straight from one work to the other. Am not sure I can handle the turnaround. I came in tired from the office, and had half an hour to shower, change – higher shoes, better knickers, slinkier suit, shinier lippy – and get out again. Must check and see whether manager actually has changed my profile on the website.

The client was waiting for me with a porn film already on. 'Ah,' I said as we sat on the bed. 'Ron Jeremy. An absolute classic.'

'So you like them big, do you?' he asked, rubbing the growing bulge in his trousers.

'I like them all,' I said. This was going to be a talk dirty one. I felt a little disappointed – I was tired from work and not sure I could summon the necessary imagination to keep up a running commentary.

'Good,' he said, unwrapping his own package. It wasn't huge, but it wasn't small, either. Just the slightly larger side of average.

I reached down and took over the wanking from him. 'Gorgeous instrument you have there,' I said.

'I like a girl who can take it all in her mouth.'

'I don't know about that,' I said, squeezing the base of his shaft. I could have taken twice the size of his, but it's good for them to think you're impressed. 'But I'll certainly try.' Some porn starlet was giving Ron Jeremy her best oral effort on screen.

'Wait. Before you do,' he said, reaching by the bed, 'have you had anything to eat?'

'Not really, no,' I said, surprised. It was an unusual client who inquired after my health.

''Cause you see, I want you to choke on me,' he said, and brought a handful of small, dry pastries out. The sort wrapped in plastic film that you get free in the first-class carriage of a train. 'And if you could retch up some food on my balls that would be perfect.'

'Do you have a drink?' I asked. 'Something to help these go down quickly?'

'And back up again.' He winked and headed for the minibar.

As it turned out I didn't have to do much dirty talk after all.

mardi, le 5 octobre

The Canadian at work, Erin, has a friend in another department, Mira, a moon-faced Asian girl. At least I think Mira's in a different department. You wouldn't know for certain, seeing as she's always hovering around Erin's desk.

They talk. And talk. And talk some more. Their conversations aren't unbearable as such, just endlessly banal. It's not even a month and already I know more about celebrity breast implants than a sub-editor at *Heat*.

The other topic of conversation is Erin's fiancé back in Vancouver. I use 'conversation' in its loosest sense here since, as a soon-to-be-married woman of the world at twenty-four, Erin typically uses the opportunity to unfurl her wisdom on the relatively inexperienced twenty-three-year-old Mira.

'It's such a struggle being apart,' Erin moans theatrically. One key element of *making friends* with women is casting everything that happens in the most tragic light possible. 'Long-distance relationships are so difficult, you wouldn't even know,' she sighs.

Oh, boo hoo, I think. *Like you two are the first ever to live apart.* Bitter about Dr C? Me? Surely not.

'We have to rely on the phone for everything now – I mean *everything*.' Erin lowers her voice a notch. 'Even the *sex*.'

And I bet he'll dump you over the phone, too, I think.

'Wow,' Mira sighs, which encourages Erin to go on about what a *romance* it is and how this experience has confirmed for her that it's *meant to be*. She swigs deeply from her ever-present water bottle. It's the sort you only ever see Canadians or archaeologists carrying around, sipping from on an hourly basis as if the conditions of a modern city are approximate to those of the Mojave. I've been to India, Mauritius and Colombia; you can bet that anyone you see there carrying a Nalgene bottle will be either on a dig or from Vancouver.

'The adversity is going to make us a stronger couple in the end, I can say that,' Erin says. When did everyone start conversing in therapy-speak? I wonder whether it's possible to go blind from rolling my eyes so much.

I don't know if it's the accent or this girl specifically, but Erin's voice has a foghorn-like quality that cuts through everything else. She took a conference call and I swear I had to almost jam my fist down the other ear to keep the honking out.

Mira doesn't contribute much. She lives with her parents, and is trying to get them to buy her a flat. If she's ever been in love before it will have been with a baby-pink iPod or a fluffy kitten. She's like a wobbly satellite to Erin's sun.

Erin's launching into an in-depth rehash of last night's phone call from her boyfriend when I put the phone down. I turn round in my chair. 'Umm, I'm very sorry, but I'm sort of struggling through something here. Would you two mind keeping the noise level down a wee bit?'

From the looks on their faces you would have thought I'd slapped them each with a rotten herring. 'Yeah, ooookayyyy,' Erin says. 'Whatever.'

'I'm sorry, I thought you said to speak up if I needed anything.'

'And?' Erin says, arching her brow. 'Did you need something?'

'Just wanted to say that it's a little distracting, is all. Maybe you could go talk in Mira's office.'

'Well, yeah, but you don't have to be such a bitch about it.'

I mumble something about being terribly sorry and turn back to my desk, blushing madly. Why does it feel like being at school all over again? It's a long, long time since I've been in the company of women.

mercredi, le 6 octobre

Am keeping a bag in my desk for after-work appointments, of which I hope there will be very few. Checked the website from home – not from work, don't want to raise any suspicion in the IT department – and the manager seems to have kept to her promise and altered my profile.

As in, the pictures are so blurred you can hardly tell the photo is human, much less a woman. I rang her.

'Darling, hello,' she whispered. 'My boyfriend is here, so I have to keep it brief.'

'Um, I saw your changes,' I said. 'Are you sure this is going to work? I mean, I can't imagine anyone booking me with a photo like that. Maybe we should consider taking me off the site altogether.'

'Listen, sweetheart,' she said shortly. 'This is what we agreed, no? If you keep changing your mind I will have to start charging you for Webmaster time. And no one wants that, do they?' Her tongue clicked against her teeth. 'I don't know why it is you're so fussy all of a sudden. You used to be one of my easiest girls.'

'I'm sorry, really, I'm just . . . you know, considering whether any future career is worth . . .'

'Yes, honey, I'll be right there!' she shouted brightly to someone else. 'I have to go now,' she hissed. 'We'll talk.'

jeudi, le 7 octobre

Sat with Erin and Mira at lunch. Erin is on a diet, so I suppose that means Mira is as well, even though she hasn't an ounce to spare. 'Doing anything interesting this weekend?' Erin asked, smiling lightly.

'Not really,' I said. 'Going Up North to visit family.'

'Wow, don't set the world on fire with your social life,' Erin smirked. Mira giggled. How did I deal with this crap as a teenager without killing someone? I looked at them, straight-faced, until Mira felt uncomfortable and stopped.

'Erin's boyfriend is coming home from Canada,' Mira said.

'So I heard,' I said. In fact, anyone within a mile radius of our office could probably say the same. 'Ooh, I'm late back to my desk.' I left the remains of my sandwich on the table and scooted off to the coffee room to read for a quarter-hour alone.

vendredi, le 8 octobre

Off to see the parents; I know they'll want the complete lowdown on the job, the co-workers, every last detail. I'm looking forward to lying in and not having to do the washing-up. N picked me up from work and gave me a lift to the train. Not without asking a favour in return, though.

The cars around us were hardly moving. 'How long do you have until the train goes?' he asked.

'About twenty minutes,' I said. 'Do you think we'll make it?'

'Probably.' The traffic on the Euston Road moved even more slowly, if such a thing were possible. 'Feel like using the torch on yourself?'

'Go on, then.' He passed me a long, black-handled metal object. It was cold to the touch and thick as my wrist. I didn't know how much I would be able to get in and said so. I pulled my tights and knickers down to my ankles and put my feet over the dashboard. 'Let me know if we pass any buses,' I said.

'Not to worry, no one ever looks.'

'Not even taxis?' I worked the torch about halfway in, but not being too wet to begin with hindered its progress somewhat.

'Maybe a bicyclist would but I doubt it,' he said. 'Ah, I've just caught the first whiff of your smell.'

We crawled past St Pancras. 'Going to stop now so I can get dressed before King's Cross,' I said, putting my feet back on the floor and extracting the torch slowly. Its rough sides scraped my lips on the way out – I'd be feeling that for hours after, I knew it. 'Do you want me to wipe it off or leave it as is?' I asked. My juices are thick and white that time of the month and clung wetly to the shaft.

'Lick it off,' he suggested.

'It would be my pleasure.'

'I love that about you.'

I made the train with three minutes to spare.

samedi, le 9 octobre

Home is, they say, where the heart is. I learned to my chagrin, however, that it most certainly isn't where the bedroom is.

Let me explain. No, there is too much. Let me sum up: I left home for good more than a few years ago, but visit my parents regularly enough for them to expect me to be around for the Really Important Things such as holidays, a bris, the final vote on Big Brother, etc. So when I came round, I was hoping (as is my custom) to stay in my former bedroom.

Alas, I was wrong. So so wrong. Because the bedroom is being done over.

Into – drum roll – a *spare bedroom*.

While no formal finishing date has yet been decided, I can see from swatches of fabric and samples of carpet and books of flowery wallpaper that the room that once contained my (beloved, white iron frame) bed and (familiar, elegant) blue curtains is being transformed into a veritable Pink Palace of girlishness.

And all this is being done some seven or eight years *after* the girls have flown the nest.

Correct me if I'm wrong – and I've no doubt someone will – but wasn't it already a bedroom? And further, wouldn't guests be just a little put off by staying overnight in what is essentially a shrine to the power of tea roses? Especially as there is currently no child in the house?

Perhaps it means my mother is expecting. Help.

dimanche, le 10 octobre

Great Pub Games #2: Obscure facts about your friends.

A4, whose own parents live nearby, came round my parents' house. We were drinking coffee, and there was nothing on telly, as usual.

A4 on A2: 'The only song he knows all the words to is "Hey, Big Spender".'

'Really?'

'Ring him if you doubt me.'

I smiled. It was good; six out of ten, at least. But as I've slept with practically all my friends, I usually win this one. 'The first time he masturbated it was into a sleeve of aluminium foil.'

'No!'

'Ring him if you doubt me.'

A4 awarded me the points. 'You next,' he said.

'Me? Surely I'll win this one?'

'Ah, but the name of the game is *obscure* facts. You'd have to come up with something I don't already know about you.'

'Yes, but that also means you have to think of something I don't know about myself.'

A4 suddenly gasped. 'Is he okay?' Which was, of course, regarding my own dear pater. 'What on earth is he wearing?'

I peered towards the shrubbery from which said parent was emerging. His silhouette, dark in the evening garden, was, indeed, odd. 'Erm, plus-fours? Bicycle clips?' (n.b. he's been known to own both)

But it was worse, far worse, than anyone could have imagined. First there was a shocked silence, then a gasp, as what I was actually seeing came into full view. A4 laughed. 'His *trousers* are tucked into his *socks*.'

Good of him not to mention the plastic aviator-style sunglasses, or the jumper with worn-through elbows, or the fact that they weren't trousers so much as tracky bottoms, then.

A4 rubbed his hands together with glee. Somehow I suspected he'd won this round.

lundi, le 11 octobre

[*David Attenborough, whispering*] In winter, the common-or-garden Female Professional Worker can be identified by her solid-colour, V-neck jumper, black wool-blend trousers and small earrings. In this way they are easily distinguished from the Female Secretarial Worker, whose winter plumage includes a skirt, flesh-coloured fishnets, and dangly earrings. Both species are observed on occasion wearing an ill-fitting jacket. By approaching carefully, it is possible to hear the chatter going on within the small groups that congregate around the kettle.

'Nice skirt,' Jasmine said as she sat down across from me. I was wearing the bottom half of my favourite tweed Austin Reed suit, a tailored lace shirt with ruffled collar and a wrap-around cashmere cardie. Office standard, by my reckoning, or at the very least a step down from call-girl attire. I was not going to start shopping in Dorothy Perkins for the sake of blending in.

'Thank you,' I said.

'My mum has a sofa just like that.'

mardi, le 12 octobre

Rubbish day at work. Squealing harridans behind my desk threatening to send brain into meltdown. Found as many excuses as possible to leave throughout the day: restocking supplies in the coffee room, mounting new jugs on the water dispenser, exchanging perfectly good computer keyboard for identical one with the IT department.

Phoned N at lunch for a good grumble. 'You know what you need,' he said.

'Not especially.'

'A threesome.'

Damn, he's right. 'Have anyone in mind?'

'Have I ever! I'm thinking Friday.'

'Not sure I'll survive until then without beating one of my co-workers to death.'

'Try. It'll be worth your while, promise.'

mercredi, le 13 octobre

When the phone won't stop ringing, I know it's one of two things: the agency or Angel. Seeing as it's been about, oh, four months since Angel's last disastrous breakup I reckon we're due. I check the phone – indeed it is.

She rings back literally minutes after calling me. I answer briskly. 'Hello?'

Angel is sniffling, possibly crying over some man, possibly

coming down with the plague. 'Hello, how are you? Been a while,' she says in a brave-little-soldier voice.

'Not too bad, at the office at mo. How about yourself?' I resist the temptation to say, And who's dumped you now? Because Angel only rings when things are going wrong for her, namely, when she's without a man in her life. This is another reason why my patience with female friends is short – a man would never ignore his friends for the sake of a shag.

'Oh, you know, getting by, day to day.' I try not to encourage her, but the story tumbles out regardless: someone slapped an order on her to stay away from his house (it's not the first time). Unfortunately he lives round the corner from her, and she can't afford to move. I see where this is going and nip it in the bud.

'Afraid I don't really have the space, but if I hear of anything I'll let you know, of course.' Also the fact that she has a tendency to sweep up my cast-offs, be they food, books or men, a habit I find disturbing. One poor gentleman last year who couldn't take no for an answer immediately took up with her after me; their affair ended badly, of course, and somehow this seemed to make her more attached to me during times of stress. God alone knows why.

She cries poor-mouth a while longer. 'Sorry, love, I have to get to a meeting, we'll talk about it over coffee soon, 'kay?'

jeudi, le 14 octobre

Text from N: just in kingston waitrose with mum, saw box labelled extra large cucumbers and they weren't kidding, humbled; thinking of becoming a monk.

I reply: Don't you dare! Or I will have to find something else to do this weekend.

N is at work and we agree to meet there. She's a real cracker, he said over the phone. The only thing is, she has to be off early in the morning.

N's working the door of the club. He points me in the right direction, and yes, he's right, this one's a looker – few years older than me, tight jeans, nice figure. Huge chest. I can see what he sees in her. I introduce myself and she buys me a drink. She's obviously had a few already. Better watch that, I think. Don't want her getting too far gone.

We dance. Scissor Sisters. They're so camp they make Dead or Alive look like John Wayne and Sly Stallone wrestling in a river of Old Spice. I love them, obviously. She's grinding into me, and from the corner of the room N is watching us.

The lights come up. We stumble towards the door. N is talking to a straight couple. I vaguely recognise the woman but can not be bothered to think on it. 'So are you going to take us home, or what?' I paw N's arm. The woman looks horrified. He laughs and says he'll meet us outside.

He's booked a hotel. She and I head straight for the shower. N watches from the door. She's even better unclothed. Mature, but not sagging. I lather her breasts then go down on her, the warm water running down her belly and over my head.

We dry each other and head for the bed. N watches me lick her out. I'm not sure if she was really that game for the threesome; she's participating, but not all that engaged in pleasing me. N arranges us on the bed side-by-side and sets to work on us, dipping his head between our thighs like a bee after honey.

But our friend has clearly had too much to drink. It's only a few hours until she has to be off, anyway. We sleep, she and N on the main bed, me on a fold-out on the side. I wake to the sound of him taking her from behind and her animal grunts. 'Want to join in?' N hisses over her shoulder.

'No, thanks,' I say and fall back asleep.

There's just enough time in the morning for a cup of tea. 'What, no breakfast in bed?' she jokes. N gives her a lift as far as the next Tube station and takes me all the way home. We spend the rest of the morning half asleep, half entwined in my bed.

samedi, le 16 octobre

Was waiting for N outside an overground station. I had just come from meeting a client out of town. A young man next to me was looking up and down the road for buses, headphones plugged into his ears, the music far too loud. I tapped him on the shoulder.

'I like that song,' I said.

'Oh?' He looked surprised. 'You like "Alice in Chains"?'

I smiled. Yoof of today can keep their Fred Durst and their Linkin Park and their Avril-bloody-Lavigne. Watered-down metal for kiddies. Back in my salad days, disaffected middle-class teenagers shuffled their ill-fitting jeans to the likes of The Mission and Sisters of Mercy. Because, frankly, baggy was just too cheerful for the pain in our souls. Sit down, sit down, sit down next to me? Begone.

The young man smiled back. 'When was the last time someone told you you're gorgeous?'

'About forty minutes ago.'

N's car came up to the kerb. 'Nice dress,' he said as I got in. 'When I drove up I thought, Well, she can't be the cute one in the dress.'

'You've seen me in this before.'

'Have I?' We'd spent an afternoon in Berkshire with a friend of his, on a boat. 'That was months ago. You look sweet, anyway.'

Went back to mine for a cuppa. He leafed through my magazines. I took off my shoes and rested my legs over his lap. We started fooling around, but his touch felt strange, almost ticklish. I was very premenstrual and slight touches were uncomfortable. But I didn't want to be treated roughly, either.

We grappled on the sofa for a bit before he gave up. 'Not in the mood, are you?' N asked. 'That's okay.'

I felt bad. After all, I'd just come from fucking someone. But work sex feels different, is not tied to interest or desire.

But I knew why I wasn't especially interested. It was not only the slightly disappointing threesome we'd had, nor fatigue from having just seen a client. 'You know what this month is to me?'

'I know what it is.' N put his arm around my shoulder. 'You're not over him, are you?' He didn't mean Dr C, he didn't mean the Boy. He meant the one before that. And he was right. Whenever I am between men my thoughts always turn back to him. I might think that this or that event has helped me move on – the shenanigans with the Boy last year, for instance – but it never does.

'I don't miss him.' N gave me a doubtful look. 'I barely remember what he was like now. I miss the idea of him.' An idea I had written off as nonsense, until I met him. The idea that there is one person you fall in love with, one right person, and you will spend the rest of your lives – or a sizeable portion of them – together. So maybe he turned out not to be the one. At least meeting him helped me believe the one might exist.

He split with me the night I thought was going to be the first night of the rest of our lives. And unlike all my other friends N never told me to shut up about him and get over it already. Because when I met N, part of what made the sex between us so explosive – and the friendship so deep – was that he was nursing similar wounds inflicted by a girl called G, who'd dumped him just as dramatically.

'You want me to stay or go?'

'I'll feel bad for kicking you out this late.'

'Don't,' N said. He dressed, picked up his bag and left quietly.

Later, I heard a drop through the mail slot. Bit late for the post, I thought. I went downstairs to check – a Yorkie bar. My favourite. N knows, he always does.

dimanche, le 17 octobre

'You coming round later?' I asked.

'Are you feeling better today?' N asked.

'A bit, yes,' I said. 'Need anything from the shops?'

'You could always go see those cucumbers for yourself. Maybe pick one out for us.'

'Yeah, I'll just nip round to Kingston and buy a single cucumber. Not suspicious at all.'

'Okay, then, get two.'

'Not sure I could manage to accommodate both simultaneously.'

'Carrot instead, then?'

'Don't get me wrong,' I said. 'I love double penetration. But when things are over a certain size, they get squeezed out. It's like I'm too small.'

'It's a question of capacity, not size. Even G had problems from time to time, and if something too big went in, the other thing would be pushed out. Unfortunately I was usually it.'

'You and she must have worked fairly hard to find something that didn't fit.' His couplings with G were near-legendary as much for her pain threshold as anything else.

'Oh, she could have done a cucumber all right,' he said. 'But possibly not the entire salad bar.'

'Chandeliers might have been too much but I reckon a bedside lamp would have done the trick.'

'A two-seater settee but not the whole sofa.' He chuckled. 'Anyway, whenever I was fisting her in front and buggering her in the rear I'd usually only last a few minutes at most.'

'Probably just as well, it's not something I can imagine anyone would enjoy doing for hours. Be sort of difficult to read your watch that way around, for one.'

'I can think of one advantage, though . . . the second hand is already in.'

'Oh, very punny.'

mardi, le 19 octobre

Manager rang early – emergency call at lunchtime. 'But I'll be at work,' I wailed. In fact, I was already late. 'I can't sneak off for the sake of a client.'

'Do you not even take lunch?' she asked. 'In, out, done. You will hardly interrupt your busy schedule.'

'No. Absolutely not. Ring him and cancel.' And yet, I thought, I probably could do it. Just. And until the first pay cheque came through, the money would certainly come in handy.

'Can't do eet, darling,' she sighed. 'He'll be in meetings all morning.'

'Send someone else.'

'You know I have no one else like you.' No one else who can be guilted into extra work at such short notice, that is. Why on earth was I still doing this? I knew the risk was high – someone might intercept a phone call, spot me going to or from an appointment, or, worse, discover my online profile with the escort agency – but I have a genetic inability to say no.

'No.' Well, maybe not.

'Darling, he's paying double. It's only a leeeetle thing. I promise it absolutely, positively won't happen again.'

I sighed. I'd argue her down another day. I had the bag tucked safely under my desk, and no one else comes back from lunch on time, anyway. I changed in the ladies' and

45

stashed the bag in a maintenance closet. Was walking out the door to meet my car when I passed a co-worker.

My supervisor Giles. Shit.

His head didn't turn – must not have recognised me.

Thank fuck for small mercies.

mercredi, le 20 octobre

We walk down to the Italian. The waiter nods at us and brings the drinks straight away. We order without opening the menus. 'Sure you don't want anything else?' N asks. 'Go ahead. My treat.'

'Aren't you the gentleman,' I smile. 'What's the occasion?'

N looks at his hands. 'I wanted you to be first to know . . . I've met someone.'

'Wow, I . . .' How? When? Our eyes meet and he smiles. 'Have you told her about me?' I wonder if it's the girl from the club, the one he was talking to when we left for the hotel.

'She knows.'

'She's cool with that?'

'As long as we don't sleep together again, yes.'

'Well. I . . .' Never expected he would find someone first. 'I'm so happy for you.' The waiter comes back with our drinks: N's a lemonade, mine a whisky and soda.

'What's wrong.'

'Nothing.'

'Look at me.' I look up. 'You're not crying, for God's sake, are you?'

'Me? Never.' I blow my nose into the heavy cloth napkin. 'It's just I'm so happy for you. You're moving on. This could be the one.'

'Statistically speaking, probably not,' N shrugs.

'I know the look in your eyes. This one's not a shag. She's different.' He doesn't deny it. 'What's her name?'

'Henrietta.'

46

'To you and Henrietta, then,' I say.
'No chance of a last go with you?' N asks. 'For old times'.'
'I thought you said you told her we were done.'
'Can't blame a man for trying,' he smiles.

jeudi, le 21 octobre

How to fuck someone and still be friends, part II

1 It's okay to cry. As long as you happen to be watching a shamelessly romantic film at the time. Then you can tell anyone who catches you that it was Richard Curtis what did it, not the prospect of growing old alone while your friends go on to blissfully happy paired domesticity.
2 Resist urge to leap straight into a rebound relationship. Also not a good time to be thinking about visiting animal shelters.
3 Do not, under any circumstances, ring your ex. Resist temptation to replace vague shame at not even being able to hold on to a fuck buddy with acute shame of acknowledging your own desperation.
4 Find replacement activity for sex. Personally speaking, the toilet has never been so clean.

vendredi, le 22 octobre

Is there any phrase in the English language more horrifying than 'work do'? If so, I can't imagine it.

It's not the prospect of seeing people I work with drunk that's appalling – I survived university thanks to late hours at the library and a tolerance for the inebriation of my friends – it's the other, unwritten rule of gathering out of hours among people you work with: someone will try to cop off with you.

After a meal during which I sat next to an impeccably groomed Malaysian girl whose enthusiasm for shopping was of such a level as to actually test my deep and abiding love of comparing handbags, some of the assembled (those who did not have families to return to, presumably, or could happily ignore their obligations for the evening) repaired to a co-worker's for drinks.

It was a mistake, I can see in retrospect. By my second year of university I had already learned the cardinal rule of going out: namely, that you don't need to. Anyone who is still around after last orders won't care what you do the rest of the night and probably won't remember you were there, anyway. I should have gone home.

But I felt buoyed by not having had too awful a time out. Maybe, I thought, I am capable of having social interactions with near-strangers that last longer than an hour. It was only later, when I went to retrieve my shoes from the other side of the sofa, that it all went terribly wrong.

I was bending over to buckle the ankle straps when I felt a hand on my hip. Someone scooting by to collect a coat, perhaps? Alas, no. It was a very intentional suggestive grab. I stood up and faced Giles.

His cheeks were flushed with wine and his tie was off, top button unbuttoned. Cripes, I thought. It's like being in an episode of *The Good Life*. I smiled weakly. 'You all right?'

'Are those what I think they are?' he asked, the hand moving round my flank slightly in the neighbourhood of the top of my stockings.

'Afraid so,' I said grimly. He must have noticed me leaving work for an appointment the other day, and I thought I'd got away with it – he must have figured it out. Please, please let this not be happening. I looked round quickly; luckily, the few people still there were too far in their own cups to notice us.

'I just wanted you to know, my partner's away for the weekend, if you . . .' He seemed to lose the rest of the sentence for a moment. 'If you wanted to share a taxi home.' I noticed with distaste a gleam of spittle on his lower lip.

Fuck, what to do? It wasn't that he wasn't attractive, he was; and it wasn't that I had anything better to do, I didn't. But say yes – and I was not filled with the overwhelming urge to do so – and it would be only a short journey to being the office bicycle. Say no, and, well, the guy sort of had my professional balls in his hand, so to speak, didn't he?

'It's not my policy to mix business with pleasure,' I said, moving away from the offending hand.

'Tell me, then,' Giles said, and teetered slightly, 'what do you mix your pleasure with?'

He straightened and I saw his half-lidded eyes roll slightly as his body swayed. I put my hand gently on his shoulder and lowered him back to a sitting position on the sofa. 'Afraid I have other plans,' I said. 'Sleep well.'

'You're a beautiful lady, you know that?' he said. He pursed his lips in a drunken kiss and slumped over.

samedi, le 23 octobre

I love ice cream like some people love oxygen.

It's also ace for a hangover. Today I had ice cream at every place I saw. That is, of course, unless I was already eating an ice cream, because stacking cones is not polite. I had a chocolate cone, mint and lemon in a cup, a luscious Spagnola cone, and vanilla.

I like vanilla. I don't tend to eat it, though, because there are so many other nice flavours in the world. But this was good vanilla and it made me happy.

I had a housemate who would only eat vanilla-flavoured ice cream. Not because it was his favourite, mind. But because (he said) vanilla tastes the least of anything, so the companies use their best ice cream for the vanilla flavour.

And the chocolate, he assured me, because it is so strongly flavoured, will be made from inferior ice cream.

Someone who believes a thing like that really does not understand chocolate. Nor the concept of food in general. He was also a vegetarian not out of love for the little fluffy bunnies superseding his desire for a juicy steak, but because, as he put it, you can feed thirty people on the grain it takes to sustain a single cow. Or something. Such people prove that taste is not an evolutionary advantage.

Woke on Sunday morning, stumbled blearily out of the bedroom, naked, to use the toilet and was startled to see a man sitting on the sofa reading a paper. But that's another story and nothing to do with ice cream.

dimanche, le 24 octobre

It was N on the sofa. He has a set of my keys.

He'd spent Saturday night at a mate's stag do, and as my house was closer to the party than his (and presumably Henrietta's), he stumbled in sometime in the wee hours and slept in the lounge. Bless. But it gave me quite a start in the morning. To be fair, perhaps the fact that he didn't burst drunkenly into my bedroom at half three and demand to come on my face proves him to be a gentleman.

I've been to a stag do or two in my time. Never in a professional capacity, though. Rather, I'm likely to be the only girl in a young man's acquaintance who can be trusted to drink pints, buy inflatable sheep and wrestle my Playstation opponents into quivering submission as well as any born male. One time the party took place at a strip club, and neither I nor the men thought anything of having a hen in the coop. If there's an etiquette to being the only XX at a traditionally XY party, it's this: don't complain, don't be the first or last to go home, and don't flirt outrageously (except with the strippers).

In fact, these rules could probably be expanded to life in general.

After breakfast we went on to a friend's birthday picnic, and in the evening to another friend's birthday drinks in a pub on the Thames. I wanted to ask him a thousand questions. Who was this Henrietta? How did they meet? Did he love her? But didn't, and he thankfully steered well clear of any mention of her. Standing on Hammersmith Bridge, after the sun has gone, thousands of spiders come out and build their webs in each of the diamond-shaped holes in the side barrier. The strings of white lights along the bridge attract insects, and we watched the spiders reap their reward for a while.

lundi, le 25 octobre

A day for strange conversations. First, waiting for the bus, a fair-haired gent strikes up a conversation as if we've known each other for ever. I can't for the life of me recognise him. Turns out he's a neighbour. Shows how much I've been paying attention. Fit as they come, too – muscular legs, nice hands, reminds me more than a little of Dr C. We exchange numbers; I've had worse starts to the day.

Giles dropped by my desk after lunch to ask about some reports I'm meant to be writing. To be honest I'm coasting through mostly on cutting and pasting from the Web, but I don't tell him that.

He didn't mention Friday night, so neither did I. He probably doesn't even remember what happened – I hope. He was about to leave when he turned back. 'Meant to mention, saw you going off to lunch the other day,' he said.

I stiffened. I should have known it. Now what? He invites me back to his office for a chat, a threat, and maybe a come-on? Can the end of my career really have come so quickly? 'Did you?' I said.

'You looked . . .' *Please don't say fuckable. Please don't say fuckable.* '. . . great,' he said. I noticed Mira and Erin stop their endless chatter to eavesdrop. 'Were you meeting a friend?'

'Er, yes, just a friend. Not to worry, he won't be dropping by the office.'

'That's a pity,' he said, smiling. 'I'm curious what a woman like you would find attractive in a man.'

I cough. Is there any way to answer that? 'Um, yes, well.' He tapped the corner of my desk and left.

mardi, le 26 octobre

Right, I've made my mind up to get out of the sex trade for good. It's time. Not just because I checked with the bank today and am now the proud recipient of an actual salary deposit. It's been long enough. I've been turning tricks for almost two years, which in straight employment is something like three reincarnations with the same company.

There's no denying I'll miss it, though. Lunchtime trips to swank hotels; dinners out with the sort of men you usually only read about in the business papers; the underwear; the sex.

So you might be thinking, Yeah, sex, taxis, stockings, whatever. But you had to live a double life and never get enough sleep. The most you've seen of London in two years is the inside of a lot of hotels. What's the benefit?

I'll tell you what it is. It's getting to see the nice side of men.

The clients, they're not all gentlemen. They're not all smart, handsome and charming – in fact, few are. They're not always on their best behaviour. But sometimes, in the arms of a naked stranger, they drop the defences they've been building up since the first time Daddy told them boys don't cry and become . . . nicer, somehow.

I get tired of men. I get tired of people in general, especially when there's so much city and so many people and so little time when your ears aren't ringing from aeroplanes or car horns or screaming in the street outside. But then someone smiles at you, and you remember that people are basically decent after all.

Like tonight. The shy fumbling, as a long-time client reached into his pocket and pulled out a tiny box. An after-thought as I was on my way out the door. A kind gesture, a trinket, the cutest little jewel – fashioned into a bee shape, with a sparkling sapphire set in the body. It wasn't a special appointment, it wasn't an anniversary. Just because he wanted to. Because he thought I'd like it. I smiled, and he smiled, and that to him was worth more than the expense of my time and the price of a bauble.

That's the benefit. That, and the agency doesn't take a cut on gifts.

mercredi, le 27 octobre

Phone call from the sexy neighbour at lunchtime. 'Can't talk, terribly busy,' he says, as if I was the one who rang him. 'But would you like to meet for coffee or something this weekend?'

'Love to,' I say. 'Not free Saturday, though.' Afternoon appointment with a client, booked before I made my decision to quit, someone who's paid for extra hours on the spot before. I planned to wear my hottest scanties and leave the whole day free, just in case.

'Sunday. I'll call you and we'll arrange something.'

'Lunchtime-ish?'

'Roger roger. Talk to you then.'

'I look forward to it.' When I hang up, Mira and Erin are giggling like I've come to school in my pants and nothing else. If that's what female friendship is like, I'm glad to have mostly opted out.

A major criticism of pornography is that anyone viewing large amounts of perversion cannot help but become used to it, then jaded by it, and then (so the argument goes) so removed from the people involved that inflicting harm on random strangers seems like a good idea. In short, that Page Three girls are the thin end of a wedge leading to secret rooms in Belgian flats.

I don't buy it. I've watched loads of porn, seen about every flavour of wank mag out there. The problem is not that exposure to large amounts of raunchy imagery encourages the viewer to objectify sex; it's that porn by its very nature is objectified. Porn is reductive. All sexual imagery is shorthand for the total experience, be it a marble nude or the sticky pages of *Hustler Taboo*. The proliferation of imagery in modern media doesn't make perverts where there were none before, it simply makes Gary Glitter's collection electronically portable.

'There are basically only a handful of porn plots out there,' I said to N.

'True. Your basic vaginal penetration, anal, oral, foreign objects, animals.'

'I'd consider animals the same as objects – the point is someone's getting reamed by something that is not human genitalia. Fisting, as well.'

'Fair enough. Then pain, rape, and restraint.'

'Often all three at once,' I point out.

'Yes, but not always, so they count as different types.' That was true – plenty of people who enjoy rape fantasies can't stomach pain; loads of people are into tying each other up on a purely consensual basis.

'Bodily fluids – should there be a breakdown within that category, or is it okay to consider bukakke and scat the same thing?' In my experience, I've found that men who like urine fall into two almost equal categories, the pissing-on and the pissed-upon. But by far they'd rather be receiving than giving in the poo department. There's a dichotomy some enterprising academic could probably turn into a thesis.

'Same thing, different levels of extreme. Someone gets covered in yuck.'

'By that criterion I don't think vaginal and anal genital insertion are technically much different,' I said.

'Maybe not, but you'd risk offending too many people by saying so.'

'Non-genital-focused kink,' I said. 'Catch-all category for men watching women squash insects, smoking fetishists, things like that.'

'What's the point if someone doesn't get done?'

'Who knows?' I counted up the list. 'Eight in total? That's not bad. After all, they say there are only five basic plots for stories. Does that mean porn is the richer cultural tradition?'

'If so, I'm a connoisseur of fine art.'

vendredi, le 29 octobre

The phone rang. I was tired. I sort of forgot that I had promised myself not to do this again, and said yes to the manager before remembering that I was meant to say no.

'Splendid, dahling. He lives in East Molesey.' Ugh. And it wasn't even convenient.

I was kneeling over the client, pulling his cock and balls. This one was a gusher; the amount of pre-come he was producing was staggering. My thumb and forefingers were already sticky with it, and a fat drop rolled down the shaft.

He reached up to stroke my face. From that angle, the soft hand, chalk-white skin, dark hair – he looked like someone else. I felt like there were crossed wires in my head, making me see ghosts that weren't there. 'Your neck,' he murmured, and I wasn't sure who was saying it. His voice was papery at that volume, very like the boyfriend before the Boy – the One.

When I was young I believed that, by concentrating hard enough, anyone who was thinking about me would be able to see for a few moments through my eyes, wherever I was, and hear and feel what was happening. When *Being John Malkovich* came out I was stunned at how closely the film resembled this half-forgotten fantasy.

I wondered who might be thinking about me, and would they be seeing this? My hands on someone else's shoulders, a dark trail of hair on the lower belly that looked far too familiar?

I rested my head on his chest. One of his legs flexed, one straight, it happened again. The ghost. It must sneak in as autumn sun slanting through the window. Hundreds of motes stirring in the slight breeze, picking up crackling bits of memory and sticking them together. I closed my eyes. At least his smell was different. That put things right.

'I'd like to see you again,' he said as I dressed. 'Call me. Not for an appointment. A real date.'

'That would be nice,' I replied, and meant it perhaps a little more than is good for me. He slipped his card into my hand with the tip. I noted the name and put everything back in my bag. 'I'll ring you sometime, Malcolm.'

samedi, le 30 octobre

I'm not a superstitious person, but my horoscope today came true!

Someone from your past is trying to make contact, it read. *Your best plan is to have an open mind in the weeks ahead.*

Hey, cut me a break. It's right next to the sudoku, okay?

I went online and checked my email – a note from L, the girl I was at school with. It was nice, for once, to have an unexpected email from someone I actually cared to hear from again instead of an ex.

At school L and I were separated at birth, thick as thieves, peas in a pod. We shared the same filthy imagination and French classes, and having discovered so, discarded the time-honoured schoolgirl tradition of passing notes for an altogether more advanced form of communication: a shared notebook of ideas. Granted, most of these were and are unpublishable, ranging from the demented (a sketch of the cartoon girl from our language texts, petting her cat's anus with her toes) to the dangerous (a full and detailed list of what we would do and to whom, given infinite time, resources and freedom from prosecution) to the frankly libellous (a portrait of our history master masturbating).

This carried on for some months when, for reasons I can only dimly figure now, I took the notebook home over the holidays and my parents read it. And were horrified. And spent about a nanosecond considering their previously liberal attitude to child-rearing before ringing L's parents. We were forbidden to associate after that. In truth, we were not any worse with each other than we would have been had we never met. It's just that we had kept a record.

Two years later we became cautious friends again in economics A levels. The other students had about as much aptitude for academic life as a salad bar. Clearly they were all going to become captains of industry some day. She chose the course as necessary to her future in law; I chose it because it was my only opportunity to nap during the day.

We told jokes in the back of the classroom; recited Billy Connolly's filthier routines. But we never, ever wrote anything down again. And we never told our parents.

dimanche, le 31 octobre

Resolved: never to pick up the phone without looking to see who's calling. Ever. Again.

I thought it might be my neighbour, calling to arrange a meeting. It wasn't. It was a call I should have known would come again. It's an unwritten rule of breakups that one of the parties involved must make ill-advised, drunken, desperate calls to the other. And no matter how it ended, who broke up with whom, it's these horrible drunk diallings that will be remembered. Whatever moral high ground the person may have had is immediately forfeited. At least that person wasn't me.

Not Dr C, though. The Boy again. Fucking horoscope.

Dear Belle

Dear Belle,
   I'm going out with a pair of best friends: one knows, the other does not. I'm having lots of sex but it does chafe rather. Any tricks of the trade to help me out?

Dear Double-Booked,
   Sorry, but has the message to lube well and often missed your household? Lube well. And often. If the front entry wears out, use the back for a bit. But for goodness' sake, girl, are you mad? You're missing the opportunity for a threesome if you don't tell the other gent what's going on!

Dear Belle,
   My boyfriend likes to rip my clothes off of me when we have sex and, though I did find this exciting the first few times, it's now working out rather expensive. How can I make him stop without seeming completely repressed? Or am I just repressed? I'm not one of those women who thinks a nice frock is better than sex, but is there a third way?

Dear Busting Out,
   While it would be tempting to lead you in the direction of some of the city's finer second-hand shops, even that can prove expensive after a few months. My personal experience with just such a man taught me to buy clothing that fastens with poppers. That, or replace all your zips with Velcro.

Dear Belle,
   I have been going out with the same girl for three years and I am really bored in the bedroom. It's crossed my mind to look elsewhere, but my heart is really in this relationship. She's sensitive and shy about sex, and I guess I just need a bit more spice. What should I say?

Dear Don't I Know You?
   Your heart may be in this relationship, but is your mouth? By which I mean talking to her about the problem instead of to me. You mention your lass is shy – but she's not too shy to have sex at

all, and that's a start. What you need is a long-term plan and patience. Some ladies respond well to having a twelve-inch strap-on and a library of porn thrown their way, and some do not. Gentle changes, slowly, over time, with a lot of snuggling afterwards. It's not much to invest if you think she's in it for the long term. And if you're incapable or unwilling to make this sort of effort, but prefer instead to whinge about it, do us all a favour and move on, eh?

Novembre

lundi, le 1 novembre

'Hey, where are you?'

'I'm at the restaurant,' I said. The waiters were starting to give me pitying, honey-he-ain't-gonna-turn-up looks. 'Where are you?'

'Kind of caught up in things,' the neighbour said. 'Can we push it back to another day?'

I squeezed a fork so hard I was surprised it didn't bend. Left deep tine-marks in my palm, though. 'Sure. Of course.'

'It's the bloody girlfriend,' he said, lowering his voice. 'She just turned up at my desk.'

Girlfriend?

'Anyway, sorry to disappoint you,' he said. 'I'll make it up to you. I'm off to a work do tonight, it's tropical themed, I'll bring you a coconut.'

Girlfriend??

'Talk to you later.' And he rang off.

mardi, le 2 novembre

Flagrant violation of company policy #1: Misuse of IT resources.

God bless the internet. How on Earth office workers managed to fill up their time in the years BW (Before Web) is beyond me. Have spent the post-lunch period downloading music and listening to it on headphones. The better to drown out co-workers' inanity, my dear. L and I found each other online and spent much of the afternoon in a chat, before deciding to meet for late drinks.

'You look exactly the same,' I smiled. Perhaps a little glossier and more expensively dressed, but L was the very image of herself as a schoolgirl. It was only now I realised how much she resembles Gillian Anderson, and I said so. She laughed.

'Cheers dears,' she said as we touched cheeks. 'I wouldn't have recognised you.'

'Really?' I'd always imagined I looked much the same as before, aging gracefully into adulthood. Maybe those tiny lines I'd been noticing lately weren't as invisible to others as I'd hoped.

'You've lost a ton of weight,' L said.

'Work stress,' I lied. Generally speaking, most of my work time is spent trying to dissociate myself as much as possible from work itself, and as soon as I'm out of the office I forget about it until the next morning. 'Sometimes you have to choose between a full night's sleep and a meal, you know?'

L nodded. We curled up with our cocktails at a corner table. 'So what keeps you busy these days?'

I'd already decided not to tell her about the small matter of fucking men for money. Not that I thought she wouldn't approve; but it's a bit much to spring on someone at a reunion, no? 'Oh, it's terribly boring,' I said. 'I'd love to hear more about what you're up to – from law to acting? Why? How? And more importantly, what are the men like?'

She laughed. 'I find the professions surprisingly alike,' she said. 'The men are like men everywhere – hopeless.' I concurred and we giggled our way through three more drinks before going our separate ways. It's a good thing, I thought, that some things don't change.

mercredi, le 3 novembre

N is very negative on the subject of pursuing the neighbour. It's not fair to the girlfriend, he says; and I agree, but don't think things are necessarily so cut and dried. Some people can get up and walk away from a relationship as soon as they think it's not going anywhere; others hang on beyond any hope of saving it. I don't want to pressure the neighbour (largely because I don't think he'll leave his girl).

In the meantime I have to deal with him vacillating between flirty and stand-offish. If this is what neighbourly relations are like, I can see why I never bothered before.

jeudi, le 4 novembre

The foot fetishists, they are tops.

I don't understand their fetish – feet are nice enough, but not that nice. But boy can I cater to it, and they certainly seem to like me.

Despite too large a fraction of my life spent in stilettos, my feet are in surprisingly good shape. Fine-boned, high-arched, uncallused and blessed with nicely shaped toes and toenails. Of my physical features I would rate the feet rather highly. I don't spend very much time on them, preferring a single lick of clear varnish to a full-on pedicure, and yet they seem to do quite well.

I met S earlier than my normal appointments. Mid-afternoon at a central hotel. He had requested no stockings, and 'pretty' shoes. Non-specific. Not a shoe fetishist, then, I wagered. I wore the violet peep-toed ones, with the open instep and little shiny bow on the side.

There is always the moment of doubt on meeting a client. Will this work? Is he nice? Is this even the right person? On meeting S, he smiled, looked me in the eyes, and his gaze dropped immediately to the floor. I knew we were on, and this definitely the man.

He led me into the suite. I sat. He poured drinks, handed me one, and sat on the floor by my chair. He was average height, slim, narrow-shouldered with a cut-glass accent and a plump lower lip. With one hand he slipped my right shoe off. He nodded, as you imagine a jeweller would on seeing a fine gem. 'Five,' he said, referring (one assumes) to the size of my foot and not the number of toes.

'Yes,' I said. He had asked, before booking the appointment.

He put his drink on the table and unsheathed the other foot, turning its underside towards him, running his thumb along its length. 'Ticklish?'

'No.'

'Good.' His warm fingers pressed lightly on the top of my foot. 'Clean?'

'As per instructions,' I said. I had worried that not wearing stockings might make them a little sweaty in transit, but if this was the case he did not seem to mind. 'Why no stockings?'

'I'm not interested in your legs,' he said, nuzzling the undersides of both feet together.

Fair enough. I'm indifferent to them myself. S removed his clothes and spent the next twenty minutes on the floor, shuffling his naked body under my feet as I held my legs bent, thighs raised from the seat. He especially lingered with my feet over his face. But he was not a toe-sucker, and seemed to prefer that I keep the feet together.

Having discerned that he didn't want me to do very much, my eyes wandered towards the window. The curtains were open but a sheer privacy curtain was drawn. There was street noise outside, but we were fairly high up, so nothing was distinct. And the sound of his back moving over the carpet. I wondered if he wouldn't get burns. My feet were over his face again, and he moved his head from side to side.

'Wmmph hmmph mmph mmp,' he said.

'Pardon?'

'Wiggle your toes.' Finally, he brought the two feet down to his crotch, cupping them round his balls as he masturbated.

'Nails,' he said. 'Dig the nails.' I dug the nails. He came. Lifting my soles off him, I could see the pink crescents some of the nails had left in his thigh. I held the feet in midair again as he tended to the mess with a baby wipe, then he dressed and poured me another drink. We turned on the television and watched a gardening show.

vendredi, le 5 novembre

Flagrant violation of company policy #2: Did not wash up own tea mug.

My approach to tea is this: as I'll be having something like my body volume in tea per day, it makes no sense to wash the mug with soap and hot water each time. It's my mug, and my tea, and I'll get round to washing up when I get round to it.

Not everyone sees my point of view on this. Came back from lunch to find mug not on end of desk, where I had left it. Searched for the better part of half an hour before discovering it half full of soap in the tea room drying rack. Returned to desk and note in a tell-tale cramped North American hand:

YOUR MOTHER DOES NOT WORK HERE
CLEAN UP AFTER YOURSELF

Idly wondered whether someone whose mother did work here would have been exempt from such advice.

'So what are you up to today?' the neighbour asked.

Trying to avoid men with girlfriends, unless it's a business arrangement? 'Nothing special.'

'Well, why don't you come round – I've been needing to get out into the hills for a weekend, and was thinking Dartmoor.'

Er, what about his girlfriend? 'What about your girlfriend?'

'She's visiting relatives in Spain.' I said nothing. Was he really going to be as casual as that, and not even apologise for not telling me about her earlier? 'Come on, it would be great fun.' Yes, indeed he was.

And yet I couldn't see that good a reason for saying no. I'd justified having married clients, after all, by thinking it was their business, not mine. And to be honest I didn't think the neighbour was particularly boyfriend material. Quite apart from the fact that he already was, to someone else. After Dr C, after the Boy, what with the thoughts I'd been thinking lately about previous relationships, it wasn't a good time for me to be leaping into something serious. So what, really, was the problem? 'I'll be over soon.'

I sat on the sofa in his flat while he packed. Photos, his and hers; books, his and hers; a double desk; little cushions scattered everywhere, definitely the girlfriend's. Resisted using the toilet for fear that I would not be able to stop myself going through their cupboards.

It was a longer drive than I thought. An hour or more out of London I started to get the familiar twitchy feeling. 'I was thinking of masturbating,' I said to the neighbour. 'But you were going to stop soon for food, weren't you?'

'I'll give you plenty of warning if I decide to stop,' he said.

'And let me know if you're about to pass any lorry drivers?'

'I will.'

Unzipped my jeans and reached into my knickers with the left hand – already soaking wet. I slipped two fingers inside, then a third, rubbing my clit with the thumb. The radio was on, some droning Radio Four drama. I turned it down. It was distracting. Turned it down again so the actors' voices were just a whisper. Closed my eyes. I don't know how long it was before I came, twitching and grunting, but the same play was still on when I finished. Pulled my hand out, licked the fingers. We stopped soon after for a cream tea.

We'll share a bed tonight, but I bet nothing happens, I think. He's a tactile creature who responds well to touch but is strangely passive. He either doesn't fancy me enough to go through with cheating, or is frightened, or perhaps a bit of both.

We sat outside a pub drinking bitter, watching mother ducks and their fluffy ducklings play in a shallow stream. He told me about girls he had flirted with, girls he had pursued. 'I believe infidelity is essential to the health of a long-term relationship,' he said. Perhaps. But he hasn't done it yet with me or anyone else. Maybe he feels he needs to establish some kind of emotional feeling for the other woman before he cheats. Which makes him rather a different creature from the clients I used to see, who by the time they book a girl have already decided to go through with the cheating, regardless of who she turns out to be. Maybe punters are punters because they went that route first and found the fallout too damaging to their primary relationships. I don't know.

dimanche, le 7 novembre

Conversations I'm glad are firmly in the past.

1 Mum, I'm not a virgin any more.
    It happened the term before I went to university. I thought I sort of loved the boy, he wrote me (very bad) songs and compared me to heroines in (very bad) books. He was ginger. It didn't last. It wouldn't have done to go to uni a virgin, anyway. My mother cried.

2 Can you just test me for everything?

Now instead of troubling my GP with a rundown of reasons (invented) of why I need the full complement of tests for sexually transmitted infections (and then some), I go to a clinic. You almost don't even have to ask. Blessed, blessed understanding.

3 Take me off the agency books, and I mean it this time.

It really was as simple as that. I called up the manager and didn't even say hello. Just that we were over and she could expect a final deposit into her account on Monday. And she didn't try to talk me out of it. Suddenly, I feel lighter.

lundi, le 8 novembre

I was still feeling buoyant about leaving the agency when I came to work. The bag under the desk – no need for that any more! No need to work extra-strength condoms into my weekly budget, nor to keep two separate underwear drawers, one for clients and one for everyday. I was whistling as I came in the office and didn't care much if Erin and Mira heard.

Giles was sitting in my chair. 'Um, good morning,' I said. As far as I knew there was no team meeting this morning and I was not behind any deadlines. 'Is everything okay?'

'I've good news and bad news,' he said, arching his fingers. 'Which do you want first?'

Was this some sort of sophisticated trap? Had my effort to extract myself from the sex trade been too slow, and someone had found my pics on the website? Was I about to be fired? Ho hum, good while it lasted, then. 'Bad news, I guess.'

'The bad news is I'm not going to be supervising your work any more,' he said, nodding to Erin, who was arriving at her desk. 'I've been transferred over to the development cluster, so this group is being reshuffled. I'm sure whoever takes over will be pleased to have such an effective team to look after.'

That makes it about two weeks until they find out I haven't

been doing anything, then. Better start looking for a new job today. 'That's a shame. I'm pleased to hear you're doing well, though. What's the good news?'

He grinned. 'Well, seeing as I'm not your direct supervisor any longer, we can have an affair now.'

I smiled weakly. I imagine the crash behind me was the sound of Erin's jaw hitting the floor.

mardi, le 9 novembre

Flagrant violation of company policy #3: Took breaks in excess of contractual agreement.

I can't help it. It's bloody Erin and Mira. Now they're telling anyone who'll listen that I'm sleeping my way through the management. It's like being at school all over again.

To the extent that I spent the better part of an hour hiding in the toilets.

mercredi, le 10 novembre

Half one this morning, a noise at the door.

It was warm. I was half wrapped in a blanket. I had been sleeping soundly, and wasn't sure if it was a knock I'd heard.

Someone outside? Checked the clock. At this hour? Went to the kitchen and looked out a small window. It wasn't the right angle. I couldn't see if there was anyone at the door. Tried the window in the toilet. Same: I couldn't have looked down without sticking my head out. Put on a white towelling dressing gown.

Crept down the stairs. Peeped out. Ah.

The Boy was outside with a rucksack. He smiled. 'Is there room in the bed? You look all fluffy and cute.'

'Mmmmphhfff,' I said, standing aside so he could come in.

'Is that sleepy for "Take me to bed and ravish me"?'

I am truly an idiot. I have no reason to let this man back in my life. But it is late, and unless the neighbour decides to make good on his sexy promises soon, I need servicing. 'No, that's sleepy for "Hurry up, before I wake up properly," I said.

jeudi, le 11 novembre

Flagrant violation of company policy #4: Had non-work-related visitor to office.

Actually, this wasn't by choice. The Boy rang at lunchtime and asked if I wanted to meet him. 'Sure,' I said. 'Where are you?' 'Look out the window,' he said.

Oh, fucksticks. He was standing on the pavement looking up, dressed in a horrible pinstripey suit and holding what appeared to be flowers. I waved limply. Mira and Erin hurried over to coo behind my back: 'How darling!' 'How adorable!'

'Nice suit,' I said when I finally got down to the door. 'What's the occasion?'

'No occasion,' he said.

'Bit outside your usual remit.'

'I'm trying to impress you,' he said, handing the flowers over. I had to admit, it was a sweet gesture. But I wasn't prepared to let my guard down just because we'd had (admittedly great) sex again. I smiled tightly and we walked off to the café.

His train back south wasn't for ages so he stayed at my office another two hours after lunch. And while I tried to explain how incredibly busy I was, with loads of work to do, he insisted on using my computer to read news headlines and made tea for everyone. Needed to use toilet but had to sit there in cramped, waterlogged agony, in case Erin decided to let on to my visitor that our ex-supervisor had a crush on me. When the Boy left I ran to the toilet, unbuttoning on the way, and plonked myself down on the porcelain to release a hot, urgent stream of piss. It was then I realised I'd neglected to shut the toilet door.

Not embarrassing at all, then.

I rode the bus home, berating myself the whole way for my poor judgment. This man had made a ruin of most of the last year of my life; what was I thinking? At home, I noticed my desk looked odd: nothing was out of place per se, but it just looked as if everything had been moved and then carefully replaced so as not to arouse suspicion.

Ugh, not again. That's my payback for a moment of weakness, then – evidence that the Boy may talk nice but hasn't changed a bit. Still jealous and suspicious where he has no reason to be. Still looking for someone he can keep on a leash, and not just in the bedroom, where it's acceptable. Too tired and fed up to consider the matter further.

vendredi, le 12 novembre

The Boy rang at suppertime. I'd taken the flowers home with me; they were in an old milk bottle. He suggested another rendezvous. I rolled my eyes but couldn't help being flattered. And in spite of obviously going through my computer, he was staying mostly in line. And the sex was awesome. I'd have to keep a closer eye on him, is all. I could handle it. 'Why don't I come visit your place this weekend?' I said.

'Why? Are you trying to keep me away from your friends? Are you seeing someone there?'

Eh? What the hell? 'No, I just haven't been out of town in ages. It would be nice to have a walk on the beach or something. Feel the fresh air.' Might as well enjoy the fact that he lives by the sea, if nothing else in this perverse arrangement.

I've found you can gauge the extent of a man's lie by the

pause that precedes it. He was silent almost a minute. 'I have some people I need to meet in London this weekend,' he said.

'Great, we can meet them together.'

He paused again. It could go either way – he could be cagey and belligerent, and blame me for starting an argument later. Or he could give in. He gave in. 'Fffffine,' he said. 'I'll meet you at the train station.'

samedi, le 13 novembre

The Boy's room looked eerily identical to when I was last there, months and months ago. The pile of unopened post on a chair, the cards stuck on the wardrobe doors – some of them from me. A bunch of flowers, dry now, I'd bought when he was laid off from work.

In fact, it was almost as if he'd packed the whole room away when we'd split and put it back together now to amuse me. I looked for signs he'd been seeing other people, and there were a few – a half-empty bottle of massage oil by the bed, a fake rose with clear plastic 'dew' on the petals – but it shocked me to realise how much of the mess was not just his, but ours. Had he really kept it exactly like this all these months? What would another woman have thought? Or did she care to wonder whose hands had once lit the lavender candles on the edge of his desk, now coated generously with dust?

dimanche, le 14 novembre

We woke early, fucked, and fell asleep again. I heard the noise of his housemates downstairs but wasn't keen to run into them. Every time his phone rang the Boy sprang out of bed and rushed up to the top floor, claiming poor reception in his room. It was odd – we were on the same network, and as far as I could tell, my phone's reception was fine.

Finally, well past lunchtime, we went downstairs. I wandered into the kitchen, and on the counter was a letter for a Miss Susie Allen. So that was her name. Strange that whoever collected the post put her letter aside, on the edge of the counter, so that you could hardly walk past without knocking it off. Strange especially considering there's no post on a Sunday.

He came into the kitchen and I held up the letter. 'Friend of yours?' I asked.

He snatched it out of my hand. 'Um, yeah, just some girl, some friend of my housemate's,' he said. 'She's off travelling and gets her post here.'

'Really?' I said. 'I would have thought she was a friend of yours. Looks like someone left it out for you.'

'No! No way. I mean, no, absolutely not. What are you saying?'

'Nothing,' I said. 'I simply wondered if it was a friend of yours.' Men are such bad liars sometimes, you have to pity them. 'Cup of tea and toast?'

lundi, le 15 novembre

Accidentally referred to the place where I work as 'my crucible' instead of 'my cubicle' during a team meeting today. Supervisor seemed not to notice. Sent off email to L first thing, telling her about it. She rang the office and didn't say a word: only laughed for five solid minutes.

Contrary to popular myth, men are from Earth. Women are from Earth.

That doesn't make the opposite sex any more comprehensible. The neighbour threw a bit of a pout when he found out about the Boy. Don't quite know why – he's the one with a partner, after all. Methinks this young man is somewhat confused. But I am confused about the neighbour as well.

Thus far the relationship with the neighbour is perfectly innocent in a quite porny way – we seem to spend a lot of time meeting for coffee and talking about sex. Rather like time with N and the As but without the baggage of being ex-lovers – laden instead with the baggage of not yet having slept together.

We were sat in a car together, eating Haribo Tangfastics. I know they're not kosher but can't resist. The neighbour pulled one of the ring-shaped jellies out of the bag, the pink and blue ones with an odd protrusion from the side.

'I wonder what are these meant to be?' he asked.

'Dummies, I think,' I said.

'That's not quite what they look like.'

I peered at the sweet. 'No, more like a rubber cock ring with clit stimulator.' We laughed.

Much later, the Boy rang. He was having a T&E moment (tired and emotional – you know, drunk). 'I feel really sick,' he said. Physically or mentally, I asked? 'Both,' he said. 'I can't live without you.'

Ho hum, tell it again when you're sober sometime. 'Have a pint of milk and a bowl of porridge and go to bed.'

'I miss you so much.'

'Drink some milk and go to bed.' I rang off. The neighbour looked at me. I dared not admit what the conversation was really about. 'Friend having lady trouble,' I said. 'It's as if I'm Florence Nightingale to the single men of Britain.'

Afterwards we were in the neighbour's car again, listening to music. He reached for my hand and kissed it. Then he closed his teeth gently round one of my knuckles. I shivered, in a nice way. 'You shouldn't do that,' I smiled. Meaning, of course, Do it again, please. I can't help it if I don't say what I mean. It doesn't make me an alien. It's part and parcel of the female condition. He dropped me slightly nearer to his house than mine.

mercredi, le 17 novembre

'I know it's a bit late,' the Boy said, 'but I wanted to give you a birthday gift.' His large hand was curled round something small. I wondered, What could it be? Surely not jewellery?

'As long as it's not something you're regifting me, or something half eaten.' This was not much of an exaggeration. The Boy has a long history of offering gifts that either obviously came to him from someone else (the half-unwrapped stoneware mug) or are partially eaten (German white chocolate). The one gift I really liked was a sheepskin for my bed; I later found out he gave an identical one to his mother. We'd had sex on it, and he gave the same thing to his mum? That's just wrong.

He scowled and put the hand back in his pocket. 'Fine, then. Clearly you don't want it.'

'Don't be silly, I was only teasing.' He wasn't pleased, though, and it took a good bit of coaxing to calm him down. Whatever the gift was it must be important to him, I thought.

Finally he gave it me. I opened the box. It was indeed a piece of jewellery.

A tiny silver bee brooch set with a piece of amber. It was rather like the one a client had given me once, only . . . not quite so nice as that one. 'I noticed you like things with insects on them,' he said. I suppose it was partly true; I think there is a butterfly-printed tea towel somewhere in the depths of my kitchen cupboards.

'Oh, this is lovely,' I said, trying to keep the disappointment out of my voice. Not that I was expecting anything better, or indeed anything at all: he'd been talking about taking a weekend abroad and I considered that gift enough. But it was the sort of thing you might have bought for a young niece, or a girl you didn't know very well; not for your girlfriend. I wished he'd kept the money and spent it on something else. 'Just the sort of thing I would have bought for myself,' I said.

But it was too late, he'd clocked the disappointment. I smiled and pinned the brooch to my shoulder. 'See? It's just right.'

jeudi, le 18 novembre

The neighbour is driving me batty. After text mini-argument (he claims too busy to meet; I reply am fine with busy, just can't take cancellations because I'm busy, too), he stops answering his phone. Resign self to fact that he has bottled out and doesn't have the guts to tell me. This morning, of course, he texts: lost phone. Okay, willing to forgive. He says he's free early this week. He came round for breakfast this morning, and we talked about weddings, which Scandinavian country has the cutest girls, and writing books. He was on a pushbike; I was feeling lazy and took the Tube to work instead of the bus.

N says of the neighbour: 'You know, if he was the woman and you the man, we'd have a term for this, and it would be Cock Tease.'

The Boy came round unexpectedly again last night and I didn't send him away. He definitely has one thing working in his favour, and that is the sex. The man has a way with a rope, especially the third time, with my wrists and ankles bound, my back on the bed. He knelt on the bed, entered me, pulled my legs towards him so they rested with the backs of my calves on one of his shoulders. I sat up slightly – the way my hands and feet were tied it was difficult not to. When he came, still kneeling, he pulled my legs in to his body, put his hands round my wrists, and picked me up off the bed. He is a lot taller than I am and very strong. A mental image I hope to remember for a very long time.

vendredi, le 19 novembre

Flagrant violation of company policy #5: Using company phones for non-work-related purposes. 'So how is the City girl,' Mum asked.

'Mum, I don't *work* in the City.' Nothing like talking to the parents to bring you straight back to the searing whininess of pubescence.

'Yes, dear.' She sounded amused. 'Will they be giving you much time off at the end of the year, or do they force all the new kids to work through New Year?'

'I get two weeks off, I think,' I said. 'I was thinking of taking the time closer to Chanukah and coming to see you and Daddy for a bit. Work the week between Christmas and New Year.'

'Oh, honey,' she said. She sounded so sad. 'The thing is, and I hate to have to tell you this way, but your father and I are splitting up. So maybe your coming for Chanukah wouldn't be the best time.'

'I'll say. I'm coming up right now.'

samedi, le 20 novembre

Something wrong with the trains; we were transferred to coaches instead about halfway. Ho hum. I don't mind so much: if you're not in first class, a train is like being in a coach anyway. But with overpriced tea.

I love the drive north. It gives me a thrill just like it did when I was little, seeing the exit that means home coming closer and closer. The countryside opening up, changing from unrelenting sprawl to discrete cities and villages in rolling fields. Passing the sign for Elland Road and the Royal Armouries, which Daddy and I always called the Royal Ovaries, because at a distance the pictograph looks like a uterus.

dimanche, le 21 novembre

The house, in fact, does not look any different from how it looked last month. 'I let him have the spare furniture in the extra bedrooms,' Mum says. 'He's living round the corner in a flat at the moment. Do you want me to drive you round to see him?'

No, not yet. I can just about hold it together in front of my mother, but I've always been a Daddy's girl, and the thought of seeing him in some poky rental makes me want to cry. 'Maybe tomorrow,' I say. We spend the rest of the day cautiously around each other: it's the first time we've really been alone together, probably since I was a baby.

'Why did you marry Daddy?' I ask.

'He always made me feel safe,' Mum says. 'And I knew we would have clever children.'

'Flattery will get you everywhere,' I say. But I notice she hasn't said anything about passion, or true love. 'Did you always know it was going to be him?'

'When you know, you know. Sometimes it happens quickly and sometimes it happens slowly.'

Or not at all, I think. She might as well come out and say, I settled down too early and this was all a mistake and I should have spent the seventies travelling Kashmir with a rucksack rather than raising children in the suburbs, but it can't be undone. 'I guess,' I say. My parents married when they were still students. By the time she was my age, my mother had an eight-year-old daughter – me. 'Would you have split up sooner if you hadn't had children?'

'Don't be so glum,' Mum says, squirting dishsoap into the sink with more force than strictly necessary. 'Your father will always have a place in my heart.' We finish the washing up in silence. I know about having a place for someone in your heart. That's where they go when they don't have a place in your life any more.

lundi, le 22 novembre

Being at home gives you loads of time to think. Luckily, there are upsides as well, as the sheer amount of brainpower I expended in the last forty-eight hours on the subject of relationships could be used to power Leeds for a week.

You may be wondering why on earth I am letting my ex back into my life after everything that happened. To be honest, I wonder why as well. It is probably a lot to do with how well he compares to the neighbour.

Boy:	Sex is reliably good, if perhaps one-track.
Neighbour:	No idea what sex with him is like.
Boy:	Does not know when to go away.
Neighbour:	Does not know when to ring.
Boy:	Lives with insufferable twats (and possibly another woman).
Neighbour:	Lives with girlfriend.
Boy:	Talks loads; says very little.
Neighbour:	Talks loads; impossible to keep up.
Boy:	Riddled with known faults and baggage.

Neighbour: Most likely riddled with unknown faults and
baggage.

Will have to sleep on this one.

mardi, le 23 novembre

I nodded at L in the coffee shop at lunchtime. She was tucked
up in a big chair, reading, a pair of oval glasses slipping down
her nose in a rather fetching manner. Sometimes I envy people
with glasses. Not so much her red hair; I tried that, it doesn't
work on me. 'How's it going?' I asked. 'Not too badly,' she
said. 'Having one of those days. I came in and scanned the
room, and didn't see any men worth my time. But now I'm
getting annoyed that not one of them is even looking at me.'

I looked around; she was right. Not a single possibility in
the room. Not even one you'd sleep with if you were drunk
and the lights in the club had just come on and they were
playing 'Time of My Life'. 'I know that feeling,' I said. 'It's
the need to have sex more often.' 'Maybe. Or maybe it's the
need to be praised as one of the world's great beauties.' L has
a hard and fast rule with men: she's hard, she's fast, and if
they can't take it she's not interested.

'You mean, keep the men in a tight, yet distinctly unbreach-
able, orbit?' Oh, to be Garbo.

'Precisely,' L said, sipping her tea. The best part of friendship, really, is the little bit of joy I get just thinking that
someone like L is out there.

mercredi, le 24 novembre

Flagrant violation of company policy #6: Took a sick day
without ringing in until after 10 a.m.

There are risks involved in promiscuity. Some of these involve viruses and I am sorry to announce I have succumbed. I have had a stinking cold since Monday – as best as I can figure, courtesy of the neighbour. My own fault, really. Although I will be dead upset if it turns out he caught it from his girlfriend.

Still, this makes a nice change. When I was a call girl there was almost no chance of taking a sick day. I remember the first time it happened, and I asked the manager if she couldn't get the punter to reschedule. She said no, and that he didn't want anyone but me, so I had to go. 'But what if I give him my cold?' I whined. 'Who cares?' she said. Considering how conscientious we were regarding sexually transmitted infections, I thought her attitude rather ruthless. I dosed myself with as much Day Nurse as I could stand and staggered on, determined to last the two hours without giving him bird flu. It remains the only appointment in which I lied and told the client I didn't do kissing; what I didn't say was that it was because I was afraid of giving him my cold. I have no idea whether it's possible to contract influenza through blowjobs.

N came round last night with Lemsip and sympathy. I was lying feebly on the sofa recounting the events of the day (which were, it must be said, few; but when you're ill they take on weighty significance). These included meeting the neighbour for a postponed, brief, and extremely frustrating coffee during which I sneezed and moaned a lot.

'Let me see if I understand,' N said, stirring powder and boiling water into a mug. 'He has a girlfriend he's not going to leave, he doesn't appear to fancy you and always cancels meetings with you.'

'Yes.'

N set the mug on the table and looked me over. 'You're getting a touch podgy,' he said.

'I would smack you, but am too weak to lift my fat arm.'

'Are you fucking mad?'

'Well, he did bring me a coconut,' I said in the neighbour's defence. 'And we had a nice time in Dartmoor.'

'A sexless nice time,' N said. 'If you're going to masturbate in front of someone you're not having sex with, I'd rather it was me.'

I thought about what N had said. Texted the neighbour late: would he like to meet for breakfast in the morning? He replied quickly: yes. So there, I thought, and went to sleep.

Woke early to another text. The neighbour. Was out for a run. Was going to a meeting after. Breakfast not possible. I groaned, turned the phone off and went to work still shivering and ill. I hope those miserable cows sitting behind me catch whatever I've got.

vendredi, le 26 novembre

Met N and A1 after work for a drink. 'Hey, sugar,' A1 said, putting his arm around my waist. 'So your Tory friend is meeting us, is he?' The first time they met A1 and N spent the entire night arguing politics, and ever since, N's been my 'Tory friend' to A1. N walked in and the two men shook hands. 'Good seeing you.' 'Always a pleasure.'

N and I were discussing the perfect mate – A1 is exempt, being married and all.

N's criteria total three:

- Ample-chested, and
- High pain threshold, and
- Gets on with his mum.

My list is somewhat longer:

- Tall and thin, or
- Tall and muscular, or
- Neither of these but physically appealing to me, and
- Nice hands, and
- Nice voice, and

- Someone who either likes to talk or likes to listen, and
- Ideally fits into my knickers, not habitually, just once or twice for effect, and
- Lives about two hours away – not more, not less.

'Hmm, I think we can say something about men's and women's relative chances of finding what they want in life,' A1 said. I glared at him. 'Of course, I wouldn't dare.'

The last criterion is important; I like my space, I like it a lot. So much so that I typically live alone in quiet areas and don't appreciate a boyfriend who just 'pops round' when he wants to.

'Yeah, if that dork keeps barging in I'd show him the door,' N said of the Boy.

'What, you two are back together?' A1 asked in confusion.

'Nothing's definite,' I said and shot N a nasty look.

'I never liked him, anyway,' A1 said. 'Not in your league.'

See, someone who lives a moderate drive or train ride away is never round your house at all times, eating all the food, leaving mysterious stains on the carpet and getting it on with your neighbour in your bed (far preferable that he plays away with his own neighbour in his own bed). On the other hand, he's not so far that he can't be there at short notice if needed.

However, this was before I moved to London. The relationship between space and time is altered here. Hauling myself from NW5-ish to a central location might take twenty minutes, might take two hours. In any normal place it would take minutes. Has someone contacted the Royal Society to investigate? Once I considered seeing a man in Leyton, and I assure you that the thought of the time it would take to negotiate that distance was a large part of not pursuing the affair. The thought that someone could live only a few miles from me and it would take *longer* than the two-hour ideal to reach him (n.b., this includes the walk or bus from Tube station at each end) was, frankly, blowing my fragile mind.

(I'm sure, in a fitter and more motivated past, I would have ignored the squillion or so people and rat's nest of streets between where I lived and where he lived and hoofed it over. But I am a spoilt lady of leisure now and demand nothing short of first-class comfort. Or, failing that, tributes of love in direct proportion to the effort I make. Such as a small island of my very own.)

Then there was the man who lived several counties away, but could drive to my house in less than two hours. He didn't survive the cutoff, either, because while he could drive to me I could not drive to him. I have no car. Before you think me unnecessarily harsh when it comes to men, I should say in my defence that it was he who ended things with me. I'm not the only one with a two-hour rule.

So I have been trying to have coffee with the neighbour, who lives round the corner from me, and it has taken us, with all the to-ing and fro-ing, about two days to meet.

Extrapolating from this, someone who lives two hours away might be assumed to reside in my kitchen.

samedi, le 27 novembre

The Boy seemed in an odd mood. 'Are you here because you want to spend time with me, or because you just wanted to get out of the city?'

What's this now? Justify your holiday? 'Um, both, really.'

He didn't say anything. Was that the wrong answer? I can not fathom men. Then he nodded, and held my hand, and we finished reading the paper. Later, I licked lemon sorbet off his body. He followed the sweet with a savoury chaser. Most refreshing.

dimanche, le 28 novembre

The Weekend, a quiz

1 The weekend just gone, I went to
a) France
b) Flitwick
c) Fulham
correct answer: a

2 I was accompanied by
a) a committee presenting me with the Légion d'Honneur
b) paparazzi
c) the Boy
correct answer: c

3 The Boy gave me, as a gift,
a) a bunch of bright orange daisies
b) a jar of jam he made
c) a sex swing he made
correct answer: all of the above

4 I came back from holiday with
a) a Tour d'Eiffel paperweight
b) rope burns
c) Lance Armstrong
correct answer: b

5 It has been _____ since I last saw the neighbour.
a) one week
b) two weeks
c) who cares?
correct answer: c

'This means we're back on, right?' the Boy asked nervously.
The train pulled slowly out of the station, and I silently said

goodbye to the trees, the houses, the sun. According to the forecast it was raining in London.

'We're back on,' I said, and he squeezed my hand. My heart did jump, I admit. And we held hands the whole way home.

mardi, le 30 novembre

A hand waved in front of my computer screen, startling me. I looked up. Giles. I took off my headphones.

'Sorry,' I said. 'Helps me concentrate on work.'

'Can we have a chat?' he said.

'Of course.'

'Good. How about tomorrow? I'll have my secretary book something.'

For a horrified moment I thought maybe he meant a hotel room. Then I realised he meant food, and smiled. 'Great.' What the hell is he after? I wondered as he walked away. A chat? Or something more?

Dear Belle

Dear Belle,

Me and my boyf enjoy doing it in the out-of-doors but we find Wimbledon a bit too dark and scary. Can you recommend a top ten list of outdoor love locations?

Dear Al Fresco,

I would do, but none of them are in London at this time of year. Have you considered a nice cosy pub toilet instead?

Dear Belle,

I've been seeing my boss for months and have just received a very generous pay rise. I can't help but feel that this is his way of saying thank you for the pleasure he derives from our liaisons. How do I maintain the upper hand while simultaneously working under him, as it were?

Dear Moral Upper Hand,

I don't understand – you feel bad about being paid for something you would have done for free? I assume from the phrase 'secret liaisons' that either he or you is attached, or you risk being fired for carrying on like this. Decide whether the risk of losing your job is worth the money (and the fun), and stay on or leave as appropriate. And if you do go, be certain he writes a damn good letter of reference. You put in a lot of overtime, no?

Dear Belle,

I'm a respectable Cambridge graduate, and recently met a beautiful girl I want to settle with. She's been honest about her sexual past and she says we must share everything. A month before we met I spent a month in Thailand gorging myself on $10 hookers. I don't dare tell her. Also, sex with the hookers was far better than with her. I don't want to upset her, but do I 'fess up and tell her my past, or just keep a cosy relationship?

Dear Love You Long Time,

There is a time and a place for honesty, and prostitution is simply not it. If having guilt-free, anonymous sex wasn't the original intent, you wouldn't have gone for a working girl in the first place, am I right? Of all the useless and overrated virtues, giving a full and total account of your past lovers and how they rate tops the list. Tell her you fooled around a bit on holiday and leave it at that – only a masochist would beg for more details. As for the other part of your question, if you want the sex with her to be better, sweetie, maybe you should remember that her experience is nowhere near that of a Thai hooker's and take the lead yourself.

Décembre

mercredi, le 1 décembre

'I hope you like Chinese,' Giles said, spreading a large napkin over his lap.

'Love it,' I said. Eating out in Chinese restaurants is a Jewish family tradition; I don't know how or where it started, but by the time I left home I'd probably had more black bean sauce than HP.

'Splendid.' We ordered. I wondered what the etiquette was: does he pay for this? As a call girl, the answer was always yes. I had no idea how businesspeople run things. Would I be expected to pick up my share of the bill? I played it safe and ordered the second cheapest thing on the menu.

'I'll be honest with you,' he said after the food arrived. 'This departmental reshuffle is not going to go in your favour.'

'Oh,' I said and looked down at the food. It smelled of hot chilli and garlic, but I suddenly felt less than hungry. Was this my last meal? Was I really going to get the heave-ho on a Tuesday lunchtime surrounded by loud men in suits?

'I don't think it's any secret that you haven't really gelled with your team members,' he said. His hands were long and elegant, but he clearly didn't know from chopsticks. He gave up and waved the waitress down for a fork. 'And since Erin has more experience and seniority than you, the only appropriate thing to do is to make her your supervisor.'

I stared at the steaming pile of rice between us.

'But I'll tell you something, and I'm counting on your discretion here,' he said.

This is it, I thought. The moment where he asks me to fuck him so I can keep my job.

93

'You're wasted in this place. Sure, you do fine work, and it probably doesn't tax your mental faculties very much. I bet in a year you'll be bored of it and looking for something new.'

Classic man move #361: Let me down easy, make it sound like it was what I really wanted anyway.

'Come the New Year, you won't see me around any more. I've managed to secure some funding, and am striking out on my own. And I want you to be there.'

'Pardon?'

'I'm offering you a job. More pay, and hopefully more interesting than what you're doing now.'

'You mean you didn't bring me here to fire me or fuck me?'

He half coughed, half laughed into his hand. 'Flattering a thought as that is, no,' he said.

Great, now I'd put my foot in it. 'You really think I'm any good?' And, wouldn't he be in trouble for poaching people away from the company?

'I think you have potential,' he corrected. 'That's a lot more than most people in there.'

'So what do I do?'

'Put in your notice but don't tell your team,' he said. 'We'll talk more later.'

jeudi, le 2 décembre

N and I went to the gym together, met A1 and A2 for a late supper at our second-favourite Italian, and repaired *à deux* to mine for digestifs and chat.

I made a note to myself, so I wouldn't forget to write it down later: *Mia Farrow must give good head.*

Conversation went along these lines.

Me: Ironically, by sleeping with men for money, I have managed to avoid anything lascivious or shady in the non-adult-entertainment industry.

94

He: A pity the casting couch seems to have passed into legend. Joan Crawford, they say, has a couple of blue movies making the rounds somewhere.

Me: Yeah. And the famous quote attributed to Marilyn, when she signed her first big contract: 'No more blow-jobs.'

He: Who said 'There goes the good time that was had by all,' and about whom?

Me: I don't remember.

He: Me neither. [n.b. the computer wasn't on and I couldn't be bothered to check. We are a very civilised *salon de jour*.]

Me: It can't have been someone who wore the label of slut with pride, like Mae West. Maybe Jean Harlow?

He: Could be. But what about Bette Davis? I bet she was one dirty fucker. Pretty in an average way, and possibly the best actress of her generation – but with that face, she so must have done anything to get her big breaks.*

Me: Well, it can't have been Katharine Hepburn or anyone like her. Ice queen.

He: I bet not. I hear she swung both ways.

Me: Ava Gardner?

He: You know that quote of hers about Frank Sinatra?

Me: About his being a ninety-seven-pound weakling who was ninety-six pounds of cock?

He: That's the one. Of course, I read once that he had the equipment, but no idea what to do with it.

Me: Honestly, why would he have to? He was Frank. And what did he do with Mia Farrow, anyway? She's like a lollipop woman. She'd break under the strain.

He: Big mouth, though.

Me: I suppose. But Mia Farrow? Married to Sinatra, Previn, Allen? Three guys at the top of their professions? And a skinny little body like that. Hysterical cow, to boot. What's the deal?

He: She must give great head.

It was said by Bette Davis, not about her.

vendredi, le 3 décembre

Being a working girl had its drawbacks, but being this kind of working girl isn't so hot, either. For one thing I have to conduct most of my business among co-workers who are significantly less forgiving than your average client-stealing, rumour-spreading, put-down-making ho. Every time my mobile rings Mira and Erin lean closer – my private life being, obviously, a topic of much speculation since that time the Boy turned up outside work.

(T)he (Boy):	What did you do last night?
Me:	Gym, food, sleep.
He:	Did you eat out or in?
Me:	Out.
He:	Who with?
Me:	Some people.
He:	Including N?

Now, he and N know each other, and everyone has assured me everything's cool. N and I are no longer sleeping together, after all. I know N well enough to know that he's telling the truth. But I'm starting to suspect the Boy wasn't and in fact is *not* cool with this.

I'm also starting to suspect Erin is taking notes, but can't be certain. I try to keep my side of the conversation as neutral as possible. Is the legit life always going to be like this? I have the sneaking suspicion that even if I jump ship there will be office politics wherever I go.

Me: Does it matter? [There is the part of me that thinks this response is probably confrontational and damaging, but it's on holiday this week.]

He: I just don't want to feel like you're lying to me.

Me: I'm not lying to you. Why does it matter whom I ate
     with?
He: Because I saw you walking with him, is all.

Okay, I'll gloss over the fact that he just *happened* to be in
London last night without saying so. He spotted us. And
instead of saying hello, and may he join us, he rings me up
the next day to plant conversational minefields? Whoah.
Fuck. Creepy. Wrong. Can I date a normal person, someday,
please? He goes on about how great Sunday/last month/
France was, and why can't I be more like I was on Sunday/
last month/France. And how he would never lie to me, and
how can I be so two-faced, and so on. Anyway, interminable
minutes more of this before:

Me: Are you really willing to lose me so you can make a
     stupid point about what a perfect person you are?
He: *(silence)*
Me: I think I have to go now.

Ah, now I remember why we split up the first time. Silly me. I
left the phone off the rest of the day.

samedi, le 4 décembre

Switched on the mobile yesterday afternoon to find three
missed calls and a dozen texts. The Boy has got out of hand,
and this has ballooned into what he is calling 'The Lie'.

    From the way he was reacting, you would have thought I'd
told him there was no Father Christmas.

    I don't really class our last conversation as a lie – more an
evasion. Can I help being on edge, especially as I think he's
been going through my things? I went out with friends, one of
them was N, and I didn't immediately ring and tell him. I

didn't tell him when I showered at the gym, either, or the last time I had a bowel movement. Do those count as lies as well? There are people who will say the concepts are one and the same. He certainly proclaims how honest he is with me often enough to have taken up permanent residence on Moral High Ground. But since he had been spying on me, and was clearly setting me up to accuse me of something, I don't feel terrible about what happened.

I was meeting L and didn't feel like ringing the Boy. Unfortunately, tact being one of my weaker suits, we did trade a few texts on my way out. So while I tried to be calm and hold back, telling him 'This is not what I need to come home to' is about as kind and lovey-dovey-girlfriendy as it got. Wittering on about these things in an endless circular discussion is not on my agenda.

I really do make a rubbish girlfriend.

And he didn't change his tone at all. Finally, exhausted by the text tennis, I replied: Good night. I hope your righteous indignation keeps you warm.

Several hours later, after spending a wholly civilised evening with L, draining bottles of white and talking about our respective holidays, I did wonder why things could be so light and easy with almost everyone else in the world. When I checked the phone later, the Boy had texted a goodnight kiss. It's something he never would have done when we were dating before. I waited only a few minutes before sending one back.

dimanche, le 5 décembre

'How's the new place?' I asked. I was holding the phone between my shoulder and ear, simultaneously installing software on the computer.

'Great,' Daddy said with enthusiasm. 'I put a poster on the wall of different types of tuna.'

Was this some sort of newly-single-man-thing? 'Pictures of tuna?'

'You know, to brighten the place up a little. In case I have people round.'

Okay, whatever. Maybe Mum never let him have pictures of fish, or something. I don't know. A little window came on the computer screen: Installation successful, restart now or later? I restarted, tried the password to hide the program, then unhid it. Perfect. From now on every keystroke made on my computer would be logged and stored, with no sign to the user – say, the Boy – that anything was amiss.

'Don't you worry, honey, I'll make you a deal, not to date anyone younger than my daughter.'

What? Date anyone? The ink on the papers was hardly dry. 'Are you sure that's a good idea?'

'Well, it would be a little strange if you ended up with a stepmother younger than you, wouldn't it?'

'Okay, number one, no one you marry will be my anything-mother, because she didn't raise me. And number two, you're dating already? Isn't there some sort of cooling-off period? Some mourning that must be observed?' I said, trying (and failing) not to sound hysterical.

'Honey, calm down. I'm not seeing anyone yet. It's a hypothetical.'

'Cripes, Daddy, don't scare me like that.'

He laughed. 'There's such a thing as being too honest, I suppose,' he said.

'I thought you always told me the most important thing was honesty.'

'It still is. But I'll give you a handy tip. Anyone who goes around telling anyone who'll listen about how honest he is, isn't.'

'That's a comforting thought,' I said. 'Nevertheless, if and when you do start dating, I expect you to be honest with me about it.'

'Well, I think we should make a reciprocal deal – I won't

date anyone younger than you if you won't date anyone older than me.'

I think I have a new contender for Creepiest Conversation In History Ever. 'Agreed.' He didn't say anything about sleeping with them for money, mind. Though I suppose that meant he could see a prostitute who was younger than me.

Okay, now I've made myself squirm twice in two minutes. New record.

lundi, le 6 décembre

I've never been the most conscientious about ringing home, but could always count on my parents ringing me when they wanted a chat. Now they both ring less often – and I can't say it troubles me. It's not that I don't care what's going on in their lives, I do; but after the last conversation with Daddy I've decided I don't want to hear about it.

'You sound a little down, honey,' my mother said.

'What, me? Oh, just things getting to me. Stressful at work lately. You know.' I still hadn't decided what to make of Giles's offer, and had only broached the subject with N, who I knew would offer an opinion only if asked.

'That's a pity. I had so hoped you'd find it less of a strain than your last job.'

Keeping in mind that supposedly my mother had no idea I was ever a call girl, I wondered what she meant by that.

'You know, right after you graduated, when you were in that bookshop.'

'Right,' I sighed. 'The bookshop. It's just different, that's all. That job was boring more than actually stressful.' To be fair, this one was pretty boring as well.

'Changing tack slightly,' she said, by which she always means changing tack entirely, 'I received the most unexpected call the other day. From your cousin, you know.'

'Which one?' I asked. There are so many I've lost count.

My mother's family are numerous and each one more fertile than the last. That she managed to keep the number of her own offspring down to fewer than five is nothing short of a miracle.

'You know, J,' she said, as if that was obvious.

'How is he?' I asked. Even though we are of a similar age, and grew up together, I had no idea what had happened to him after I went to university. I knew he hadn't, and that was all – the rest was implied with whispers and gestures, the sort of thing usually reserved for instances of cancer and divorce. From the emphatic nature of the signals I'd guessed he'd married a cancer-ridden divorcee, or similar.

'He's well, and living in Central America of all places,' she said. 'Mexico, or was it Belize? Anyway, you'll be happy to know that all his problems with the law over that drug-dealing charge are long behind him and that he's really cleaned up his act. Been off the stuff for a year, he says.'

'That's great,' I said. He'd been dealing drugs? I'd had no idea; clearly the Jewish matriarchal sign language has evolved to include such things and I simply have failed to keep up.

'You should ring him up sometime,' Mum said. 'You two were always so close.'

'Were close. I wonder what we'd have in common now.' Apart from making a living on the fringes of legal society, I mean.

'He seemed to think you should go out and visit,' she said. 'I told him your work kept you very busy, though.'

Hmm. Late winter in rainy, crowded London or holiday in the sun? Maybe instead of following Giles to his new company, what I really needed was some time off to think about it. Somewhere warm would be nice. 'Actually,' I said, 'I think I may have some extensive holiday coming up.'

Silly idea, really. Tempting. But silly. Yes. Silly.

mercredi, le 8 décembre

Saw a little girl – maybe ten years old or so? – in Brent Cross yesterday, wearing a pink shirt that had a picture of a bunny and the message ' Get Lost'. Was tempted to offer her money for the shirt.

jeudi, le 9 décembre

Not being a call girl any more has its advantages and disadvantages.

Advantage: leg coverings. No matter how long the coat, how clingy and luscious the skirt, how reliable the stockings, you will catch a chill. The top half is usually underdressed, too (shockingly few punters request cardies), but not to such an extent as the lower half. These days I could go out in cords over tights if I liked, all tucked into fuzzy boots, with no ill consequence save my own sartorial embarrassment.

Disadvantage: transport. Though underdressed for a cold night, one does usually get from point A to point B in a taxi while working the sex trade. Now I stand at a cold bus stop, or sweat down the back of my jumper on an overheated Tube train, and wonder why people choose to leave home at all.

Advantage: selective party attendance. No longer am I required to make someone else's night sparkle. Granted, I spend a lot of time reading in the bath, wondering whether I am still capable of making my own nights sparkle, but at least I don't have to feign interest in work-related conversations while my drunken client staggers into the women's loo. At times my work role was more babysitter than sexpot.

Disadvantage: spending money. Giving lavish gifts is the high point of winter, as is drinking bottle after bottle of pricey fizz – largely to distract the population from the cold. The benefit of hourly, cash-in-pocket work is being able to hit the shops on the way home. And possibly even emerge with a gift for someone.

Advantage: throwing away the fuzzy red knickers for ever. Whoever decided sexy women and Father Christmas were a logical cross should be strung up.

Disadvantage: having to buy my own champers.

Advantage: sunshine. Since a British winter has, on average, about fifteen nanoseconds of daylight from now until March, I spent a lot of previous winter days asleep after late nights out – and never seeing the sun at all.

Disadvantage: personal grooming. I'm no couch potato, but then again, knowing significantly fewer people are going to see me wearing less than three layers this winter is no incentive to keep up with sit-ups, waxing or the like. Sometimes I worry the Boy will tell people my previous occupation – then relax, because the state I'm in, no one would believe it.

vendredi, le 10 décembre

'You can't be seriously considering it,' the Boy said, flipping through old magazines. We'd just come from the shower, where we'd had a lovely fuck. It was like when we were a new couple, it was that good. We'd started by lathering each other, then I fingered his pucker while sucking him off, then he'd taken me up the arse. 'That would possibly count as the most irresponsible thing I've ever heard in my life.'

I shot him a look. This from someone who spent the last three years 'in between jobs' while I was paying a small fortune in taxes? *Typical attitude of his class*, I thought. *They can coast indefinitely and never look the worse for it; but if you're middle-class and take a sick day you're shirking duty to God and country.*

'Besides,' he said, 'no one really does the whole gap year thing any more. That's so ten years ago.'

'Except Susie, of course,' I said.

'Pardon?'

'Susie. Your friend. You know, the one who has her post delivered to your house. You said she was off travelling, right?'

'What are you implying? She's just someone I know. It's not like I'm sleeping with her. I mean, she's fat and smokes and reads *Heat*. She's just keeping a few things at my house, and that's it.'

Wow, methinks the man doth protest too much. 'Mmm,' I said. 'Well, it's a tempting offer. I'd love to get some travelling in while I'm still young. And I haven't seen my cousin in so long. We used to be very close. I hardly feel connected to anyone in the family any more.' *That's it, play the filial guilt card, he can't possibly begrudge me that.* I despise myself sometimes.

samedi, le 11 décembre

The Boy was hardly out the door when I checked the keystroke logs on the computer. I had been at work most of Friday, so he'd had a wide-open opportunity to snoop on my computer.

And he took it, that much was clear. He'd been careful to erase his history in the Web browser so I wouldn't know, and had made a more-or-less good effort to replace everything on the computer desk just where it was, so it appeared he hadn't even turned it on. But he hadn't known about the keystroke logger and I could see everything. He'd checked up on my diary, then cycled through my recent Web activity. And then—What ho? What is this?

Checked his email – password easier to guess than I would have imagined, not that I'd have to guess it now. And then. His own anonymous blog, publically posted on the internet for anyone to see.

I logged on and had a look – and my heart sank. Oh, he was

still seeing Susie, all right. She was away in South-east Asia visiting her dad, but they were definitely still on as far as he was concerned. I guess it was nothing I hadn't already known, in my heart of hearts, but still it stung. He even posted some of the things she'd been sending him, comparing the way she was to the way I am.

That was the horror of it: seeing her most recent email, and how banal it was. She had had food poisoning. Her father's new wife is only a few years older than she is. Had he received her gift in the post yet? If not, never mind. Looking forward to seeing him soon – maybe he could fly out in January?

Love, Kitty.

And that hurt. To find Susie calling herself by the same pet name he'd always used for me was a painful thing to read.

But not as much as finding out about all the other girls.

dimanche, le 12 décembre

Recipe for relationship failure:

Take one large resentment. Age well over time. Marinate with many and detailed notes on what a horrible person your girlfriend has been. Season with endless rehash of her prior job. Stir well with accusations of her cheating to take the focus off your own extracurricular activities, which turn out to be many and varied.

Keep online diary recording your chunterings and conquests, which she finds.

Prepare self for when she opts in favour of extended holiday abroad.

lundi, le 13 décembre

It's the time of year for one of my favourite things: port with cheese. Granted, this could easily be done year-round – cheese already forms a large part of my diet, usually in pickle sandwich form. But there's something so succulent about port and cheese when it is, to paraphrase Donne, the year's midnight.

It remains one of the great disappointments of adult life that the best port list I ever laid eyes on was in the first-class section of a rather nice airline (rather nice, because they upgraded me). Unfortunately it was August and I couldn't bring myself to spoil my winter treat. Also, port on an aeroplane? No, really . . . port on an aeroplane?

It's a truism that food and sex are not only similarly pleasurable, but also may be enjoyed together. Countless Mills and Boon novels and the entire oeuvre of Mickey Rourke have told us so. Usually I would agree, but in the case of port and cheese, I must strenuously argue against. As a prelude to sex, yes, a thoughtfully selected 1985 vintage and some Dorset Blue Vinny can be as potent a seduction tool as a Barry White album. But in the bedroom itself? Never.

Please allow me to qualify the statement. Bailey's is a perfectly acceptable tipple to lick out of the small of a lover's back. Drops of whisky are like a particularly erotic perfume and I've certainly had a gin cocktail, if you know what I mean. But port? In front of the fire, in a small glass, and quite emphatically sitting up.

And, if things with the Boy continue as they are now, possibly the only satisfaction I'll be enjoying over the coming holiday season.

After lunch I pop by Erin's desk to 'borrow' her stapler – mine has been nicked by Jojo, the Malaysian in Personnel. Erin's still at lunch. When I put the stapler back it moves the mouse, and her computer screen comes back to life. A chat window is open.

The employees all use a messenger program to communicate between offices – it's more convenient than phoning and, I've found, saves time when asking questions. Erin's been chatting with Giles, I see. He's almost always online.

< **GilesTheMan** > hey sexy
< **canadienne** > Still thinking about this morning ;)
< **GilesTheMan** > my fingers still smell of you
< **canadienne** > Off to lunch now . . . maybe organise a 'private meeting' later?

My face goes beet red. Not embarrassment; anger. Stupid, stupid girl, I think. And then I wonder how much of this goes on with the Boy and Susie when I'm not around.

Idiots, I think with real hatred. *Every one of them*. Erin and the Boy. Susie and Giles. What is wrong with men? Why do they need to lie, run around, and generally hurt as many people as possible in pursuit of nothing better than a screw? If they really need to get their end away, why can't they do it with a whore?

I'd seen the Boy's pictures of Susie online. She was very young, flat-chested, with short, spiky hair and glasses. The sort of girl I would have pegged as a lesbian, Hey, calm down – I went to a girls' school. But in spite of the fact that I knew I was prettier, that he thought her stupid and hated her smoking, it wasn't much consolation. It made the whole affair, in fact, slightly worse.

And that's what I think about this discovery: how can Erin be involved with Giles? How could someone as singularly annoying as her, as rigorously average, be hanging off the end of his cock for fun? How, in any sort of fair world, does this happen?

My heartbeat is thick in my ears. If it was another place, another time, I'd wait at her desk until she came back and smack her one. Now I just imagine doing so, over and over, and the adrenalin makes me feel ill. Back at my desk I open a chat window and type in a message to Erin. *You idiot*, I write. *Do you want to tell your boyfriend or shall I?* Shall I? Shall I blow the whistle on Erin? Shall I email Susie and tell her what her so-called boyfriend's really been up to while she sends back world-weary missives from the Let's Go! circuit? But my finger hovers over the return key that will send the message, seemingly endlessly, and I find I have neither the hate nor the guts to send it, in the end.

mercredi, le 15 décembre

Met a gentleman late, at his house.

It was an old client. I was there on business.

I needed the money to offset costs for the rest of the month. I needed to go out and relax with an old friend, someone I knew would not judge me. I needed to feel wanted without the problem of having to establish that it was just for companionship and sex, not for ever. And N was busy with his new girl.

Was it cheating? Yes, it was cheating. I'm a fucking hypocrite. I wouldn't have rung the client, wouldn't have even thought of it, if not for that diary. The Boy thought my going to dinner with N justified a drama? He can take a fucking flying leap. What's sauce for the gander is sauce for the goose, you know. I found myself on the other end of the client/whore relationship for once. I needed a quick release, no strings attached. I needed N, but he was off with his new girl, and I didn't want to have to make that call, anyway.

I needed to get the Boy off my mind for a few hours.

The client, M, is older, short but elegant. An ex-jockey who works in the City and keeps a mews house for the weekdays. Likes: white wine, white knickers and light domination. Dislikes: talking about his family, meeting before 10 p.m., paying in small bills. I always left M's house with a fistful of pinks.

He didn't ask questions when I rang him. He said he was free and he'd see me at ten. He handed the cash over. We got straight down to business: brief kissing, his eyes closed, mine open; I stripped slowly, shoes first so we were on eye level. Kneeled to take him in my mouth briefly, looking up to meet his eyes. Stood up and he turned me round. His hands were small and rough; he caressed my bottom and bent me over the sofa. Usually he likes me on top, but this time we didn't even make it to the bedroom. He asked if he could come on me – I said yes; he pulled the condom off and ejaculated on the small of my back.

We were lounging on the floor, half dressed, when he finally asked. He'd rung the agency a month ago; they sent another girl in my place. 'So why all of a sudden, out of the blue like this?'

I shrugged and drained my wineglass. He refilled it. 'No good reason,' I said.

He nodded. The details weren't important. If there was something in my voice, or in my eyes, he let it go. And then the oddest thing. He started telling me about his family, here was a picture of his wife; about his daughter, an artist. He had saved clippings from the paper where her work was mentioned; here was a black-and-white photo, of a curly-haired Jewish woman. His daughter.

Who was older than me.

At the end of the appointment I went up for a shower. Next to the bath was a hairbrush, and wound through it long, dark hair. Just like his wife's hair. Like his daughter's. Or it could have been another call girl's.

'Love is patient, love is kind,' I said to the wet tiles. I

wondered, if I were a wife, how much I would want to know. How much I would be able to forgive.

jeudi, le 16 décembre

It's been a difficult week and I can barely stand to look. But I manage somehow to obsessively read all of the Boy's past emails and his weblog entries. It's a tangled web indeed; he's been a very busy boy. As near as I can reckon, the list of objectionable women in the Boy's life runs roughly thus:

1 Sierra Hohum. Bland, blonde medic who happily admits to not knowing the names of the heart valves. Extremely jolly-hockeysticks. As far as I can tell, he simply idolises her, but she hasn't slept with him. I met the girl several times and was never particularly impressed. Men treat her like some exceedingly rare jewel; can't figure why, since I was at school with six-hundred-plus identical models.

2 Susie. The dark horse. Clearly their relationship is ongoing while she is away in Thailand; less clear is why he lies about that. Possibly something to do with her mother retiring to Costa del Croydon while her father goes off to marry a Thai lady. Or is that ladyboy? Maybe because he constantly refers to her as 'a bit thick' and clearly finds her smoking unattractive. Either way, not the sort of girl he would introduce around at home.

3 Georgie. Like Sierra Hohum, but fan of sci-fi. And will deign to fuck him, judging from email she sent asking whether he avoided catching anything while she had thrush, since her boyfriend seemed to be having odd symptoms. The very thought of people of that class passing round the same STIs to each other makes me retch. Why are men always suckers for a posh accent, pear shape and pashmina? Smokes as well. Clearly he's disgusted by the habit, but can overlook such small defects.

4 Lena. Frizz-haired stick insect I caught him in bed with over a year ago. 'Nothing happened, she was just sleeping next to me in her underwear,' he claimed. His email begging her to give him another chance tells another story. She clearly wised up and moved on. Therefore, in his parlance, 'the one that got away'. Often wonder why I didn't move on, too.

5 Jo. Large, frumpish first girlfriend who is ten years his senior and would happily drop everything – job, boyfriend, house, identity as an autonomous human being – to be back with him. According to him they did it eight times a night, so either she is made of asbestos or she has very low standards for effort.

6 Me. I hate myself for even letting him back in the door tonight. I'm tired and stressed and don't know what to do. Curiosity truly has, if not killed the cat, at least left it significantly grumpy.

vendredi, le 17 décembre

'Girl, you look hot!' Angel said. I was a little apprehensive about introducing her to L, but as it happened they were in the same college at uni, so I needn't have worried. They both knew the Boy, of course.

The Boy smiled, but it didn't go to his eyes. 'You're wearing that?' he'd said as we left the flat. I was dressed in a strapless black minidress with metallic patterned stockings, pink cashmere knee socks and a pair of black stilettos. It was an attention-grabbing outfit and I knew it.

'I thought you liked this dress,' I said. We'd bought it together ages ago; he'd snuck into the changing room to fuck me while I was trying it on.

'Bit OTT for someone else's birthday,' was all he said. There was an accusation implicit in his voice, but fuck it, I thought. I haven't done anything wrong. It's just a friend's party.

Angel was feeling a little fragile and unable to 'deal with public transport', as she put it, so we took her car. It being central London and a Friday night there was not only no such thing as a spot to park, but no possibility that there would be any time soon. We circled further and further away from our destination, trapped in the one-way system. I gritted my teeth and tried to smile. This was going ever so well.

Finally the Boy lost patience and jumped out. 'You stay right here,' he yelled. 'I'll find a space and come back to get you.' Eh? With what, your bat-sense? He slammed the door and jogged off.

'God, I thought he'd never go,' Angel sighed. 'He just talks and talks and never lets anyone have a word in.' *Pot, kettle and black*, I thought, *but she does have a point*. 'Did you see when we were at mine and my housemate was making fun of him? He didn't even notice.'

I nodded. Part of what I had once loved about the Boy was his odd anachronisms, the way he was always up for company, always jolly. But now it seemed like his constant chatter was blustering against some inner void, more annoying than entertaining. He hated anything with a sad ending, never read any of the books I gave him and was enthusiastic about a film as long as it involved a mothership landing during the third reel. Quiet contemplation and being alone were anathema – his mobile was such a constant companion it might as well have been grafted to his ear. The silly turns of phrase I once thought funny turned out to be the common parlance of other men of his class, something I soon realised and used to my advantage as a call girl. He wasn't as sharp as most of the people I knew: unable to speak any foreign language or play an instrument even badly, not a good cook, not well versed in science, modern culture, current events, or . . . anything much apart from sailing and skiing, in fact. Worse still, his wide-ranging ignorance seemed to be a point of pride. Among his crowd this was pretty typical; they enjoyed success without much talent, intelligence or hard work. Among my friends it was embarrassing.

Fucking hell, I seethed. Why am I settling for this moron?

Just as he disappeared a modern miracle occurred – a car pulled out of a space literally metres away. Angel took the better part of a lifecycle parallel parking the car, but managed it in the end. She and L disappeared into the club while I went to find the Boy.

He'd gone. I rang his mobile – straight through to answerphone. Must be on the phone to someone else. I turned a corner, and another, and another, until I wasn't sure if I could find my way back and finally found him walking along, looking at the pavement, deep in conversation on the phone.

He rang off quickly as I approached. 'We've found a spot and have gone in,' I said. 'Who were you on the phone to?'

'Uh, no one,' he said. 'What's your problem?'

'Pardon?'

'You're being short with me. I don't know why you're being like this, and I think I'm going to go home.'

I was confused. Clearly, he was lying about something – he rarely took notice of my moods enough to discern annoyance short of a nuclear explosion. Something else must be going on. 'Come on, nothing's wrong. I just don't want to miss much more.'

He stood firm, arms crossed over his chest. 'You're acting like a freak,' he said. 'I can't deal with you, I'm going home.'

I sat on the kerb. It was cold and my skirt was short; I didn't want to think what I might be sitting in, either. 'Suit yourself,' I said. 'Obviously you have a better offer elsewhere and you're trying to get out of here by blaming me.'

'I don't understand why you always do this to me,' he said. *I always do this to you?* I thought. *It's my friend's birthday we're ruining. Not one of yours. Not that you would ever invite me along, anyway.* 'I need to be with a woman I know I can trust. You're a complete mess.'

'Really,' I said. 'Why don't we just knock this on the head, then? I'm sure you'd be better off with Susie. Or Georgie.'

He was just about to start off again – *I told you for the last time I'm not seeing Susie, she's just a friend, etc., etc.* But he stopped himself. I could tell he wondered how I knew about Georgie, but didn't dare ask.

He sighed. 'If you never acted like this I wouldn't even be tempted by other women,' he said.

'Don't blame me. If you weren't tempted by other women I wouldn't be acting like this.' It felt like my arse was freezing to the kerb. 'I'm going inside to see my friends,' I said. 'Feel free to join me or go elsewhere, as you wish.'

He came back in after half an hour. *On the phone to one of your harem no doubt*, I thought. We left L and Angel and took the night bus home. A man across from us eyed me up the whole way while the Boy stared grimly into the middle distance. Yes, I thought, my eyes playing over the man looking at me. I should definitely get away. Ring J in the morning. Tell him I'm coming, and I'm bringing a bikini, and I mean business.

The Boy left in the morning.

samedi, le 18 décembre

The thing about the Boy is, I have a giant weakness. For his brothers, I mean.

No, not in that way – though they are all attractive enough. He has three brothers, and apart from the one just younger than him, whom I've hardly ever seen and who thinks I'm a slag, I adore them. The youngest two are growing into extraordinary young men, particularly the second youngest, Magnus, who is like a younger version of the Boy. Except a bit cleverer. We have similar tastes in music. And he has some idea how to be economical with his words.

So I was only a little surprised when he rang during the week – he was meeting a ladyfriend in town before Christmas, but wanted to come up the day before; could he stay at mine? I said yes, the sofa is always available to friends and asked where his girl lived. Magnus didn't know what area of London she was in, but had a street name – I looked it up – luckily there was only one street by that name, and it was near the Kensington Olympia Tube station.

He arrived late, so I threw together some pasta and sauce. We ate and drank beer while watching *Spinal Tap*. In the morning he took advantage of the shower and I asked what time he had to be off.

'Not until late,' he said. I suggested we might visit Greenwich – it is one of my favourite places, and I hardly ever have an excuse to go. Plus there is the bonus of seeing the tourist sights by riverboat. It always feels a bit inauthentic going to the Tower of London when you actually live here; viewed from the water, however, you don't look so much the grockle. Magnus agreed. We would pretend to be tourists for the day.

He texted the girl and we took the Tube into town. I noticed how easy it was to spend time with him not talking; a relief after the constant chatter of his brother. *Ah, if only you were five years older*, I thought. But then that wouldn't be possible, and if it was, ethical. I have learned from experience not to sleep with the brother of someone you've already bedded.

We were waiting for the riverboat when he received a text reply. 'Fuck,' he said, and walked off to make a call. He came back with a black look on his face.

'What's wrong?' I asked.

'She doesn't live in London any more,' Magnus groaned.

'What, she just moved?' No, he said. She hadn't lived in London for ages. 'But you have an address, right? We found it on the map.'

'I guess there must be another place by the same name . . . in Nottingham.'

I was helpless with laughter. 'You mean you managed to organise a date without even knowing where the girl lived?'

'Well, we did it all by text. I haven't actually seen her in a year, so, you know . . .'

'What do you want to do?'

He looked at his watch. 'Let's go to Greenwich. I'll get a train later.'

Even though it was cold and windy, he insisted on sitting on seats on the deck. No one else was there, and it had an amazing charm, like London was all ours. I didn't have to pretend to be ultracool and could openly stare at the sights. The King's Reach, the Tower, the *Golden Hind*, the *Belfast* . . . slowly giving way to warehouse conversions around Canary Wharf, then there was the Dome, and finally Greenwich. As the river-boat came up to its pier we saw a man out in a rowing boat, battling the weather and the wake of the boats passing through. 'Madness,' I said, pointing him out to Magnus. 'He must love it,' he said. My fingers and ears were aching from cold, but I was enjoying the day too much to mind.

We went to the Maritime Museum, and I spent ages staring at a giant propeller. What did it come off? How fast did it go? It hardly seemed possible that humans could make and use something so fine and so big, but then I'm aware that there are many other human talents widely divergent from my own more modest ones. We went on to the Royal Observatory, and went for a drink. He asked what I was doing for the holidays: packing mostly, I answered. Put a few things into storage, shop for a swimsuit. No point seeing my family for Chanukah with the divorce and all. Maybe going to Yorkshire to see A4's family.

'You're not coming for Christmas?' Magnus asked.

'Your brother didn't invite me,' I said.

'Really? Mummy told him to ask you. You should come for New Year, at least.'

'I doubt I'd be the most welcome guest,' I said. 'Your brother didn't exactly leave on good terms this week.' I wasn't going to go into the details – Magnus was a friend, but he was a brother first.

He smiled and shook his head. 'You must know what he's like by now. Act in haste, regret at leisure. He'll have been in tears before he even got to the M25.' I nodded and half hoped he was right. But we didn't speak of it again, just went for eel, pie and mash before taking the riverboat back to London. They only had jellied eel that day, not stewed, so I had pie and mash. I escorted Magnus as far as the train station and wished him luck with his lady in Nottingham.

lundi, le 20 décembre

Giles and I met again for lunch. This time I chose the venue: a small Polish restaurant I know well, where the tables are close enough for everyone to hear your business but no one cares enough to notice.

He looked over the menu, amused. 'I'm afraid I'll have to leave the decision in your capable hands,' he said. I waved to the waitress and ordered us both *barzcz* and the huntsman's stew.

'So what have you brought me out here for, then?' he asked, as a smile of amusement flickered across his face.

'I'm sorry to do this to you, but I don't think I'll be able to join you in the New Year.'

'You've decided not to leave your job?'

The waitress plopped two bowls of soup in front of us, cerise where cream had been stirred in. I asked her for some rye bread and she nodded. 'No, I've just reconsidered my priorities,' I said. 'I'm going to do some travelling, really think about whether this is what I want to be.'

He sipped the soup and smiled. I don't think he liked it. I love *barzcz*, the flavour but not the smell. Beetroot smells of sheep shit and dirt to me. But it tastes like rich, sweet heaven. 'It'll be a pity to lose you,' he said. 'You have abilities that will be difficult to replace. Frankly, I'm surprised the company haven't made you a better offer to stay on.'

'There's been no offer,' I said. If he was hinting, he needn't have. Jojo in Personnel accepted my resignation with the same aplomb I delivered it and no one had said a word about it since.

He quit the soup after three spoonfuls. 'I do hope you decide to come back,' he said. 'For purely selfish reasons. You'd be an asset to any firm lucky enough to get you.'

'I would have thought you found the talents of some of my other co-workers a little more compelling,' I said, raising an eyebrow. 'Erin, for instance.'

He smoothed the napkin on his lap. 'Be that as it may,' he said, 'there are some people I find I can . . . collaborate with . . . on an occasional basis. That isn't the same as respecting their professional talents.'

Good on you, I thought. At least you haven't denied it. But I wonder why he bothers with a workplace affair? If he was a friend, I would recommend he spend his time on call girls instead.

Who knows, maybe he already does.

mardi, le 21 décembre

I love A2 and A3, they're mad fun. In a sort of grumpy-double-act way. A3 took the train down from Macclesfield and we went for an Indian, a pre-Christmas, pre-leaving treat.

The problem with A3, of course, is our unresolved issues. A2 can handle me as much as he likes; we've seen each other naked and cross-dressed and with a giant corkscrew dildo up each other's arses. With A3 it's different: someone who's never known you that way takes every touch much more meaningfully.

After the meal we were joking and throwing the mint wrappers when A3 put his hand on mine. 'Now then, quit it,' he said in his thick Northern burr. I have to admit, it sent a shiver through me. He has that power, even if he doesn't know it.

It was like the first night Dr C and I slept together, when we were all out in a group beforehand: A3 stroked my hair, and the intimacy of it, the deliberateness, unsettled me. Even hours later, sated and tired in Dr C's arms I could still feel it.

I felt half guilty, but was sort of glad to be leaving him.

mercredi, le 22 décembre

Went to Covent Garden at lunchtime for some shopping. Had to remember am on mission to procure gifts for other people, not myself – will be limited on the journey to J to what I can carry from the airport.

The atmosphere is festive – fairy lights in the shops, incessant jangle of 'Do They Know It's Christmas?' at all hours of the day, charity muggers in overdrive. There is a gilded carousel outside the Royal Opera: *Leisure Events Proudly Presents London's Victorian Golden Gallopers For Your Pleasure.*

I remember seeing Covent Garden for the first time as an adult – or rather, not seeing it, being then in thrall to a lover who enjoyed walking me through the streets blindfolded, guiding me over puddles and leaf-slick crosswalks. With eyes closed I can sometimes still hear his dry voice announcing obstructions in my ear (steps leading up, uneven stone pavement) and, being new to the South, I learned the smells and sounds of London before seeing it. We spent our little money recklessly, on baubles and silly clothes. The wine velvet dress we bought together and I wore without him, a week later, to a Christmas meal with friends in Yorkshire. When I rang him that night, merrily, to say a stranger had said to let him know he was a very lucky man . . . 'I know,' he said, the disembodied voice as if we were walking around town together, his thin hand hovering at my waist. 'I know.'

He left me the next year and London has never seemed real since. I am free to look at the streets now, eyes open, but it's like walking a film set.

jeudi, le 23 décembre

Public transport is ace; truly it is. There being, of course, no other choice when one does not drive. It's like it or lump it, and I do so like it.

Unfortunately, as in all the best affairs, the love is not requited. Such as at Christmas, when the train companies revoke all the cut-rate tickets, so the charge of riding an overcrowded carriage, standing up, from London to York is roughly equal to the cost of going private on a kidney transplant.

Then the train, which is already running at a deficit of one carriage, is called upon to make an extra stop to collect the passengers from another train which was cancelled.

Finally, said train is then itself cancelled; making the final stop not the city you were hoping to turn up in, but a village about twenty miles away, as it is now late and the train needs to get back to a depot in London for the night so can't possibly go on any further, requiring that the people meeting you are a) themselves armed with non-public forms of transport, and b) willing and able to trek to the middle of nowhere to collect you and costing in petrol an amount about equal to the original cost of the train ticket.

Which A4 was. Public transport, truly a modern miracle.

vendredi, le 24 décembre

'What up,' my cousin J says as if we'd never stopped talking. The line sounds clear, as if he's just round the corner.

I smile. Has it really been so long? Almost half our lives? It has. He says he is well and certainly sounds it. I don't know if the gentle waves I can hear in the background are real or my imagination.

'So are you coming out or what?' he asks. There's no

pressure there. He's so laid back it's like asking someone over for coffee. I can't help but envy the obvious calm in his voice, and tell him so.

'Serenity, girl,' he says. 'It's the journey, not the destination.'

Well, whatever. I start unloading about work, about the Boy, and he interrupts me. 'Hey, just do what you got to do.' I remember when we were young, he so wanted to appear hard and took to talking street – absolutely ludicrous to anyone from our neighbourhood. But I guess, thinking about what I've recently learned of his past, it fits now. He's earned it. 'Just come crash at mine for a while and get some sun. You don't have to decide nothing.'

Oh, but I already have.

samedi, le 25 décembre

Some things never change. A4's mother will always pay over the odds and roast a turkey, even though no one in the family except A4 eats it. I have a single slice of the breast, but to be honest, I don't much like it, either. Everyone else has chicken.

A4's sister-in-law will always scowl at me until I produce my usual gift for her, handmade rum truffles and a mix CD.

A4's brother will grumble if anyone gives him a combination Christmas and birthday card. His birthday's on Boxing Day, but don't you dare buy him a single gift for both occasions.

A4's auntie will nag us both about why we're still single, and why don't we just get back together already?

A4's mum will drink too much and insist on everyone singing carols, and when they refuse will sulk and take unflattering photos of the family as they pass out on the sofa, one by one.

I wish my family never changed.

dimanche, le 26 décembre

When I get up A4 is in his appointed spot, by the television. News is on, not unusual. What's strange is his stillness. I look closer. A giant wave, a tsunami, has wiped out most of South-east Asia.

'Jesus,' A4 says. Being of staunchly Catholic stock, it's odd to hear him utter even this mild blasphemy. 'You don't know anyone out there, do you?'

Apart from Susie? No.

lundi, le 27 décembre

Took the early coach back – no trains. Was tempted to fall asleep, but instead watched mist lifting off the fields. Rail lines along the road joined and parted again, malevolent silver, like mercury. The closer we came to London, the more snow was on the ground. And finally in London it turned to oily slush. Winter wonderland. Wondered how long it would be before I saw it again.

Spent the day packing boxes. Or rather, spent the day wondering just how long I can leave it before starting to pack boxes.

'I'm going to miss the hell out of you,' N said over late drinks.

'Same here,' I said. 'And how's it going with you and . . . ?'

'Henrietta,' he said. 'I don't know. We'll see.'

'Something wrong?' I asked. I'd been so wrapped up in my own drama I had no idea what was going on with N and his girl.

'No, not really,' he said. 'Just get the feeling she might be bored and preparing to move on.'

'She'd be a fool,' I said, putting my hand on his.

'Well, like I always say, there are two kinds of women in

the world, stayers and goers. She's a goer. If she doesn't think I'm The One, it's just a matter of time before she's out the door, and probably sooner rather than later.'

'I'm sorry,' I said. He shrugged. 'Which am I, if you don't mind my asking?'

'Oh, you're a stayer,' he said. 'But you spend a lot of time trying to convince yourself otherwise.'

mardi, le 28 décembre

It must have been Magnus's doing. That's all I can come up with. Either that or he was right – as soon as he left the Boy regretted what happened. He rang to say he was coming to visit, and invited me home with him for New Year.

I checked the Boy's email. Susie wrote to say she will be coming back to Britain because of the tsunami, and she'll arrive in London on the 30th. I can see that he replied, and wonder why he decided not to spend the holiday with her instead.

We meet A1 and his wife for dinner. Our respective mates are told to secure a table while A1 and I go to find a cashpoint, as the restaurant he chose doesn't accept cards. The fresh air is crisp and takes my breath.

'I didn't expect to see him with you again,' A1 said as we were walking back.

'To tell the truth I didn't expect to be with him again,' I said. 'But here we are.'

'Is it going better this time?'

'Not really,' I said. 'But I'm going to stick with it. Find out for once what lies on the other side of the first crisis. See what all the long-term couples are on about.'

He smiled sadly and patted my shoulder. I remember being at his wedding, and how my heart fell when he said his vows to his wife. I didn't expect it, didn't think I'd feel that way on the day, didn't imagine I'd be stood there wondering what it would be like to be in her shoes. We both know it ended for good reasons: he met me too young. I didn't know how to hold my temper then. Still don't, much of the time.

When we got home the Boy seemed a little tired, but I mounted him on the sofa and fucked him hard. I tasted the beer on his breath and myself on his cock. And all I could think the whole time was: *Is this better than Susie? Can she make you come like this?* I'd never fucked with so much resentment, not even when a prostitute.

Sometimes I wonder if I met everyone in my life in the wrong order.

jeudi, le 30 décembre

The Boy was out in the garden with his brothers and I was inside, on the computer, chatting to A4.

> <luvlyjubly> How is it with the family?
> <belle_online> Almost bearable. Thank fuck for his little brothers.
> <luvlyjubly> Is it a nice house?
> <belle_online> As far as these places go. They've stuck me not just in another bedroom, but in another wing.

The Boy's parents had kept his room just as it was when he left for uni, with bunk bed, a stuffed elephant and old water-colours he did at school on the wall. He still received post there, as well. I idly picked up a short cardboard cylinder on the desk and twirled it round.

> <belle_online> Anything special planned for new year?
> <luvlyjubly> Same as last year, going to P and R's for drinks.

<belle_online> How many people are they having over?

<luvlyjubly> Not too many, it's usually about a dozen I think.

The postmark and stamps on the tube were odd, covering half the surface – where on earth had that been posted from? I opened the tube and extracted a rolled piece of card. It was calligraphy of some sort, drawn in wide brushstrokes. The characters were unfamiliar, not Chinese, something else. I looked closely at the smaller writing along the bottom, scratched out in English. The Boy's name. And Susie's. And a love heart. My stomach turned.

<luvlyjubly> How about you?

<belle_online> I think we're going to the fireworks with his brothers and parents. Though considering his dad that implies an all-night brandy-drinking sesh afterward.

I looked again at the postmark. She must have sent this as a Christmas gift, before she knew she was coming back. I rolled the paper and put it back in the tube.

<luvlyjubly> Well, I don't envy you there.

<belle_online> As well you shouldn't.

I left the computer and went off to listen to music. Billie Holliday. The down-turning strings, the voice cracking, always just behind the beat. Unbearable, given the circumstances, but somehow nothing else would do.

vendredi, le 31 décembre

The tender could only hold three people at a time, so the Boy rowed his parents out to the boat first, then his brothers, then came back for me. I hadn't brought wellies so had to borrow an old pair of the youngest brother's. They were several sizes too large, and damp, to boot – my feet were already freezing and I reckoned the rest of me would join them shortly. But I'd had a few whiskies before we set out and was counting on a kiss at midnight, so it didn't matter awfully.

In the dark the Boy's face seemed shockingly young. 'I'm really looking forward to this,' he said, but his smile was more of a grimace. 'I've always had such wonderful memories of us sailing this boat together.'

'I'm surprised you remember,' I said. He was right; it was a good time then, before I started working with the escort agency and before he started fooling around. For a moment I almost remembered what it felt like, being dizzily infatuated and so happy I thought my face would crack. The first time I met his family his father urged him to marry me. He didn't – but I sometimes wonder how different the last few years would have been if he had.

The Boy flicked the oar and the tender turned so we were crossing the current. The lights offshore brightened the faces of his family, now standing on the foredeck the better to spot the fireworks when they started.

'Of course I remember,' he said. 'You're the only girl I've ever taken out on the boat. I think of it as ours, somehow.'

Now this really rubbed me up the wrong way. I knew for a fact it wasn't true. In his Web diary he had pictures of his large ex, Jo, weighing the inflatable rubber tender down at a dangerous angle on the way to the mooring. The diary also made reference to showing a Japanese girl the finer points of seamanship from the main bed of the berth. He'd promised Susie a thousand times in email that he'd take her sailing round the Isle of Wight when she came back. Why did he have to throw out such an obvious lie? I had been enjoying myself until then.

More to the point, why didn't I call him on it? Maybe it was guilt about prying into his diary. Maybe I thought it would all blow over. Or maybe, somewhere, I still felt a little bit bad about his having to date me while I was turning tricks, even though it shouldn't have made a difference.

Shouldn't have, if we'd been honest with each other. If he'd told me right away that he had problems with it, instead of acting like an arse whenever I spent money, and then fucking around on the side.

'Really? I figured it was a rite of passage for all of your kitties,' I said curtly. We reached the yacht in silence and Magnus helped me aboard.

Dear Belle

Dear Belle,

I'm a strong, outgoing, feminist kind of girl, but have a boyfriend who views me as an object. We went swimming the other day and he went into a strange mood afterwards. I eventually dragged it out of him that he was really embarrassed about the size of my thighs. I couldn't decide whether to laugh or cry. Ditch him?

Dear Tender and Juicy,

Sorry, but was he not already familiar with the sight of your thighs? If anyone is going to treat you like an object, please make it someone for whom a generous girth is a pleasing thing. There are men in this world who will worship your thighs like the temple pillars they are. So dump this fool and go find one. Now.

***

Dear Belle,

I have finally found a boy I like. Trouble is, he has a broken cock. By which I mean he has a constriction in one of his tubes which means he can't come. I suppose I shouldn't really mind, seeing as he can do other stuff. But I want the whole shebang. And it would require years of surgery. How long can a girl last when she isn't getting her dessert?

Dear Traci Lords,

Unless a protein facial is your kink of choice, I don't see a problem here. It isn't as if he doesn't want to come with you – he physically can't. And barring the condition causing him serious pain, it's not an issue I would force. Chances are he's already rather gun-shy (so to speak) about it. If a faceful of salty spray is an absolute must for you, take him on holiday to the Western Isles and do it on a rocky beach.

***

Dear Belle,

I am a circumcised teenage virgin and would like to know what kind of reaction I could expect from a girl upon her discovering my distinct lack of foreskin. Would you be so kind as to hazard an informed guess, so that I can prepare myself for any likely outbursts on her part?

Dear The First Cut Is the Deepest,
   Personally, I prefer uncut, but it seems that most ladies if given a choice like a man who's had the chop. They seem to think it's more hygienic. Any initial reaction you get will probably be more curiosity than horror, and I wouldn't expect it to harm your chances of receiving regular blowjobs. In fact it may enhance them.

━━━━━◆━━━━━

Dear Belle,
   My boyfriend is wild in bed but a Conservative at the ballot box. In your experience, is politics a good way to tell whether you'll have a stud or a slug in the sack?

Dear Swing Voter,
   Political leanings have nothing to do with quality of sex. There's a persistent image of Tory men as more kinky, but trust me, sexual perversion knows no political, racial or cultural bounds. But I have to ask: is he thinking what you're thinking?

Janvier

samedi, le 1 janvier

Resolved: to put an end to sleepy-sex.

Everyone has an internal sex clock; my alarm sounds about twice a day. While the half-asleep roll and shag can sometimes be an efficient way to hit the snooze, it should by no means form the majority of couplings. Even tense periods in the relationship are no excuse: if the sex is all we have, we should be trying, damnit! I fear complacency is setting in. Sometimes I can't remember if we actually had sex or I just dreamed it. Considering my plans to leave in the next fortnight, though, this won't be a problem much longer.

Resolved: to organise and categorise sex toys.

They're everywhere: in the bathroom cupboard, a box on top of the wardrobe, or at the back of the closet. While the concept of a dedicated piece of furniture specifically for vibes, whips and the like smacks a little of saddo 'lifestyler', there has to be a better storage solution than this. Also may be restrictions on number of dildos one can take in carry-on baggage these days.

Resolved: to stop fancying men of inappropriate age.

While men ten years younger than myself are available and seemingly everywhere, they have little to offer apart from relative firmness of the flesh. Charming eighteen-year-olds are simply not going to deliver the goods I require without serious tutelage. If the boyfriend doesn't pull it together, hopefully my age cohort is capable of something else worthwhile. Though perhaps the possibility of pulling anyone while away is too horrible to think about yet.

Resolved: to reintroduce my feet to high heels.

Yes, the pavements are deathtraps in winter. Yes, there is

no good reason to wobble about in strappy sandals, given my current lifestyle. The popularity of Uggs attests to the fact that women prefer comfort to style. But strangers whistling at you is a solid defence against the chill of winter, and it never happens in trainers. Also, I plan to be clad in more weather-appropriate shoes when I go to see J, so this may be the last outing the old stilettos have for some time.

And seeing as my sexual activities will probably be severely curtailed in less than a month's time, here are a few suggestions for you, Dear Reader:

1 Change the time of day for your lovemaking
   If you always leave sex till the last thing at night, odds are the variety is suffering for it. Granted, with demanding jobs and children underfoot, finding the time can be difficult . . . but then, who said pleasure comes easily? Schedule a lunch-time quickie with your lover, or call in all your favours to organise a midweek day off.

2 Have an open mind
   If one partner refers to various sex acts as 'the thing we seldom do' or 'the thing we never do', there's a problem. Yes, you might want a tame massage while he wants a no-holds-barred dungeon scene, but isn't give-and-take what strengthens relationships? Do everything once before you decide – twice, just to be sure you weren't doing it wrong. If you don't like it, at least you've tried.

3 Talk to your friends . . .
   . . . honestly. Sometimes it can be liberating to hear people say what they do in bed. And explore your own sexual past – is there something you used to do, and miss? Are there ways and means of getting your current partner to change the routine? Friends are also a great source of information, such as where to obtain props (of both rugby and sexual varieties).

4 Make mistakes
   As the sages say, 'tis better to have fisted and failed than never to have tried at all. Or something. What would you

rather have, a bank full of racy memories to rely on when you're drooling on your deathbed, or a spate of predictable, though tasteful, reminiscences that are all the same?

5 Watch porn

I don't buy this debasement-of-women nonsense. I don't buy the white-slavery argument. The vast majority of erotica does not harm anyone and buying a Jenna Jameson video doesn't bankroll pimps in Prague. Watching porn will not make you a sociopath. There is something for every taste at every level of raunchiness. Even if what turns you on is watching fully clothed men rub against lamp posts . . . If a kink exists, the porn is out there. Find it.

dimanche, le 2 janvier

I have begun to wonder whether it's not too early to go under the knife.

I know: someone who traded on her naked body for a living really has no right to be considering cosmetic surgery. Especially before middle age.

I blame television. And the holidays. Sat around with little to do but eat my body volume in mince pies, the television became the staple entertainment of the month. I emerged the other side with not just a half-stone of holiday weight, but a shocking addiction to makeover programmes.

You would think, as a former call girl, that having naked pics on a website up against the best airbrushing has to offer would have burrowed into my self-esteem years ago. But no, it's the sight of middle-aged housewives undergoing dodgy rhinoplasty that has me wondering whether Belle's still got the goods.

Until now I had always been happy to accept what I was given – we can't all be born Angelina Jolie – and make the best of it. Granted, my parents are both attractive people and

I'm fairly sporty. My breasts have so often been described as perfect that I believed the hype. But now it seems beauty is not just about genetic good fortune and what is easily achieved through diet, exercise, hours of painful waxing and installing flattering lighting throughout the house. Anyone who considers herself perfectly sexy straight out of the box is clearly in the minority.

Watching these shows, I'm horrified. Nothing is sacred, no fault too minor to be laser-sculpted into oblivion. Even labia aren't exempt from the surgeon's knife. I can only imagine the effect this will have on call girls. How long before agency websites start including genital close-ups, and women with pert and juicy lips will have to go to great lengths to assure jealous friends theirs are real? Perhaps it's a good idea to stay retired.

lundi, le 3 janvier

Every couple enjoys a certain amount of private code-making; it's part of the pleasure of having someone in your life. Over time the stilted, awkward get-to-know-you conversations give way to a sort of shorthand that only the two of you understand. It's part of what holds two people together, lets each know the other thinks they're special. It's the little things that keep a long-term relationship afloat.

Here are two of ours:

1 'I believe you' is simply a more polite way of saying 'Enough already.'

'Er, honey, it seems a little strange to me that this girl Susie has her post delivered to your house, sent you love calligraphy from her holiday, and is storing things in your bedroom while my spare belongings are relegated to the damp basement. Oh, and you call her by the same pet name you used to call me. You wouldn't happen to be sleeping with her, would you?'

'Of course not! How could you possibly think such a thing? I would never cheat on a girlfriend! You are such a hypocrite!' (ad nauseam)

'I believe you.'

2 'Mmm' means 'You're wrong/ignorant/laughable, but I can't be bothered to labour the point.'

He: Wind farms are a real blot on the landscape. I can't imagine why we haven't gone completely to nucular power yet.

Me: (softly, eyes closed) Nuc-le-ar, dear.

He: Pardon?

Me: Nuclear. You said nuc-u-lar.

He: (after long silence) Sorry, but I can't tell the difference between what you said and what I said.

Me: Mmm.

mardi, le 4 janvier

'You, my dear, are positively jet set these days,' L said.

'Oh, darling, don't I know it. What with that EasyJet trip to Prague last year and all. And not forgetting the Eurostar.'

'Care for some company on your sojourn?'

'Really?'

'I was thinking of taking a few months off later in the year. Asia, don't you know. But I reckon after the tsunami and all, it might be a better idea to go elsewhere.'

'Really? Shouldn't you be looking for, you know, work or something?' Bit of a moot question. Her mother has a collection of Jags. And no visible means of support. I guess L is simply carrying on a proud family tradition.

'Job, schmob.' L waves her hand. 'It's all a cover for being a lady of leisure.'

'All right, then, you just say when. Mi casa and all that.'
'Oh, I will,' L smiled.

jeudi, le 6 janvier

It's late; I daren't look at the clock. My theory of getting too few hours of sleep is that if you never know exactly how under-rested you are, you won't feel the full effects of staying up later than you should. But I've been thrashing about for hours doing nothing more than making the sheets damp and I know I'll wish I'd taken a sleep aid come morning.

Thin shafts of streetlight poke between the curtains. I'm alone with my thoughts, never a good pairing to begin with, far worse now. Am I making the right choice in leaving? And when I leave, will I be single – or not?

I know what the answer should be. I know what the magazines and website quizzes say. But I can't escape the feeling that under the bravado of the media is an unspoken struggle that every woman, someday, will likely go through. How many wives of my clients spent nights like this? I have a few phone numbers – women who found my number jotted somewhere and phoned me to make accusations. I saved all those numbers in my phone as 'Don't Answer', 'Angry Wife' and so on. Can I ring them up now, ask how they did it, how do you deal and when do you know not to?

When does love trump good sense, and for how long? The Boy rang me late, whispering; I imagined a sleeping body in another bed somewhere, maybe sleeping through his phone call to me, maybe not.

I thought he might be calling to wish me luck on my last day at work. As usual, we wallowed in the minutiae of his day until I was grumpy about the state of our relationship.

'Why do we go on like this?' I moaned. 'We only really like each other about half the time. Perhaps less than that.'

'We're tied up in each other,' he said. 'We share too much

to just walk away.' And though it was a simple-minded thing to say, especially considering where I thought he was, it was true. My love for him had yet to die, and I didn't think I could bear leaving him before it had.

As N said, I'm a stayer. For my sins.

vendredi, le 7 janvier

There is very little to signify my last day at work: handing in the identity card that opens the outer door and the key for the door to the office, packing my sparse belongings in a box that has been provided, and even though it is barely larger than a shoebox it dwarfs the few things inside: a few pens, a half-used notepad and a reference book. There's nothing of interest on my computer, but I upload my work files to the company server and reformat the disk anyway. At lunch someone takes my chair away; it's been bagsied by a pregnant woman in Billing. Every time I do something I think, *This is the last time I'll use the toilet here. This is the last cup of tea.*

'Are you gonna need this?' Erin bangs her fist on the top of a filing cabinet at the end of my desk. I shake my head. I only ever used it for storing my work bag, when I still had appointments.

This is the last time I'll hear Erin's voice.

This is the last time I'll walk out this door.

'Hellooooo? You fergot yer mouse pad!'

'Keep it,' I say, back to the window. *Okay, that was the last time. With luck.*

samedi, le 8 janvier

I don't consider myself sentimental – not when there's a big floppy sop like the Boy to compare myself with – but I had to make certain before leaving that the few things left at my mum's house that still mattered to me would be safely stowed away until I came back, including:

- the bootleg Material Issue T-shirt a friend sold to everyone in A-level art instead of doing her projects,
- every broken pair of earphones, because you never know,
- a museum-sized hoard of costume jewellery I never wear – again, you never know,
- an entire roll of blurry photos from the week I met A3,
- two Ikea lamps I never remember to buy replacement bulbs for,
- all the notes from my degree (a surprisingly slender collection, that)
- two pairs of slippers, though I hate slippers, and
- countless CDs yet to be transferred to MP3.

It's all about legacy, innit

dimanche, le 9 janvier

The Boy met me at home just as I was taping the last of the boxes shut. Anything that was left had either been in the flat to start with, was going to a charity shop or was being squeezed into my luggage for the plane.

'I presume you'll need me to take these in for a few months?'

'No, I've already made arrangements,' I said. A4 was hiring a car and after I'd gone would be coming round to check the post, drop off my keys with the estate agent and take my things to his.

'Oh, you should have said,' he said. His face drooped. I suppose he'd assumed I would be asking him for last-minute favours; it never occurred to him that I could be more organised than that. And there were plenty of good reasons not to keep my belongings at his. For one thing, I knew the cupboard under the stairs in his house was already full of boxes of Susie's crap and that, due to the tsunami, she was coming back earlier than expected; for another, I knew he couldn't be trusted not to go through my stuff.

'Not to worry, he offered,' I said, referring to A4. 'Anyway, I want to spend the time with you rather than spend it moving boxes.' And if we happen to split up soon, at least I won't have to collect my boxes from your house – or send someone else to do it.

lundi, le 10 janvier

The Boy and I planned to go out but we had to change tack. The hurry of packing had left me a little worn, and I was feeling fragile and on the edge of getting a cold. My throat was raw and my muscles had the feeling of meat left too long on the bone. I didn't feel bad about changing plans – it wasn't very nice outside, anyway. He doesn't take not getting his way very well, but even he understands that not to make a show of sympathy is a bad idea. 'Is there anything I can do to make you feel better?'

Sex for starters, I thought. I smiled weakly. 'The muscles in my legs are aching. You could massage them.'

The Boy frowned. It's not what he meant. I'm usually not bad at translating from Man to English, but assume by his reaction what he really meant me to answer was *No, love, you go do something else, I'll suffer in silence.*

I'm not the sort of girl to suffer in silence. I pouted and

indicated the massage oil. He poured some into his hands, rubbing them together so it would warm. He then applied himself to my left thigh, slowly at first.

'You can go harder,' I said.

By the time he was massaging my right calf, my foot resting on his shoulder, he was stiffening. When he reached the toes of that foot he was hard. He shifted so he was coming out of his shorts, put my other leg on his shoulder, and scooted up the bed until he entered me.

'You go on top,' he said.

'I haven't the energy,' I protested. Plus, I loved the way his cock felt inside me at this angle. He reached down and grabbed my breasts roughly, harder than he ever had, hard enough to leave marks. I love that. I ground myself into him and felt his shorts – still on him, pushed to one side – sodden with my juices. He came, then coaxed me to orgasm before taking me the same way again.

We drank the red I was saving for something nice, and ate crisps, spreading crumbs all over the floor. His hands danced under my white dressing gown. We fucked again, him leaning me up against the sofa, then over the boxes in the hallway.

No sense getting too much sleep the night before I leave.

mardi, le 11 janvier

'What can I do to bring you back?' the Boy murmured into my hair. Pedestrian traffic to the ticket hall parted around us.

'Stay faithful,' I said. There was no reply and we held each other quietly for a moment in the noisy airport; after all, what could either of us say? He believed nothing he did should ever be questioned. I believed he'd be in someone else's arms within an hour of my departure. I knew from the website that Susie had come back from Thailand and was disappointed he hadn't collected her from the airport. The only way for this farewell, this moment, to exist was by our unspoken mutual agreement not to challenge each other's untruths.

We played the goodbyes just as they should be done, with long kisses and clinging at the point of separation, and yes, once past the whisky stands of the duty-free and the purgatorial waiting area I allowed myself to cry.

But not for that long. Sometime tomorrow me, my bikini and two suitcases will be in another country where it is sunny and warm.

mercredi, le 12 janvier

The drive from the airport is a long one. In the dark I have no sense of where I am now: only that it's warm and the air is heavy, smelling of the sea.

Air travel is a sort of miracle, isn't it? Just this morning I was freezing cold in London. Now, even stripped down to a T-shirt and trousers, I feel too hot. I can't stop my head swivelling as we drive from the airport into town, trying to decipher the bright signs, the unfamiliar road markings, the voices on the driver's radio.

I'm the last person to be dropped off. The van drives away from the dark bungalow. J had said the key would be under the mat, but when I check, it isn't. Great.

'*Buenas noches,*' a low voice comes out of the trees.

'Hello? Is anyone there?' I can't see anyone, but the bushes rustle ominously.

'Good evening, are you cousin?' A small man shaped like an inverted triangle steps into the garden and points at his chest. Tomás.'

'Hello, Tomás,' I say, setting the bags down and reaching out to shake his hand. He doesn't offer it and my arm drops back down.

'I have key,' he says. 'Your cousin thought maybe safer.'

'That's great.'

'You speak Spanish?' he asks, with a little hope in his voice.

'I'm afraid not.' He nods as if this is the expected answer. I feel a bit of a twat. 'But I'd love to learn.'

Tomás beams. 'Tomorrow maybe I come by?' He opens his right hand and gives me the key.

jeudi, le 13 janvier

It's late when J finally turns up. Or rather, it's early: by my reckoning it was somewhere between half three and the dawn chorus. Not that there really is such a thing here – with insects singing all night you hardly notice when the birds wake up and join in.

I stumbled out of the bedroom. 'Oh, wow, here you are,' J said, as if I'd just come back unexpectedly from a trip out of town. He was a lot taller than the last time I'd seen him, and a lot more tanned. His eyes looked tired and a little crinkly. 'I didn't wake you, did I?' He leans in for a rough hug. His shoulder is huge and freckled and smells of soap.

'Don't worry about it,' I said. 'You all right?'

'Wicked,' J said. 'How's the crib?'

'The crib is fine,' I smile. 'Did you have a nice night?'

'Yeah, good, actually. A mate of mine just bought a DVD player so I went round and we watched scary movies.' In person his voice sounds a lot less affected, a lot less street; but I also notice it's diverged significantly from mine; it sounds quasi-Jamaican, sing-songy.

'If you go to bed now you'll have bad dreams,' I taunt.

'Good thing I'm not going to bed, then,' J said. 'How about some coffee?'

'Rule number one,' J says, flopping on the bed while I grind my teeth into stumps, 'is that nothing around here works. I have a mobile, so when the landline's down – and it usually is – you're welcome to it if you need.'

'Ta,' I said. Actually, I made it online for a brief time before the connection inexplicably failed. I'd forgotten how long and slow the Web can be on a dial-up. But it wasn't the country's dodgy infrastructure that was getting my goat. It was the Boy, who according to his recently updated weblog had gone straight from seeing me off at the airport to Susie's bed. And he was upset.

Not because I left; because Susie had evidently gone off him sometime between leaving for a year out and seeing an entire island washed away. She was refusing to have sex with him. If I hadn't cried I would have laughed, or something like that.

J leaned over and switched off the monitor. 'That shit's a waste of time,' he said. 'You want to go to the beach? Drive somewhere? You need to go shopping?' I asked him what we had to eat and he shrugged. 'I'm no cook. Come on, let's go get you something.'

We walked round the corner to a grocer. I blinked against the strong tropical light, eyes watering. J took off his sleek sunglasses and put them on my face. I noticed he had tan lines at the sides of his ears from the glasses. But they helped.

'Rule number two,' J said. 'Let's get this done and dusted first – no alcohol in the house. I don't go out to the bars, so if you want to go, ask Tomás to take you. Some of them are not nice places for women on their own.'

'Okay,' I said.

'And if you have prescription drugs, put them out of sight,' he continues. 'It's a daily struggle for me to stay clean, so I need to know you're on my side.'

'Of course I am.'

The grocer was an old man, fat, and spoke to us in English.

'That's nice,' I murmured to J. 'But shouldn't we be at least trying to speak Spanish to him?'

J laughed. 'He doesn't speak any more Spanish than you or me. Almost half the people here don't. He's Greek. Rule three: most people here are tourists. Even the locals.' I selected a few strangely large citrus fruit, a can of beans, bread and a weird, star-shaped fruit. J carried our bags home.

samedi, le 15 janvier

J left me a bicycle and a note with instructions to find my way around. I smile: I didn't learn to ride a pushbike until I was a teenager, and it was J who taught me.

All the houses are small bungalows with improbably lush gardens. There are a lot of shops, I notice, and a lot of pay phones. An oddly high concentration of dentists (at least, I think they're dentists' offices).

I need a hat. After half an hour the back of my neck is prickling hotly. I've never burned easily; on the other hand, a Yorkshire summer consists of about a net hour of direct light every year. And while an occasional trip to the sunbed was de rigueur for a call girl, I hardly went often enough to build up a base tan. Happily, this is the tourist section, and as far as straw hats go I am spoiled for choice.

dimanche, le 16 janvier

We leave the doors open when someone's home, because it's hot. Tomás lets himself in. The screen door shuts loudly behind him, a hollow aluminium clatter. I jump up from the computer, where I've been agonising over the Boy's weblog again – should I post an arch, suggestive comment, or otherwise let him know I know?

146

'Oh, hi!' I say. 'I thought you were corning around days ago.' Tomás shrugs. Punctuality clearly isn't a priority. 'You going to teach me Spanish today?'

He laughs. 'You think you can learn in one day?'

'Probably not,' I smile. He helps himself to a fizzy drink from the kitchen – it's frighteningly green and, I guess from the label, supposed to taste of lemon. Today,' Tomás says, flicking on the television and sitting on J's sofa, 'only watch Spanish television.'

'Okay,' I say. 'Anything in particular?'

'I came over to watch the sports. You mind sports?'

'I don't mind,' I say. Lesson one consists of catching up with the football. Which is pronounced futbol. This may take longer than I hoped.

mardi, le 18 janvier

Phone message in the morning from the Boy on the landline. I do the maths: he rang about 4 a.m. UK time. Sigh. Try not to take it personally. I ring back.

He doesn't ask about the flight, or how I'm settling in. Probably just as well; apart from 'long' and 'fine', I haven't much to say. He natters on about friends or something – it all seems so far away now.

'When is a good time to ring you?' he asks.

'Mid-afternoon, I suppose,' I say. 'If that's not too late for you.' I don't mention the timing of his last call.

'Good, I'll ring you tomorrow,' he said.

'If the phones are up,' I say.

'If the phones are up. I really do miss you and love you, you know.' I put the phone down. Why the renewed enthusiasm? I wonder. Susie must be serious about the embargo on fucking. I have to admit, the thought makes me smile, even though I know he won't like going without sex for long. And knowing what a reserve of girls he has standing by, he won't have to.

Tomás invited me round for a meal just after sunset. He's in the kitchen chopping and slicing with the speed and scant attention of a pro. 'Are you a chef?' I ask. He shakes his head. He preps and waits tables in his brother's restaurant on the beach.

He goes through the names of the vegetables – *zanahorias* (carrots), *cebollas* (onions), *hongos* (mushrooms). I ask him for a piece of paper, so I can write them down, but he says no. 'You want to speak Spanish,' he says 'you learn by doing.'

I nod. He offers a beer, which given the lack of alcohol at J's seems like a flood after a drought. I have just one, thinking it might not be a great idea to go home smelling of beer.

Tomás produces a lot of food – far more than two people could eat, surely – and though I have no idea what most of it is, I eat loads and it's all tasty. So he's cooking as well as teaching me a bit of Spanish – wonder what's in it for him? A girl could certainly get used to this sort of treatment.

'Is it okay?' he asks. I nod, and ask him how to say something is tasty.

'*Este está sabroso*,' he says slowly. I repeat it. Is this a date? I wonder. He's not my type. On the other hand, the language barrier means only essential conversation is exchanged – a relief after the non-stop wittering of the Boy. And his gentle openness is very different from the clients I used to see, who usually kept their guard up as long as you possibly can with your clothes off. He's not at all like I imagined Latino men, not conceited or chauvinistic that I can see, and that is awfully sexy.

Corner shops abound here. They are called *bodegas* and sell everything from cans of tomatoes to phone cards, just like at home. Even the Greek grocer offers aspirin and cut-price coach tickets on the side. But my favourite by far is the corner shop you can't go inside. It's shaped like a giant T, made to be driven or walked up to. You tell the man inside the shaft of the T what you need, he tells you how much it costs, and the transaction is conducted through a tiny window. Like when the garages at home lock up the walk-in bit after 10 p.m., except without the danger that implies.

The man smiles at me through the tiny window.

'Where are you from,' he asks as he goes to fetch my drink.

'England,' I say.

'England? I have a cousin who lives in London,' he says. 'Is that where you are from?'

It's close enough and not worth a mini-geography lesson. 'Yes,' I say.

'You come here three days in a row for a chocolate milk,'

'*Me gusta leche chocolatada*,' I say slowly. Okay, I probably sounded like a complete tit there. But I reckon it's use it or lose it.

He smiles indulgently, but continues to talk to me in English. 'You have a boyfriend?' he asks.

'Yes, in England,' I say, losing the energy to try the Spanish for that.

'He left you here on your own?'

'I'm afraid so.'

'He's a confident man,' he says, handing the drink through. I am straddling the pushbike so almost drop it, but manage not to.

'*Yo la tengo*,' I say, smiling. I've got it. He smiles, too, and I ride away. Two. Whole Sentences!

Apart from J, Tomás and the man trapped selling chocolate milk from a giant T, no one takes notice of or speaks to me. In this way it's a lot like London. On the other hand, I do go around in a hat and giant sunglasses, whizzing past on the rusty bicycle, so there aren't many opportunities for chatting. But you get to see a lot this way, and figure out the local tribes.

Type 1: Resentful local. Speaks Spanish about you in front of you, on the (usually correct) assumption that you don't understand. Often to be found working in restaurant kitchens, probably spitting (or worse) in your soup as we speak.

Type 2: Invisible local. Who are they? Where do they live? Whose offices are in the shiny-windowed buildings scattered through town? No one will say. Possibly conspiracy of some sort, though unless involving coconuts I don't see what it could be.

Type 3: Long-term resident. Also known as 'Gone native'. Has tanned self to deep shade of shoe-polish brown. Has mastered six words of Spanish to be used at all opportunities and without embarrassment. Does not own socks; is in fact close to forgetting what they are for. Rides bicycle.

Type 4: Recent convert. Has bought a wardrobe of vomit-patterned shirts and is determined to wear them all in effort to enforce 'relaxed' lifestyle. Has mastered six words of Spanish to be used at all opportunities, but still apologises for not knowing more.

Type 5: Honeymoon couple. From daybreak to 11 a.m., horrified by the other people populating the carefully selected location of their dream holiday – the brochures never showed quite this much vomit. From 11 a.m. to next morning, too drunk to notice.

Type 6: Tourist. Called 'tourons' by the English-speaking expats. You know, as in 'tourist' + 'moron'. Tourons drink a lot. They scream a lot. Pay for things you can find for free on the beach. Consider volume of hot chilli intake at mealtimes to be in direct proportion to level of manliness. Bit like being at home, really.

lundi, le 24 janvier

I love J, I fucking love my cousin. How did I manage so long without him in my life? He is so the man, for reasons including, but not limited to:

- His taste in music fucking rocks. That is to say, he owns all the CDs I never quite got round to buying. All of Dr Dre's solo releases? Check. The entire back catalogue of The Donnas? Check. Granted, these were probably all purchased with drug money, but I don't think that makes it ethically wrong to borrow them.
- He uses my face creams. Without asking. This might not seem like a good thing. But you expect male relatives to ridicule your collection of toiletries, not raid it. One day I came home and he was on the sofa, watching the football, face slathered in a pore-tightening clay-and-sea-mineral mask. Okay, so he was probably using twenty quid's worth of product without my permission. On the other hand, he's not asking me for rent. It seems a fair exchange.
- He loves scary movies. I love scary movies! At last! Someone I can watch them with! More gore = more better. Apparently Tomás has a wide collection of horror films as well. Ace.
- J is an unashamed consumer of junk food. I have always felt that one of the privileges of being an adult is the ability to eat chocolate for breakfast every morning and porridge be damned. J lives the dream.
- J makes faces at me whenever the Boy calls. Inevitably I

start giggling. 'What's going on?' the Boy asks, worried. 'Oh, nothing,' I say. 'Just thought of something funny.'

- He completely understands when I don't want to return the Boy's calls for a few days.
- J loves hugs. In fact, his sense of personal space is distinctly un-British. I don't know, maybe that's something you pick up in prison.

mardi, le 25 janvier

Over at Tomás's for supper with J and some random girl. J doesn't introduce her as his girlfriend so I don't assume she is. I just hope she's not a screamer; the walls at home are thin.

The sky is still light long after the sun goes, and it goes here far later than it does during British winter. I love the twilight, the open windows and ceiling fans, the sound of insects in the half-night. The food is excellent. J brought over a few things, and I admire the gusto with which he eats everything from crab to sausage. He never asks what is in anything and never appears squeamish. I love that. I like the food, too, but am a bit more cautious, finding J's habit of eating everything with his hands a trifle disconcerting.

Growing up, we rarely ate anything explicitly non-kosher, so things like lobster and pork were relatively unusual to me as an adult. I can't get over the ingrained response that there's something wrong with this kind of food. It tastes great, but unlike with sex, I can't quite let myself go all the way.

Missed call from the Boy when we come home. I check the clock and figure it's too late to ring back; anyway, I'm not long for the waking world. I bid J and his lady goodnight and toddle off to bed.

She is a screamer.

I woke up in a right mood. J threw the phone in my lap on his way out the door. 'If you're not going to ring your man, ring your mum,' he said. 'And when I come back, either be somewhere else or be smiling.'

'Yes, sir.'

Mum let the call go to the answerphone before picking up. 'Hello, honey,' she said brightly. 'What are you doing? I've just come back from a date, would you believe.' I made a gagging noise. 'He's a lovely man, I'll have you know.' I gagged harder.

'I've been thinking about things since you and Daddy told me your news. It's really a huge life change, you know. Puts things in perspective.'

'Oh, darling, don't take it too much to heart,' Mum sighs. 'It was coming for a very long time.'

'Yes, but it's got me thinking about family and things. Heritage. Stuff like that. I've been thinking about going back to kosher.'

Mum chokes on a laugh. 'Are you kidding? Please tell me you're kidding. Unless of course you've met a single doctor on holiday by the name of Cohen, in which case tell me you're not kidding.'

'I haven't met a nice boy. I'm not kidding. I've thought about it, and I'm serious.'

'Please, think about it some more before doing anything rash. When was the last time you were in shul?'

'Er, some time ago.' As in when Wet Wet Wet were in the charts and I thought blow-dried hairspray was a good look. 'But don't you think I should go back?'

'Religion isn't something you pick up and put down like a fashion. People die for these things. Plus you love shellfish and going out on Friday nights. What are you going to eat there if you go kosher? Seaweed?'

I hadn't thought of that. 'I won't miss the food,' I say. 'Besides prawn crackers smell of foreskin.'

'The fact you know that would tend to indicate this isn't a good idea, honey.'

jeudi, le 27 janvier

I try ringing Dad and reach his answerphone. I check the clock. Surely he should be home from work by now, maybe settling in front of the news with a bite to eat? 'He's probably out with a lady,' J says. 'Or in.'

'Ugh, don't say that. It chills me to the bone to think of my parents screwing other people. Thinking of them having sex with each other was hard enough.'

'They're grown-ups too, Boo. They're allowed a sex life.'

'But do they have to make it so obvious?'

'Goes with the territory,' J says. 'I've had longer to get used to it.' His parents split before his first birthday and J was raised by his mother. They lived off benefits and the generosity of others while she trained to be a nurse. His father was rarely in the picture, if at all.

'I bet your mother doesn't tell you about her dates. It's as if she thinks we're sisters now instead of mother and daughter.'

'No,' J says, idly picking at his nails. 'She tells me about her multiple orgasms.'

'Okay, you have officially won the Creepy and Wrong Award for the day.'

J smiled. 'Was it even a competition?'

samedi, le 29 janvier

Tomás's brother owns the restaurant he works in. Is good because Tomás usually has something extra sent out for us that doesn't make it to the bill. I've already learned the Spanish for 'You don't have to pay' (*No tiene que pagar*). Is bad because Tomás's brother is hot. Distractingly so. Enough to turn a girl's mind away from her nominal boyfriend.

It makes me feel a touch of sympathy for Tomás, who is lovely and kind and never in a million years would I find him physically attractive. To grow up in the shadow of someone who is . . . well, let's not mince words here, godlike, must be frustrating.

Of course, Tomás does have one up so far: for all the smouldering looks the brother and I have exchanged, he does not speak or understand very much English. I may have to put a little more work into my study. Although asking Tomás what the Spanish is for 'Your brother is so fucking fit' might not be a good idea.

lundi, le 31 janvier

Odd, odd conversation with the Boy. Something has clearly unsettled him – Susie, I'll bet, or some other bit of brainless fluff – and all he does is ask me, over and over again, if I care about him (yes, or, if I'm being honest, sometimes) and if I'm sure (as far as I'm willing to tell him, yes). I ask if he's okay. He doesn't answer, just says 'Good, because if anything ever happens – if anyone ever rings you about something weird – I just want to know . . .'

Well, whatever. But it puts an odd thought into my head. What will happen if and when the Boy and I split up for good? He was relatively low-key about our last breakup: of course he went and told anyone who'd listen what a rotten human being I am, but at least he didn't tell everyone everything. For instance, Magnus is not aware, as far as I know, of my former profession. But I shudder to think what might happen if he did tell.

It frightens me so much that I'm a shaking wreck when J

comes home. 'I want to ask you to make me a promise,' I say to him. 'If anyone ever rings here, anyone you don't know I know, don't tell them I'm here. Don't let on you even know me.'

'Are you in trouble?' J says, taking my elbow and leading me to the sofa. 'Because I hope you know that I will support you whatever—'

And I suddenly realise how ludicrous this is, worrying about such stupid things to someone who's been an addict, been a drugs dealer, been to prison. To someone who literally hit rock bottom – thankfully, before he died – my problems are small beer.

'I'm sorry,' I said. 'It's nothing . . . it's nothing that level of serious. I'm not ready to tell you yet.' It's not because I think he would object, disappear from my life, or judge me. He's been honest about his past and expects nothing in return; I'm just picking the moment.

I talk around the subject, drop oblique hints, and decide to leave it for another day.

J smiles gently. 'You don't have to tell me anything,' he says. 'And remember, you're my cousin. Whatever happens, I got your back.'

Dear Belle

Dear Belle,

I have found a stash of porn under my girlfriend's bed. I can't mention it because I shouldn't have been so nosy. But looking at the guys whom I presume she is fantasising over has left me feeling a little inadequate in the bedroom department, and a bit demeaned. Can you give me some tips about how to make myself into her dream porn pin-up?

Dear Double Standard,

You haven't said so, but I'm assuming you're the man in a hetero relationship.

In which case, HELLO? You probably download more porn in a week than she's ever seen in her entire life. Do you think she feels entirely comfortable with the thought of her man ogling a picture of some double-D implanted 'model' being fisted in both holes?

Porn is fantasy and (usually) strictly that. No one expects to win an Oscar, but I bet you've practised an acceptance speech at some point, am I right? Porn is on the same level. And often, it's so overtly out of the realm of normal human experience that no one – not even the consumer, provided they're normal – expects the things that happen in porn to come to pass. In fact, I believe porn is far less damaging to your self-image than glossy magazines, because nothing in porn expects you to actually be Jenna Jameson, whereas every shot of every seventeen-year-old model (male and female) advertising wrinkle cream demands a standard that can never, ever be met in the real world.

You've nothing to fear, and I wouldn't mention it to her unless she does first. Unless she starts hanging out with Ron Jeremy, in which case I would worry.

———

Dear Belle,

I am plagued by desire for a lover to write Shakespeare's sonnets all over my body during foreplay. The trouble is I always go for hard guys who wouldn't be caught dead reading poetry and get a bit snippy when I bring out my Arden edition. Can you suggest some poetry that would not compromise my lovers' masculinity?

Dear Sei Shônagon,

Have you considered Philip Larkin? Even the densest knuckle-dragger can probably spell 'fuck'.

Février

mardi, le 1 février

Oh, for fuck's sake! So that's what the Boy was on about last night? That's what had me so worried?

Apparently Susie's chucked him. He must be worried she'll contact me or something, and then his world will truly come crashing down. Well, let it come if that's what happens. I'm ready for it.

mercredi, le 2 février

Tomás is clearly working on expanding his English vocabulary, just as I am trying to get to grips with a Spanish one. So maybe he's just trying out different words to see how they sound – even if the results aren't entirely accurate.

Today he called me 'wholesome'.

I know, I'm just as surprised.

jeudi, le 3 février

Belle's Guide to Your Holidays, part 1: Shopping

From this point on, you must resolve to never spend money on holiday again. Apart from the essentials, of course – room, board and condoms. This is for the simple reason that all products for sale in the coastal regions of the world have no use.

Take, for instance, the attractive bottle stopper tastefully emblazoned with the name of your holiday destination. So perfect as a memento of your trip. *So* useful for saving the remains of a bottle of wine. Sorry to burst your bubble, but national binge drinking trends show we haven't had leftover wine since rationing ended. Plus, used wine always smells of bread and tastes of dishwater the next day. The wisest move you could make would be to leave that silly thing gathering dust on a shop shelf rather than your own.

Other typical holiday purchases are so ludicrous in their intentions that I think we deserve a collective MBE for services to optimism. But be honest – you'll never wear that sarong back in Huddersfield, straw bags only go with swimming costumes, and the local aperitif tastes of petrol. Also, the real currency exchange rate is nothing like the quick and dirty approximation you've been using while making these purchases, and you'll return home to find not only have you paid seventeen quid for a shot glass that can't even go in the dishwasher, but that the people at NatWest know it.

The tourist shop itself is a masterpiece of modern capitalism. Seeking an authentic native experience there is something akin to doing your weekly shop at Fortnum and Mason. The grumpy harridan at the till is no more selling lovingly handcrafted local antiques than Asda is. You know how cringe-worthy it is to see a group of tourists stumbling out of a Wee Scotland Shoppe on Regent Street, bags bursting with tartan tablecloths? Think of those poor souls and step away from the tchotchkes.

And whatever you do, however you choose to spend your money while on holiday, do not have a tattoo or piercing done. At least you can be rid of a regrettable T-shirt easily.

samedi, le 5 février

The tourist boat outing was my birthday present to J. Twice-daily tours out in the Gulf, no guarantee of seeing dolphins but a possibility. It reminded me of going to Greenwich with Magnus. The sort of thing you only do when someone else buys the trip for you, so I did.

The sky was blue, bright and heavy. The rows of grey fold-down seats were empty. There was a woman standing near the rail, looking down, watching the bow cut through the water. She smiled at me. J was busy taking photos with his hands; neither of us had a camera. 'Man, I should have brought a camera!' Then a few minutes later: 'Damn!'

The woman was wearing a flimsy dress and an open coat. I knew that dress from Topshop last year, knew she had to be British, too. She said her name was Vic.

'Aren't you hot in that?' I asked.

'Not really,' she said. I reflexively looked at her chest. Large breasts, and no, I couldn't see her nipples. She caught me and laughed. I smiled and shrugged. She wasn't embarrassed.

Vic stepped off with us at the end of the two hours and we three walked together as far as the turnstiles. She mentioned her hotel name and room number, and I thought she was friendly. J wanted to go for a meal where Tomás worked, so we did, and I promptly forgot her.

mercredi, le 9 février

Ugh. Ugh, ugh, ugh. They say knowledge is power but I'm not convinced. Discovered an email the Boy sent to Susie today, after an apparent attempt at reconciliation:

> oh, little lass, hope the smell of me on your pillow convinces you to open your heart and your loins again. [Loins?? Cripes.] when are you coming to visit? Cannot forget the memory of you greedily ridding me [sic.]. You will have to help me get fit again, in any way you choose.

Went for a run on the beach. On the way back could see my footprints from the way out, the depth and vigour of them, each a well waiting to be filled with unspoken hatred.

samedi, le 12 février

J and Tomás went night fishing together. I said I wasn't feeling up to it but really I had sort of had it with practising my broken Spanish for an evening. I was bored and restless and decided to go to one of the hated tourist bars instead. I perched on a stool and wondered when my going-out uniform of tight jeans and silky top started to look too conservative. Everyone around me was pouring out of Day-Glo bikinis.

Vic, the lady from the boat, was there. I didn't recognise her at first, the hair was different, worn up. She smiled and talked to the man next to her. She had a wedding ring, he didn't. Friend? Lover? Husband? I lay across two empty seats, head on one hand. Vic looked at me and smiled. We started chatting. The man looked dejected – not her husband, then. Nothing to worry about, she giggled at him, just catching up on girl talk.

'I thought I recognised you.'

'You never rang.'

'Would it help if I said you looked fantastic?'

'Maybe.'

'And your handbag is great, too.'

Once upon a time I swore I would never sleep with a married person, but time and a job as a call girl changed that. And tonight I was feeling turned on and mildly malicious. The Boy's words to Susie running a circuit in my head: *cannot forget the memory of you greedily ridding me*. Well, great, thanks to that email I'll never forget it, either.

I was tired of reading about the Boy's conquests. Tired of his ringing up every night hinting about my helping with the air fare. I never asked him to come.

'I didn't think so. Just making certain.'

I closed the door softly, but knew from the absence of lights that J was still out. 'A shower?' I asked. 'I know I need one.' My clothes were a heap on the floor before she even had her shoes off. The bathroom was small with large mirrors.

Vic came in a few minutes later. She was naked and glorious. 'Mind if I join you?' Of course I didn't. I asked if she wanted a cooler shower – I like it very hot. She said she was fine. There was a squeezy bottle of shower gel, I squirted some out, and soaped her.

She looked better with her clothes off. She wouldn't stop kissing me. I held her face and it was small, fine-jawed; I wondered if it felt strange to her, having a woman's face so close to her own. My tongue felt every inch of her face, neck, shoulders. Her ears were tiny and soft. Closer now, in the light, I could see the tattoo on her shoulder was a lily. Why a lily? It didn't seem the time to ask. I licked down to her chest. She had the kind of nipples that stand right up, the kind perfect for nibbling.

Water and steam filled the room quickly. On my knees I soaped her torso, those unbelievable breasts, So heavy they slid out of my hands. The tiny scar inside her hip, the gently purple-grey stretch marks. Her legs were long and still thin. I was jealous and aroused at the same time. She had natural pubic hair, though, and it spread through her inner thighs. Vic pulled my hair, but I stayed down. Spread her legs and felt her with a finger. Her labia were dark and prominent, she was starting to swell and flush. I washed her carefully. Just touching, just exploring. Bent down so low I could see her reflection alone in the mirror. Her face was a picture, a mixture of surprise, curiosity and pleasure.

'Look at me.'

'I am.'

'What colour are my eyes?'

'They're perfect.'

We dried each other and went to bed. She was small and girlish, and looked years younger without the makeup. I always feel conscious of looking like a teenager even now. I knelt between her legs and she raised her hips towards me, a question in her eyes. She was willing and ready, but what now? She said it was her first time with a woman.

Between her legs, I had a strange drunken flash, a sort of gynaecological moment. I was about to screw someone's mother. Hadn't done that before, not to my knowledge. A new milestone. Then the moment passed, and I was in that hairy thicket, and her hands were at my hair again, but leading me down instead of up.

What can I say? This isn't a sex education course. You know what's down there and what to do. Or maybe you don't, and are looking for pointers. Afraid I can't give you many. Sorry, but it's just that I was born with the equipment and have been test-driving my own for some time now. Clitoral stimulation, oral pleasure? Not even the introduction. I can make a woman come with my pinky, the back of her knee and a well-timed exhale. You'd be carpet-bombing her pussy for days with no result.

If it makes you feel any better, I truly do believe that men should be allowed to give other men blowjobs on a strictly friends basis. After all, how could a woman really know how a man wants it?

'Don't you ever leave me.' The things we girls say when we're drunk.

I smiled. 'I'm right here.'

'What about tomorrow?'

'We'll see about tomorrow when it comes.'

She was happy to kiss me, she seemed fascinated by my breasts, far smaller than hers. She asked me to show her how I masturbated and looked at my cunt for ages. 'I want to see how you look when you come,' she said, and I laughed.

We held each other for a long time, though it was late and we were both tired. Her legs were wrapped round my left one; my right hand was buried in her thick hair. She smelled dark and warm like mushrooms. The moisture between her legs was dripping down the back of my thigh.

Eventually we went to sleep, spooning together in the bed. It was warmer in the room than she liked, so the covers were off. When morning came, I got up to shower and boiled the kettle. When I came back she was still half asleep.

'Coffee or tea?' I asked.

'Is there real milk?'

'Yes.'

'I'll have tea, please.'

Sitting on the edge of the sofa, I watched her drink the hot tea in tiny sips. She reached over and put the television on. Cartoons and news. I was worried about her turning up at the hotel and the children waiting for her. Watching their mum stagger in hung over, hair in all directions, would probably scar them for life. Then again, it was a holiday.

'Any plans today?'

'I'm going to stay in and order up scrambled eggs, salmon and champagne. We only came here for the kids' sake, after all. I need some holiday as well and getting sand in my hair is not my idea of a good time.'

'Travelling the world with room service, though. Sounds like a good reason to have children.'

'It's only once a year. Usually it's me up in the dark, pouring Cocoa Pops down their throats.'

'That sounds pretty good, too. Would you like a taxi?'

'I'll take the bus, thank you.'

'I'll walk you to the stop.'

dimanche, le 13 février

Hmm, maybe, considering my general interests, it might be to my advantage to learn more words in Spanish for sex acts.

Would have to ask Tomás. Scratch that plan.

The Spanish is coming, but slowly. Today I learned the word for Jewish (*judío*) and asked Tomás about his religion (Catholicism, naturally). I think if I was ever a Christian that would be the flavour I'd choose. The celibate priests, the Vatican, the changing of wine into blood: I find it difficult to buy the general theory underpinning the activity, but damn, they do have all the best kit. I struggle for the words to tell Tomás that being Jewish is as much about the culture as about the belief. He nods. He gets this.

Do I miss home? Tomás asks.

'Not really.' I have always felt a stranger in a strange land. The fact that people here know I'm a tourist from a mile off doesn't bother me because, I realise, I'm used to the same treatment at home.

I can pass on looks in England until someone asks my name. 'Where are you from?' they say. Here, I tell them, fruitlessly. I remember a shopkeeper in Yorkshire who balked when he ran my debit card through. I asked what the problem was. 'I'm looking for a wedding ring,' he says. 'Er, why?' I asked. But I knew. It's the surname, not even remotely anglicised, which doesn't match my face. And then my mother went and gave me an equally odd first name to match.

The counter staff at the Polish deli back in London never addressed me in English; with the name and the looks they assumed – almost correctly – that I was one of theirs. A career in MI5 was always out of the question; my grandparents are all foreign-born.

At least here the disdain locals feel for tourists is above board. Young men in low-riders can't decide whether to whistle or hurl abuse when they drive past me. I can deal. I can deal with looking different and being treated differently. What I can't take is back home, where lip service is paid to multiculturalism but you can still say someone has 'something of the night' about them with impunity.

Nothing rankles quite like when friends claim to know what it is like not to feel English because their granny was born in Edinburgh. Fuck that noise. My relatives came from countries which have since burned out of existence; they spoke Yiddish and Hebrew when to do so was to risk death. I've been to Henley, been to the polo, been chatted up by viscounts and kissed by OBEs. None of it matters. I am not English to them. How I cringe when the Boy talks about the family he wants us to have and uses the term 'hybrid vigour' as if I was husbandry stock.

I say to Tomás – in English – that being a tourist is not a strange concept to me. And that I feel bad for him, watching the place where he grew up being invaded by drunk tourists. He smiles and nods, but then says, 'It gives us work,' and the conversation ends there.

jeudi, le 17 février

Belle's Guide to Your Holidays, part 2: Sunshine

If evolutionary biology is to be believed, the native residents of warmer climates typically have darker skin and hair than their northern counterparts as a response to constant, unrelenting UV exposure over the aeons. Conversely, people bred in cooler climes lost the pigmentation for dark hair and skin long ago.

This is clearly poppycock. For one thing, I've lived in the North of England, and there is no such thing as a natural blonde in Newcastle. Furthermore, even the most limited exposure to cultures abroad will reveal that people who live in sunny places never go out in the sun. Ever. It could be thirty degrees at Easter in Seville, and the local girls are wearing nothing more revealing than a long-sleeved top, jeans and a quilted gilet because it is 'still winter'. I can not understand the ruckus surrounding the wear of traditional Muslim dress in schools, except perhaps that it was a bit daring compared to what the usual schoolgirl sports and therefore at risk of inflaming the male teachers' desire.

Sun cream is famously expensive on holiday, and this is less to do with fleecing the tourists than because there is no local demand for the product: the women go about swaddled in enough layers of fabric to give a Saudi woman pause. It is widely cited that the average Briton will suffer more sun damage in two weeks' holiday than they would the entire rest of the year. I daresay that's still more than the local population will experience, sheltered as they are in cavernous churches and under innunmerable café awnings.

Doing as any normal British person would do, namely, tearing off your clothes and falling asleep on an exposed piece of ground the moment the temperature climbs above, say twelve degrees, immediately marks one out as a tourist. Even wearing a straw hat will indicate to the locals that you ain't from 'round 'ere'. Pity the poor English lass who succumbs to dipping her cramped white toes into the balmy Med, for she will be followed by catcalls of 'Hey, inglesa!' or 'Hey, Inghilterra! Daveeeeed Beckham!' wherever she goes.

dimanche, le 20 février

J, Tomás and I were flopped on the sofa on the lanai. Now, how cool is that? Outdoor rooms complete with power supplies and, here at least, a television. You couldn't do that in Britain. We were eating pizza and watching a schlocky horror movie. Not just a mildly tasteless film, but really quite appallingly so – the sort of film where blood spurts with the energy of a thousand suns.

The phone rang. J went to answer it, came back outside and flipped the receiver towards me. 'For you,' he said. It could only be the Boy. Ugh. I hadn't told him about Vic and didn't think I was going to – it felt good to have a secret.

'Hello, little kitty,' he said. I hate that name now. 'Wow,

sounds like you're having a good time. Are you lot having a party or something?'

No, you fool, we're having a bondage-themed orgy with the Colombian national athletics team. I'm being spit-roasted by Olympic hurdlers as we speak. What do you think? 'No, the neighbour came over for supper, that's all.'

'I have some great news,' he said, voice trailing off in that way that you use only with little children when you're about to take them somewhere they don't want to go, such as the GP, as in, 'Weeeeee're going for a caaaaar riiiiide todaaaaaaayyyyy!'

'What's that?' I said, as yet another nubile teenage girl was beheaded by the chainsaw-wielding antihero. I wondered vaguely whether Susie had responded yet to the Boy's sad little email begging her to have sex with him.

'I'm coming to visit next month!'

Question answered, I suppose.

mardi, le 22 février

Now, as a native of Britain, it is hardly within my rights to criticise another country's cuisine. After all we have made a national pastime out of fashioning suet into various shapes, and few native recipes do not require a process of boiling, then frying, then boiling the food again.

But it has occurred to me that, quite apart from the profusion of glorious fruit here, the food does seem to only consist of four things: pulses, tomatoes, rice and chilli. Sometimes cheese. And having discerned this, I reckon it will save me a lot of time in the future.

Thank goodness. Means Tomás and I can proceed to a new topic in Spanish.

'So should I book a flight via Canada or via the US?'

'I have no idea,' I said. I was outside on the sofa, bare feet, watching ants make a steady trail from the definitely-out-doors of the back garden to the semi-outdoors of the lanai. I pointed to them when J walked past, deep in conversation with his Screaming Lady on the mobile, but he just shrugged.

'Does one take longer to get through customs than the other?' the Boy asked.

'No idea,' I said. 'America, probably.' In fact they'd gone through my luggage when it was in transit here, which I discovered only on opening a suitcase on the third day to discover a friendly note from the Department of Homeland Security inside letting me know that, for the sake of public safety, they'd had a good paw through my knickers, nothing to be alarmed about.

'Oh, kitty, I am so looking forward to seeing you,' he said.

'Please don't.'

'Pardon?'

'I hate it when people recycle pet names.'

He was quiet. I could all but hear the wheels turning. What the . . . ? Does that mean . . . ? But in the end he must have decided that questioning me might lead to an argument, because he didn't follow it up. But he did find a reason to be off the phone pretty quickly.

Okay. Now, J is my man, and I love him to bits, but some things do rankle:

• The Screamer. I mean what is it with her? Yes, sex is fun. Yes, it is exciting. But we just spent all evening watching horror films on video. Don't let's feel the need to recreate the audio experience in the bedroom afterwards.

- Socks. Are men not familiar with the concept of putting them away? He seems to manage to guide most laundry in the direction of the basket under the bathroom sink. The socks, on the other hand, seemingly possessed by a rambling spirit, manage to evacuate themselves from the other clothing and are scattered about the house. At last count I spotted six (none matching).
- Hair on the soap. I've stopped waxing as it is no longer related to steady employment, so this is not an issue where I can claim superiority based on a lack of body hair. But somehow my pubes manage not to burrow into the soap. Unless of course they belong to the Screamer, in which case eww.

dimanche, le 27 février

Food and drink are not my strong points. Yes, I enjoy them as much as (and sometimes more than) the next person, but am not particularly knowledgeable about which beverage goes with which meal or the difference between sardines and pilchards. Come to think of it, does anyone really know?

But I am, slowly and with Tomás's help, trying to improve my cooking skills. Not out of any attempt to impress, mind: it's more so I don't end up eating salad cream sandwiches every night when I go back to the UK. That's not out of desperation; I genuinely love salad cream. The fact that it's such a slap in the face to po-faced GI dieters is simply extra.

And I must admit, learning under such a talented and patient cook is a bonus. We've already tried out dozens of things for me to cook when the Boy is here that I can't wait to try.

I went back to Jo's and we stayed up drinking; it was just like old times. Her boyfriend kept ringing but she just ignored his calls. It felt so good to know she preferred me over him. I sort of felt sorry for him but not really. Later we were in bed and I had an erection all night. I know I could have had her at any time but didn't.

I see the Boy paid his bloaty ex a visit. Clearly hoping to get a little ego fluff before coming to see me.

Fucktard. I went out and laid a gorgeous woman and you dry-hump a beached whale.

The thought didn't make me feel particularly better.

Dear Belle

Dear Belle,

I am a gentleman of 74 and I have been seeing my ladyfriend, Doris, for almost six months. I would very much like to take her 'up the Garry' but am unsure how to approach the subject. Should I buy her chocolates and then ask her politely while in the boudoir, or do you favour the approach whereby I slip it in, pretend it was an accident and gauge the situation by her reaction?

Dear Dark Knight,

If your ladyfriend is of a similar vintage to your good self, there is positively no way she would believe that the ramrod banging on her back door arrived there by accident. My advice would be to broach the subject outside the bedroom, perhaps during a quiet, romantic (and suitably expensive) dinner, whereupon you produce documentary evidence to your freedom from all known diseases and assure her of your patience, good humour and familiarity with all the modern forms of lubricant.

Dear Belle,

I am desperate for my boyfriend to have a back, sack and crack. It's not fair – I Brazilian myself regularly but he won't do me the courtesy in return. How do I persuade him?

Dear Mrs Sasquatch,

Having your Brazilian is one thing, but the sheer acreage covered by a B, S & C is equivalent to waxing you, all your female relatives and every woman you meet today baby-smooth for the next three weeks. Why not just pick one of the three? I'd choose back, if you are a girl who is into aesthetics, but sack is probably the connoisseur's choice.

Dear Belle,

I'm a married accountant. A recent late shift at the office led to some under-the-desk filth with a sixth-former on work experience. I'm racked with guilt – and now the little witch is blackmailing me for her silence. What do I do?

Dear Twisted Knickers,

I'm afraid it's pay now or pay later, dear. Obviously the honourable thing to do would be to refuse the former object of your lust her illicit payday, and take the consequences whatever they may be. Or if domestic harmony is more your speed, go ahead and shell out, but don't expect that having found your weak spot she will actually let the matter drop. The choice is yours. And next time you're afflicted with an unruly swelling, may I recommend either taking matters into your own hands or letting a professional see to it?

Mars

mardi, le 1 mars

It's so wrong. I know it's wrong. And yet I can't help myself.

I fancy the pants off Grayson Perry.

Of course, in the case of the famously cross-dressing Turner Prize-winner, they would invariably be ruffled pink pants. For Mr Perry is not just a transvestite but a grown man who enjoys dressing like a little girl. And that is a twist so far up my alley it's ringing the bell right now.

People with sexual kinks can often tell you when and where they began to fetishise – a young boy discovering his mother's shoes in the closet, for instance, or a teenaged girl pinching herself hard enough to draw blood while masturbating. Mine may not be quite a lifestyle choice, but it certainly looms large in my sexual closet. And my preference for men dressed like girls had a genesis, though it started much later than childhood.

I'd always been attracted to cross-dressers. One of my strongest erotic memories was making out with a boy from school in a purple crushed-velvet dress on Halloween. Once I dated a Norwegian because he occasionally wore a black maxi-skirt. But the desire didn't fully flower until later. It was with A2. He was tall and undoubtedly masculine, but also thin-framed and long-haired. And he looked the business in Petit Bateau.

For a time, when things between us were good, it was our mutual obsession. Midweek blues thwarted by going out on knicker-buying missions. He in the sleeveless frock, me topless in a tight pair of boy's briefs, watching lesbian porn together. We joked that he was a gay woman trapped in a man's body and that I was a gay man in a woman's. It wasn't true, of course. We just liked frilly pants. A lot.

Alas, it came to an undignified end. I showed less and less enthusiasm for dressing up, as a result we had sex less often, and eventually, not at all. I felt terrible about it but could never explain. It was far easier to let him think that I had bored of the game and it didn't turn me on any more. Or that, as he slowly gained weight, his figure didn't cut quite the dash in a red silk G-string that it once had. But the truth was far worse, something that could never be spoken.

I simply could not go on fucking a man who had better legs than I did, and the stockings to prove it. It just wasn't seemly.

mercredi, le 2 mars

<TheBoy> I don't know what to pack. Do I need a suit?

<belle_online> No, just a lot of shirts and shorts. Swim trunks. Don't forget suncream.

<TheBoy> I was hoping to get some sun . . .

<belle_online> You'll burn in about a nanosecond

<TheBoy> what about insurance?

<belle_online> pardon?

<TheBoy> travel insurance

<belle_online> I wouldn't bother but it's up to you.

How tiresome! I know this is the first time the Boy's been abroad without his family for purposes other than skiing (and, by extension, having gluhwein-fuelled sessions with brainless totty), so he needs plenty of hand-holding. On the other hand I also know this holiday is taking the place of the one he didn't have in Thailand with Susie, so I'm not as excited about the prospect as he imagines I should be.

\<**TheBoy**\> How about my driving licence, and do I need any vaccinations?

\<**belle_online**\> contrary to popular belief you *can* drink the water, I wouldn't bother

jeudi, le 3 mars

Surprise envelope in the post. The Boy drew me a card! I check the postmark – sent almost ten days ago.

It's a little comic starring two cats. The first one is flea-ridden and scraggy – above it he's written *Me: fed up, tired out and generally pooey.*

Then another cat, a ball of straightened fur, thousand claws flying in the air like a spiky ball. *You: lonely, grumpy and full of hiss.*

Then the last sketch, which looks surprisingly similar to my room here, of two cats curled together on a bed with white curtains open and sunshine through the window. *Us: blissed out and back together.*

It's lovely and sweet; he really is clever with a pencil. But the fact that I can't be certain he drew it for me in the first place makes me very sad.

vendredi, le 4 mars

Belle's Guide to Your Holidays, part 3: Hot Spots

Is there anything more appalling than a so-called tourist hot spot? I mean, apart from Friday night on the BBC?

At the height of the season there's one thing you can guarantee about going out in a foreign city, and it's that the clubs will be lousy with English-speakers. Also that you will have just missed the live band but the wet T-shirt contest is due to start any minute and a group of drunk American teenagers are nominating you.

Tourist spots are meat markets which make Smithfield look like Tesco Metro. You could set a watch by the drunken men who wobble past and offer you a drink or a dance: by my reckoning, about one every four minutes.

Your choices are limited: accept, and you're press-ganged into the sort of memories that make people choose holy orders upon return to jolly old Blighty, or refuse and be accused of lesbianism.

It's a pity, really, because the men have not picked up on the subtle dress code of the tourist club. Women in T-shirts and shorts are not interested in your advances. Women wearing the square root of an inch of Lycra are. If in doubt, check the lower back for a prominent tattoo, or as my friend L calls it, 'the tramp stamp'. You're as good as in.

One gentleman recently approached me and would not be rebuffed. 'Sorry,' I said. 'I'm not looking for company. Why don't you try some of the others?'

'Because you got it going on, and you don't even know it,' he says.

Oh, I know it all right. You don't charge three hundred an hour without some confidence that you have at least a little something going on. But still, I was wearing more clothing than all the other ladies in there put together, and I didn't even have trousers on. When I pointed this out he accused me of Sapphic tendencies and lurched away.

It's when the lights go down and the dancing starts that things turn from horrifying to truly purgatorial. Drunken girls writhe against random crotches to the strains of the Pussycat Dolls. I can't help it, it makes my stomach turn. Don't get me wrong. I love dancing. I love sex. I love strippers. I love that I can choose to do any of those things. What I hate is the alcohol culture that makes us act like twats abroad. What I hate is the skeezy cunts in Fred Perry shagging vodka-blind Top Shop girls up against a public wall in San

Pedro. What I hate is the knowledge that in two weeks' time these same people will go home with sunburns, sarongs and an undiagnosed STI for the NHS to take care of. And when Emily tells her future husband how many men she's been with, she won't count these holiday fucks. She won't stand by her own actions. She'll judge me and people like me for getting paid to do something she did for free.

samedi, le 5 mars

'How about you?' Tomás's friend, a man with sideburns so black they looked drawn on, asked me. 'What's your seduction music?'

'The usual things,' I said. 'Bill Withers, obviously. Isaac Hayes's *Hot Buttered Soul*.'

The fellows nodded in appreciation, but the truth is, I don't believe in seduction music. If Suede has to do your work for you, doesn't that indicate your partner is better off having a crack at Brett Anderson?

I won't deny that some music is inherently sexy. I love Air and Jeff Buckley – nothing gets me wet quite like the first six tracks of *Grace* – but any lover lazy enough to stick that on as a half-arsed prelude to fucking is about as likely to get the good stuff from me as John Prescott is.

When I was a sex worker things were different: men were paying for a full-on experience, and if frilly lingerie, bubble baths and Morcheeba did it for them, I could suspend disbelief for an hour and play along. But at home I like nothing more than the sounds of two bodies together.

The lad I dated at school habitually played U2 whenever we set out to do the dirty. I don't know why, apart from a suspicion that he (incorrectly) thought his parents wouldn't figure out what we were up to in his room. I can't believe some of my first non-self-induced orgasms were obtained listening to Bono's voice. It's positively shameful.

A4 ruined Bob Dylan for ever when he revealed that a mate of his from uni – a skinny ginger bloke who buys hair gel in bulk – played 'Lay Lady Lay' every time he brought a girl to their flat. Every time I think of it, the thought of some over-earnest undergrad spinning that tune makes me cringe. Big brass bed indeed.

But I suspect the fellows actually weren't lying tonight when they listed, among other things, Enrique Iglesias and Cat Stevens as their choices for music to make love by. If nothing else, on the off chance I actually end up pulling any of these gentlemen, I will be sure to avoid the one who listed 'Parachutes' as the most genius sex platter ever. Because there is excusable bad taste, and then there is Coldplay.

dimanche, le 6 mars

The Boy's plane is late. I tried to check the status online before leaving but the connection was down. Gives me a little time to wander around, not that there's much to the airport.

When the plane unloads I scan the crowd: there he is. He looks drawn, but that's not surprising. Including flight changes the journey took sixteen hours. He jogs slowly towards me and picks me up. We kiss. He smells different.

'Wow, it's hot,' he says. We haven't even left the airport yet, and that is air-conditioned. And it's only March. I smile. 'Bring sunscreen?' I ask.

'No, I brought after-sun instead.' I knew he wouldn't, so I bought sunscreen anyway. Factor 30. Will have to sneak it into his food, or something.

There are probably a thousand ways to tell a local from a tourist here, but this one works without fail: see who's on the beach in winter.

Reliable sunshine never occurs in Britain. In fact, it never occurs in most parts of the world. That's why so many people travel here. But for the locals it's a bit chilly, and they wouldn't be seen dead on the beach before June.

I'm willing to suck it up – the weather is great, and I'm here because the Boy is here, enjoying the sun, having fun and so on. The water is off limits, but the sand is warm and welcoming.

I never expected, though, that if I took him to the beach he would do something which made even the hardened tourist-watcher wince. Something which even the half-irradiated Canadians and clueless Germans found beyond the pale. Something which, should archaeologists discover written evidence of this culture in a thousand years' time, will surely have gone down as one of the more memorable events in local history.

He went for a swim. In winter. In the ocean.

No one swims here. The beach, especially at this time of year, is for seeing and being seen. For one thing it's cold in the water – far colder than the Gulf Stream-warmed coastal waves of Britain. Also, the riptides are so fierce you can find yourself halfway to drowning in about three seconds. There are signs posted everywhere. Surfing at one's own risk is just about tolerated, but swimming, never. You'd be mad.

'Well, what are you waiting for?' he yelled. I lowered my sunglasses and the entire population of the beach stared at us in horror. 'It's bracing!'

I'd forgotten what it's like to be part of a couple. All those annoying habits that can be kept at arm's length over a transatlantic telephone line are suddenly right up in my face. Such as:

- The snoring. Really, why do men do this while women don't? Although, considering how few women I've shared regular sleeping arrangements with, perhaps I'm generalising.
- The inability to make decisions. 'Would you like me to cook something, or shall we go out?' And he just sits there, mouth agape for several seconds, before saying he'll do whatever I want to do. Well, if I wanted something in particular, I wouldn't have asked, would I?
- The man stuff. You know when a man comes onto another man's territory, how they have to be competitive and determine supremacy? The Boy actually offered J an arm-wrestle within twelve hours of being here. Luckily J declined and laughed it off – he probably would have won, anyway.
- The ignored advice. I told him to bring suncream. He didn't. I offered him mine. He didn't use it. He got burned within an hour and is now hobbling around like Ranulph Fiennes straight out of a desert marathon.
- The fucking phone. I came up behind him to ask a question and saw him tapping 'Hiya lass, not to worry, arrived safely, miss you!' into the hated thing. 'Who are you texting?' I smiled, pretending not to have seen the screen. 'Uh, um, m-m-my brother,' he stammered.

mercredi, le 9 mars

The Boy's sunburn is not improving. Note to manufacturers: after-sun is all a bit of a scam, innit?

The choices in such a situation are: he wears clothes that cover the burn, and complains endlessly about the pain of fabric against skin, or he doesn't, and risks more burn. And I don't want to go into the sexual contortions necessary to avoid rubbing the burn – because while I like it a little rough in the bedroom, and the Boy loves dishing it out, he most emphatically cannot take it. You'd think he was being flayed alive from the sound of it.

At least it's payback to J for my putting up with the screaming lady.

jeudi, le 10 mars

'You're not taking him on the bus,' J laughed.

'What?' I said. 'It's the easiest way to get around, and it's cheap.'

'It's cheap for a reason,' J said. 'Those people are crazy.'

'If you don't think we should take the bus while he's here,' I said sweetly to J, 'the least you can do is loan him your pushbike.'

Now, calling J's glorious machine a pushbike is an understatement along the line of calling Harvey Nick's a corner shop. It's a titanium-framed beauty, and clearly cost thousands – or possibly was extracted from someone in exchange for drug debts. I don't like to ask.

'No. Fucking. Way.'

'Pweese?' I put on a baby voice and batted my eyelashes, just like I'd seen the Screamer do to him once.

'Fine, okay, whatever,' J grumbled. 'But don't you two go and do anything stupid!'

I knew of a river, starting from springs inland, that ran as far as the sea. It was supposed to be a great place for swimming and canoeing, the fishermen were always talking about it, and I'd even heard that if you went diving in the limestone source you could find arrowheads. I reckoned if we set off early enough we could cycle there, hire canoes and paddle down it and back up, then cycle home.

'What should we do?' the Boy asked, about the bikes. 'Chain them to something?'

'It's that or take them in the canoes,' I said. The Boy considered this seriously. 'Of course we chain them up.'

'I'm a little worried about your cousin,' he said. 'What if they get nicked?'

'Not to worry, he's a lot more laid back than he looks.'

The Boy disappeared to find a good place to hide the cycles while I paid a bored-looking woman for canoe rental. I went down to the edge of the springs. The water was glass-clear and smooth; thick, long grass swirled in the currents.

Hmm, he's taking his time, I thought. I pulled the canoes down to the edge of the water, went back up for our bags of food and water. Waited a few more minutes: no sign of the Boy. Retrieved the paddles and sat on the ground. Still no Boy.

I bet he's ringing some girl, the cunt. It put me in a very black mood to think of him sneaking off to whisper sweet nothings to some slag while I was all but turning cartwheels to keep him entertained.

By the time he came back – some twenty minutes – I was not in the mood for our outing any more. 'Oh, why do you always have to be this way?' he said, trying to put an arm round my waist. Why do I always have to? Is he actively trying to make me angry? I turned away. 'I just wanted to ring my family before the battery runs down. I didn't know the charger wouldn't work here.'

Like fuck, I thought. The sooner that battery goes dead the better.

samedi, le 12 mars

The Boy loves food. Correction: the Boy loves large amounts of food, he's not picky. Magnus poked fun at his eating habits when I visited at New Year – they were arguing over who should have the last of the lemon cake, and as the Boy had had a slice already and Magnus hadn't, you would have thought it was clear cut. But no, the Boy insisted everyone had already eaten more than he, at which point Magnus pulled a face and imitated his brother's voice with surprising accuracy: 'No bulk, big sulk.' Everyone laughed and the Boy reluctantly gave up his claim.

In fact, he has probably the worst palate of anyone I've ever met. Nothing is salted enough, and a slow-simmered white wine sauce, in his opinion, holds nothing against a jar of shop-bought Bolognese. At least he's easy to please, and once you have the bulk equation cracked, it's smooth sailing. Also it saves money as Michelin stars are mostly lost on him.

Unfortunately the Boy doesn't like the local food. In spite of his brawny appearance, he is the sort of man who goes into a curry house and asks for extra-mild korma. Luckily there's not just local food on offer here: the tourist restaurants cater for less robust palates. Well, I think, if you can't take the chilli here, I can't imagine what you would have eaten with Susie in Thailand.

We were walking back from the Greek grocer when he noticed something on the ground. 'What's that?' he exclaimed.

'It's a starfruit,' I said. Now that I'd eaten loads and knew that they grew everywhere, I was no longer surprised by this weirdly geometrical fruit.

'Can you eat them?'

'You can,' I said, and picked it up. The tree was only feet away. This one must have just dropped; it was smooth, with no insect holes or bird-pecks. 'Want to share?'

He reached out. 'Do I peel it?'

'No, skin and all. You can eat the whole thing.'

He bit into the fruit gingerly. 'Oh, wow,' he said. 'It's like a lime-flavoured plum.' I started to walk away. 'Wait,' he said. 'There might be more.'

dimanche, le 13 mars

Which part of 'That feels good' – in the sexual context, of course – is so difficult to understand?

When I was paid to sleep with people, being told 'That feels good' was a green light, a signal that I was on the right track and, if lucky, could expect a generous tip or a repeat customer. Therefore, when someone told me in no uncertain terms that something felt good, the last thing I would have done was stop doing it.

But now that my services are available to one person only and on a strictly voluntary basis, it seems 'That feels good' means the opposite of what I thought it did. Because as soon as I say something feels good . . . the Boy promptly stops.

I can't imagine why. Perhaps he thinks I mean 'That feels good – but it could feel better,' therefore concluding that doing whatever he is doing, only faster, harder, and in another location altogether, is the way forward. Or maybe he's a stubborn, contrary type at heart, the sort of person who will suggest going to the cinema just when you say you want to stay in, and 'That feels good' is an incentive to do the complete opposite.

I've tried several times to remedy the problem. First I

stopped saying anything at all, but that led to the assumption that I wasn't enjoying anything.

So I moved on to the subtler approach: squirming and groaning with pleasure, for instance, instead of vocalising my approval. He thought I was being ticklish and stopped. So no gain there.

Maybe the problem is a lack of specificity? I could be saying 'That feels good' when he's doing more than one thing and so, confused about which 'That' it is and how 'good' it's feeling, he stops one in order to concentrate more fully on the other. Except if so, it's always been the wrong thing.

And while some people like a bit of direction – harder, there, more, now – it can be a touch deflating when your partner comes over all Orson Welles on you with 'Do the windmill thing with your tongue again, but more slowly, and not pinching at the same time, please, and for goodness sake don't breathe on me unless it's a dry breath and not a damp one. Starting when I tap you on the shoulder, okay?'

Or maybe – gulp – he's become so accustomed to other women that he can't remember what feels good to me. The weirdly fussy way he's been handling my nipples might support this. I don't like softly-softly when it comes to breasts; I like rough handling that leaves evil-looking marks and probably comes within Geneva Convention definitions of torture.

The thought drives me round the bend: I've kept multiple lovers at the same time, and in the line of work had to deal with the unrelenting newness of many clients, night after night. It's not so hard to figure out what a stranger wants, whether he likes blowjobs shallow or deep, with light teeth or without; whether the cheeky finger up the backside is a welcome intervention or no. You get used to adapting to the signals, and by the end of the hour should be fucking him just the way he wants to be fucked. If not you haven't done your job. So to a so-called partner, reading your signals should be second nature, right?

Maybe we've been apart too long.

There's an island off the coast that's only accessible by ferry. So we hire a vehicle for a few days. The Boy presents his UK licence and about seven thousand other forms of identification, in the hope that some combination of them will be suitable, as my Spanish is far from good enough to deal with questions. It all goes smoothly, and the keys to the car are soon in his pocket.

He wonders why we didn't hire a sailing boat, some nice compact little cruiser, but I assure him that it was prohibitively expensive. Besides, the car will probably be drier and more comfortable. With the back seat down, the area in the car would be larger than my bed. So we pack food, water, clothes and armful of bedding. Then it's just us and the open road.

Us, the open road, and every other tourist who reckoned negotiating a completely unfamiliar highway system would be a doddle. No one respects the signs here; I reckon they don't even know what they are. Cars are undertaking left, right and centre.

We stop at a layby where two men are sat on the edge of the open bed of a truck. The hand-painted signs nearby advertise their wares: meat. It looks like – no, on closer inspection, it is – they're cooking something over coals in an old oil barrel.

We buy two of whatever they're selling, and take off. Steering with one hand and eating greasy pork (I think it's pork; it had a trotter) with the other might seem dangerous, but in fact we're swerving no more madly than everyone else.

The Boy makes a manful effort to get through all the food – truly, this is his talent – but in the end gives up, declaring it 'too greasy'. Wow, I think, that's a new one.

We stop again an hour later and feed it to the grateful seagulls.

We reach the end of the ferry ride just in time to find out the campsite is full. The Boy's worried; I'm not. We can always find a place close by on the mainland. That leaves a few hours until the last ferry back.

The island is long and thin, a barrier island. We start walking, barefoot, on the beach with everything back in the car park. It's longer than I imagine, because almost an hour later we're still walking. I suggest we turn round or we'll miss the ferry. The Boy guesses it can't be much further.

We meet a family on bicycles coming in the other direction. I ask how far it is to the end of the island. They say they don't know; they didn't make it that far. I thank them and tell the Boy we should really go back now. He winces. There's a thorn in his foot, and he can't walk very fast.

All our food and water is back in the car, miles away. He's limping badly. I stop and try to extract the thorn. It's tiny, and we have no magnifying glass or tweezers. Eventually I do extract it, and he's grateful, but it's taken almost half an hour. 'Like drawing a thorn from the paw of the lion,' he says. By now there's little chance of making the ferry. We have a wind-up radio and listen to it for a bit. There isn't much radio reception. A Shakira song comes on, though, and I sing along, dancing circles around the (very amused) Boy.

'You must be delirious with thirst. Usually you'd be in tears by now.'

The bottom of my feet feel like they're on fire, but it's worth it. We make it back to the car park and the ferry is long gone – so are the people. Ours is the last car left. We could try to camp somewhere, but fold the seats down instead, and make a feast of tinned beans and tortillas before falling gratefully asleep.

'We can't leave without a swim,' the Boy insists. We'd woken to the sound of tapping – a bird was attacking its own reflection in our wing mirror. We washed at a standpipe and went to watch the sunrise.

'The riptides here are lethal,' I say.

'Are you saying you're scared?'

'I'm saying you're welcome to risk your own life, but not mine.'

He jumps right in. With the position of the sun, there's so much light reflecting off the water I can't see him. What if something happened? I look around. There are a few people on the horizon, fishermen probably. No phones for miles; the first ferry hasn't come yet. How would I raise the alarm?

I sit and worry my nails for almost an hour until he returns, covered in goose pimples and jellyfish stings. 'Actually, I'm glad you didn't come,' he said. 'Did you see that? I almost didn't make it.'

'Turn round and look, I couldn't see anything. I was worried you might drown, you fool.'

He looks down and sees my raw fingertips. 'Oh, poor thing,' he says, and kisses my head. 'Let's get the ferry and some breakfast – I'm ravenous.' His skin is still damp, and cold to the touch.

I shake my head. 'Not just yet,' I say, indicating the car, where the back seat is still down and our bedding from the night still strewn. 'I think maybe you need some more intensive warming up.'

jeudi, le 17 mars

I'm a woman. As such, I am privileged to enjoy certain prerogatives. One of them is to have arbitrary rules of conversation that are indecipherable to men. There are lines, and then there is between the lines, and that's where I prefer to conduct things at times. I know it's not fair, but then men get to pee standing up. Throw us a bone here. Gentlemen paramours and relatives, take heed.

The Commandments go roughly thus:

1 I am the woman, the one in charge of the conversation. Thou shalt not have any subject changes unapproved by me.
2 Thou shalt remember the first ten minutes of the morning and keep them holy. The period before my first cup of tea is not suitable for chat.
3 Thou shalt not refer to sporting analogies too often.
4 Thou shalt not interrupt *The Simpsons*, even if it is dubbed into Spanish and the only thing I clearly understand is Mr Burns saying, '*Excelente*.'
5 Thou shalt not covet another woman's rack unless I have mentioned it first.
6 Thou shalt not refer to PMT, even if I am clearly experiencing it.
7 Thou shalt not pronounce the word 'controversy' with undue stress on the second vowel. Do you know how annoying that is to everyone else?
8 Thou shalt not use the word 'hypocrisy' in conversation. Thou art not twelve any more. In writing thou shalt not spell the word 'hippocracy'. That would be a government run by horses. There are online dictionaries, and thou shalt make use of them.
9 Thou shalt not expect conversation when I am reading, even if it's only the paper or the back of a packet of rice.
10 Thou shalt not talk to me through the toilet door. Ever. That's just wrong.

vendredi, le 18 mars

We were walking the beach, looking for turtle eggs – Tomás had dropped by with a sheet on how to identify the nests, what to do when you see one, and so on. Unfortunately, most of the locals think that the appropriate thing to do, on finding the delicate nest of an endangered animal, is to collect the eggs for overpriced tourist drinks or to set their dog on them. But we are undeterred.

By 'we', I mean me, of course. The Boy was jumping up and down in the surf, more interested in jellyfish than eggs. Fair enough, I guess. It ties in with his sci-fi obsession.

He shrieked suddenly, and I jumped; I thought maybe he'd been attacked by a flotilla of jellyfish (what to do in such an event? Is it true what they say, that weeing on it works?) or had his toe crunched by a crab, which had happened to me the week before and he showed absolutely no sympathy for, just laughed and laughed, 'You should have seen the look on your face!' I sincerely hoped it was the crab.

'You have to come see this,' he said, waving his big freckled arms at me.

Whatever it was, it was difficult to see in the water, and I wasn't about to go beyond knee-deep. I saw the Boy bend and scoop something out of the water, and bring it ashore.

It was an alien. At least, that's my professional opinion. Having read comics since a young age I feel fairly well qualified to identify them on sight. It was floppy and mango-sized, with a frilly edge, leaking copious amounts of evil-looking purple fluid.

'I think it's a sea slug,' he said.

'I think you're mad to pick it up.' But worse: he leaned closer and sniffed it. 'What on earth are you doing?'

'I don't know,' he said. 'I think it's dying.'

'We should put it back in the water,' I said. We walked round the corner, to a cove, where the current was weaker. I found a medium-sized rock and dug it into shallow, warmer water; he laid the giant purple slug behind it. There was still purple ink dripping off the Boy's hands. He suggested I tough it. I'm not usually squeamish, but I believe in the power of species evolution, and if purple inky things from the sea raise a strong repulsion somewhere back in my reptilian brain, I'm willing to bet there's a good reason why.

We waited ages, until it didn't seem to be moving any more. The sun was going away, anyway, and we had a long cycle home. 'You don't think we could eat it?' the Boy said as we left. 'Everything else here is edible.'

'A purple slug? Yeah, just throw that under the grill,' I said as we pedalled away.

samedi, le 19 mars

'Theory,' J says suddenly. We're watching a horror flick on the sofa. Or rather, J and I are watching; the Boy is hiding behind my shoulder and trying not to whimper too loudly. 'All the nipples of the world can be put into three categories.'

'Are we talking just women's, or all nipples in general?' I ask as the nubile topless lovely on screen meets a most undignified end thanks to an axe.

'Women's only,' J says. 'We have your basic standy-uppies, big roundy ones' – at this the Boy pokes me in the back, and I poke him back harder; I mean, J and I are close and everything, but there is a line – 'and puffies.'

The lifeless body of yet another C-list starlet hits the tiles. 'Puffies?' I say. The film slows and shows her jiggling flesh as it settles in a pool of fake blood.

'Definitely,' J says. 'Practically a textbook pair.'

199

dimanche, le 20 mars

Now Slug Beach is the Boy's favourite place here. Pity; I was sort of hoping that my swimsuit might inspire him to spend more time in bed. I, at least, have been going without sex while we've been apart. But we've barely finished fucking before he wants to be back on the shore. So far today he's found:

- A horseshoe crab. Is there anything on this Earth that looks less like it comes from it? We turned it over on the sand – for all their armour, they're not especially fast, or threatening – and he poked its belly. At least I think that was its belly.
- One of those fish that puff up and are spiky. It was in a fisherman's bucket, and he was about to throw it back, but not before the Boy had a good look. It had puffed itself up after being caught and the man told me it would deflate once back in the water. It looked at me with flat black eyes and I shrugged. When he threw it in, it bobbed on the surface for a moment like a child's beach toy, then deflated and swam away.
- More shells than we can carry. Also found some shark's teeth. The Boy suggested I make them into necklaces for his brothers. I laughed. What does he think this is, *Castaway*?
- Birds. Now that we've started counting, we have seen seventeen varieties of bird that we don't recognise and one we do: curlews.

lundi, le 21 mars

The Boy's mobile must really be dead now, because I haven't seen him using it and he's been asking for access to the computer. I sigh, warn him about the intermittent service, and leave him to it. I return a few minutes later to get a bit of newspaper from the room.

He reaches across instantly and turns off the monitor. I look at him. 'Why did you do that?'

'Umm, umm,' he says. There really is no explanation, is there? He was either snooping around in my things or writing an email to another girl. Twat. When will men realise that if you play it cool, you can get away with a lot more?

mardi, le 22 mars

Note to self: don't go through a man's wallet. Ever.

I couldn't help it. Especially after the computer thing. The Boy was outside, talking to J, and his wallet was splayed open on the table. Just a quick peek, I thought. I suppose I shouldn't have been surprised, but I found a condom inside.

And extra-large? Is he kidding? I've seen the literal length and breadth of men's cocks in my time and there are few that can't be contained in the average-sized Durex. There's a good case for smaller condoms for smaller men, but extra-large? You're being had.

He came back in, without J, and I threw it at him. 'What's wrong?' he said.

'Condoms in your wallet?'

'What? This? It means nothing. That's f-f-f-f-or . . .' I could see him straining to think of something plausible. 'You know, in case we're trapped somewhere and need to carry water.'

'Really? I would have thought the spermicide might adversely affect the taste,' I said bitterly.

'Oh, why can't you stop this?'

'Stop this? You have a fucking condom in your fucking wallet. You are fucking writing secret fucking emails to God knows who. You're the one who needs to fucking stop.'

'Enough with the language,' he said, and turned away

smugly. Ooh, I hate that. My use of expletives is a greater error than finding condoms in his personal effects? Fine, then, I won't talk.

Ten minutes of silence truly unnerves him. He decides to try a softer approach. 'Please, I forgot it was in there. It's probably been in my wallet for years. Please believe me.'

If there's anything you should never believe, it's someone who begs to be believed. 'The date on it would indicate otherwise.' I'm a past master at keeping tabs on condom expiry dates. This one came out of a packet purchased last year.

'If I was cheating on you – which I would never do – you must know that I'm not the sort of person who uses condoms, anyway.'

Oh, I know that all right, and it chills me to the bone. The privileged classes incubating chlamydia between themselves like it was some sort of private club. If I wasn't already in the habit of being screened for diseases at regular intervals – considering my past, you can never be too careful – that would have sent me straight to the clinic. 'That. Is not. A comforting. Thought,' I said between clenched teeth.

'Please, just look at me.'

'I can't look at you,' I said. 'You don't use condoms? Could you imagine if I told you the same thing? That makes you lower than a streetwalker in my opinion. And that's a considerable insult to streetwalkers.'

'I'm not the one who took money for sex,' he said with real bite in his voice.

'Really? Then perhaps you should have done, because the number of girls you've been running around with, it might have been a very lucrative sideline.' He started to open his mouth. 'Don't deny it – I've read your email.'

He says nothing. There, I've said it. I haven't admitted to the diary, but I've said it. He isn't certain whether that means I read his email yesterday, or in general. He says nothing.

I straighten my shoulders and wipe the tears from my

cheeks. 'I don't care where you go, but get out of my sight for the next few hours.'

'You're chucking me out? I'm in a strange country!'

'I care? Get out,' I said. 'Don't come back before supper.'

mercredi, le 23 mars

In fact, the Boy didn't come back until well after supper. I was in bed, reading; he slipped into bed next to me. We said nothing for the longest time. I thought if we did I might cry.

'Please, I'm so sorry. I don't know what would happen if I lost you.' I notice he didn't apologise for any wrongdoing in particular, but it's enough. It's more than he would usually offer. Eventually we kissed and made it up, very gently so as not to wake J.

In the morning I was still sad and distant. The Boy was much more subdued than usual. Tomás invited us over for lunch, and we went, the Boy occasionally reaching over to stroke my fingers while me and Tomás chattered in half Spanish, half English.

Suddenly the Boy grasped my hand. 'Is that his cat?' he whispered loudly.

'It is.'

'That has to be the fattest tabby I've ever seen.'

Tomás noticed we were talking about the animal and brought her over. 'Look, she has a trick,' I said. Tomás brought out a piece of meat left from lunch and put it on the chair where he was sitting. The cat waddled over and sat, looking up at the chair. I tapped the wood.

The cat looked at me, looked at the meat, then looked at me again. I tapped the chair and she emitted a mew. Finally I took the piece of meat and put it on the ground, and she ate it.

'So what's the trick?' the Boy asked.

Tomás and I smiled. 'That's her trick,' I said. 'She looks

at you until you give her food.' The cat rolled over, happy to be the centre of attention, and her fat belly fell to one side.

'Cripes,' the Boy said. 'That's no cat, that's a land seal.' He laughed and I suddenly felt much better.

jeudi, le 24 mars

We're walking on the beach at night, me with shoes in one hand, hanging on to his arm for support. We're both a bit tipsy. We've just had a huge seafood meal at Tomás's brother's restaurant and are feeling a bit jolly.

'How about a roll in the hay – roll in the sand,' he says suggestively.

'Have you ever had sand in the crack of your arse?'

'Not yet.'

'How about here instead,' I say and drag him under the pier. We do it standing up. At least, he's standing; my legs are wrapped round his hips and my back is rubbing against what might be, I think, a barnacle. Or broken glass. Whatever. I don't care.

He comes loudly. We rearrange our clothes and walk on. 'Laaaaaaaand seeeeeal,' he sings, going deep, his big chest booming with the sound. It disappears into the road of waves. He turns back toward the pier and tries a falsetto. 'Laaaaaaaaand seeeeeeeal!'

'Are you for real?' I say, but it's sing-songy, and we laugh.

'Come have a feeeeeeel . . .' He pirouettes in the foam at the edge of the water. 'Of my beautiful land seeeeeeal!'

I fall over laughing. He instantly pounces and starts kissing my neck. I can't stop laughing; I'm spluttering now, it's actually hard to breathe. 'You're making me squeal,' I gasp

He raises himself on his arms. The curls of his hair move slightly in the wind. 'I haven't heard you laugh so hard in such a long time,' he says.

'Marry me, and we'll have a litter of props,' I say and pull him back down.

'If I didn't know you were lying to please me, I'd say yes,' he says.

vendredi, le 25 mars

I wonder why women have the reputation of being the more demanding of the two sexes. From my standpoint, men are the fussiest little fusspots on the face of the earth.

Yes, we ladies go in for hair-based rituals, obsessive shoe collection, and bag hoarding. But when it comes to the meatier subjects, men are just big girl's blouses.

Example: pain. Ask a woman for a list of the most physically painful experiences and you'll get an answer like childbirth and pubic waxing, in that order. Men, on the other hand, find shaving cuts an ordeal. Shaving cuts. A wee blade getting a touch too close to the skin.

Male egos require constant stroking. Every task is an achievement, every success epic. That is why women cook, but men are chefs: we make cheese on toast, they produce *pain de fromage*.

The Boy claims the domestic high ground because I once burned a powdered custard (which he has not done, according to his blow-by-blow of my cardinal error in the hated weblog, 'since the age of twelve'). Hold me back, Heston Blumenthal. I being capable of faultless hollandaise, the intricacies of mixing pink powder and hot milk don't seem worth my while. And I bristle at the feeling I have during this visit, that by shacking up with me for three weeks he's auditioning me as a cohabitee. Frankly, I could give a monkey's for playing housewife.

And then today he turned an all-white wash of mine shocking pink in J's washer. So much for being a paragon of the home arts. Obviously, he being a man and therefore having a man-sized ego, we will never bring it up again.

samedi, le 26 mars

I'm torn. I'm ready for the Boy to leave, but worried as well. There's so much we haven't had the time to do while he was here. We stay up far later than usual, having sex and talking – not about anything serious, nothing heavy. We're both aware that the luxury of having the other around all the time is about to end.

And the sex is changing. When he came here it was quick, fast and urgent; we'd both been looking forward to it. Now it's taking longer, we're going more slowly, it's less about instant satisfaction and more about building up . . . I don't know what, really. Nice memories to take home. Something like that. He holds me for ages afterwards. Is this because he wants to have something to remember me by, because he doesn't expect to see me again?

'When are you coming home?' he says as I put the light out.

'I don't know,' I say. I don't miss England, to be honest. I miss my friends, I miss my family, I even sometimes miss him but I don't miss home. 'Soon.'

dimanche, le 27 mars

His luggage has expanded; he's taking back a dead horseshoe crab in a shoebox. 'Do you really think they'll let you take that into the country?' I ask.

'Worth a try,' he says. And I send him home with sunscreen – for next time, I say.

The flight leaves on time, everything goes smoothly. It's still morning, and I am stood in an airport, alone.

Sunny day. Think I'll go to the beach.

lundi, le 28 mars

J's not a man of many words. Or rather, J's not a man of many serious words. He just looks at me and cocks an eyebrow. So much has happened the last few weeks and we've had no time to sit around and chat. I feel I have some explaining to do.

'I know, I know,' I say by way of apology. 'You don't have to tell me.'

'You're going to have to pick his pubes out of the soap yourself, okay? I ain't going near that shit.'

mardi, le 29 mars

Archaeology should be undertaken with care. Especially when it's your own.

I was clearing out old received emails and discovered a wealth of files I had forgotten about. Many things I had either put out of my mind or buried so deep they were unrecognisable as mine.

Pictures of myself with a series of regrettable haircuts, work from my student days – was I smarter then, or just more focused? – remnants of email and photos of past lovers. Trawling through the past took the majority of the evening.

It's the old photos that have the most power. Squinting in a bit of sunlight on holiday in Rome, yes, but more specifically, someone you were intimate with . . . well, being intimate.

There aren't many of those, mostly because I'm very tight-fisted with homemade erotica. Sure, I've stripped off and done unspeakable things to strangers, but let a beloved snap a pic? Almost never. One reason I've been reluctant in the past to produce homemade porn is because once it's out there you have no control over it. Literally none. And whoever sees it will think of you whatever they like. The recipient is free to post the pics all over the internet, mull over them wistfully some time after you've parted ways, or – worst of all – erase them.

I'm not normally a hoarder. I don't save cards past a year unless they're handmade by the sender, or extraordinary. But faced with what was a set of, frankly, badly posed and poorly lit shots of myself and an ex in flagrante delicto, I could not bear to send them to the trash bin. Even though he was modelling a rather fetching pair of my knickers. Especially as it's someone I haven't seen since the split. I'm frightened that if I never see a photo of him again, like the information I happily spilled with seemingly no mental effort in student assignments, I might forget he existed.

As if that could happen. He really knew how to wear women's underwear.

mercredi, le 30 mars

I lay on a wooden bench by the beach reading. A man came up to me – fifties, local, smart suit and sunglasses, probably a business owner – and looked at the cover of the book (Seneca, *On the Shortness of Life*).

'Very interesting,' he said in English. 'Are you comfortable here? Enjoying yourself?'

To be very honest, I was half thinking about falling asleep but feared sunburn. 'Yes,' I said.

He smiled and extended his hand in a friendly manner. 'Please continue,' he said, and walked away.

Seneca goes on at length about states of exile and how, when he is at peace and has the necessities of food, shelter and so on, a man should feel as at home anywhere in the world as he does in his own country.

A theory to which I heartily subscribe. Nevertheless, my heart did flitter a little to hear 'Come Up and See Me (Make Me Smile)' playing from the sound system of a tourist bar.

Dear Belle

Dear Belle,

On my second day at work at a major TV company, they made us all tell a whole room of people our sexual fantasies. This was supposed to be for some new TV programme. As you can expect, our bosses exempted themselves from this activity. There is still resentment among us and we feel a bit 'molested', even though we are all grown-up men and women. I worry that now my bosses are looking at me in a different way. But I am also consumed with a desire to humiliate them in return. What should I do?

Dear Show And Tell,

Eww, that steps over the line even for me. Now, sexual harassment being part and parcel of my chosen profession, I can't claim to be au fait with the proper authorities on these matters, but doesn't that squeak in under the rubric of some variety of assault? You should speak up sooner rather than later – unless you found yourself turned on by a certain co-worker's admissions, in which case I'd persevere in hope of the perverse.

Dear Belle,

My boyfriend likes to be fellated for hours (well, it seems like hours) at a time. Can you pass on any tricks to make him come quickly? I'm getting jaw-ache.

Dear Tetanus,

A mint or an ice cube held in the mouth may give him pleasure; it may have the added advantage of numbing your mouth. Sloppy wet hand action for a few seconds while your mouth takes a rest occasionally is usually acceptable, and if all else fails, stick your finger up his bum. He'll either come quickly or demand you stop – either way, result!

Dear Belle,

I met my girlfriend when she and I were both drunk. All subsequent meetings have ended up with us both in the same state. When drunk she is wild, passionate, free and abandoned.

However, when sober this is not the case, as she is an able student of biochemistry and bores me senseless. How should I proceed?

Dear Dick,

Either turn up at hers consistently armed with a bottle of fizz, or be resigned to dating less intelligent girls in the future.

Avril

N and I had a game: managerial-speak clichés. You take an old saying and make it new again, all through the judicious use of the thesaurus and a heavy helping of what I believe they call 'thinking outside the box'. It's a cheery waste of time I've passed on to J now. For someone who's never held an office job he's surprisingly good.

We sat in the garden, he with sunglasses and wind-up radio, me puzzling through a women's magazine in Spanish. Luckily, most of the words for cosmetics and sexual practices are the same.

J: If you can't tell your arse from your elbow, that would be a clear case of arse/elbow distinguishment issues.

Me: Alternatively you could say you have forest/tree distinction concerns.

J: A bird in the hand is worth two in the bush – bird number to bird location valuation ratio.

Me: Don't count your chickens before they hatch – be aware of pre-born chicken accountancy concerns.

J: Experiencing canine/feline precipitation.

Me: By the way, does it ever rain here?

J: Almost never. But when it rains, it pours. I mean . . .

Me: . . . at the point in time when atmospheric moisture is detected, it will inevitably be a not inconsiderable amount.

J: Can't make an omelette without breaking a few eggs?

Me: The disjunction between culinary outcome and the propensity to maintain eggshell integrity.

J: Speaking of which, are you cooking tonight, or are we going out?

Me: The likelihood of porcine levitation indicates that perhaps the latter outcome is more probable.

J: Fair enough. Hand us some of that suncream, will you?

dimanche, le 3 avril

I'd been expecting some webcam action with the Boy but the internet connection makes cans on strings look like a good idea. There are alternatives, such as chatrooms, but he's proving reluctant to use instant messaging. This is ostensibly because he's not very good at spelling. Still, at least we can have phone sex. Even though J wonders why he keeps finding the phone in the bathroom.

mardi, le 5 avril

According to his weblog archives the Boy makes fun of me for not liking jewellery and flowers, which defies explanation in my book.

Clarification: I don't want jewellery and flowers from a lover. As treats I buy for myself, fine; as gifts from friends, acceptable. But something about the obligatory roses on a birthday or bracelet on an anniversary leaves me cold. Now, gifts from clients, that was another matter.

There's a particularly filthy image A2 sent me in email. It's a parody of those horrible print ads for jewellery. It shows a woman in silhouette, lips clamped round what you can only assume is her partner's love machine. Below, the picture of a particularly large diamond, and the slogan: '*Diamonds. Now she'll pretty much have to.*'

Yes, I admit I sniggered more than may be ladylike. But it's also a depressing thought. Are men still resorting to buying expensive baubles to ensure their ladyfriends perform a service which – may I be frank here? – should be more or less expected in any normal sexual relationship?

Or are women who actually enjoy sex in the minority, and I somehow missed the memo on requiring a down payment for play?

If so, it makes me wonder why some women are so quick to criticise prostitutes, when it appears their main motivation for sleeping with their lovers is collecting gaudy jewellery. Methinks the ladies do protest too much.

Closer examination of the archive reveals that Susie was exactly opposite to me in this regard. She demanded holidays abroad, expensive meals, the lot. Greedy cow. A2 rang to see how I was getting on, and I lamented this fault. 'I should have at least insisted on trinkets and tributes with most of my boyfriends. They must have thought I was a cheap date.'

A2 never bought me any regrettable rings during our time together. His gifts tended more to the hard-bound variety. Though he did once part with the better part of a grand to procure a handbag I adored, and, what's more, did this without my ever hinting for it. 'But getting earrings wouldn't improve your relationship,' he said, quite reasonably.

'True, but at least I'd have something to show for it.'

Well, I have a handbag, anyway.

mercredi, le 6 avril

I miss sex when I'm alone. But while nothing is as good as the feeling of fucking someone else, of having your tongue entwined in another woman's fragrant fold or being filled to the rim by a hard cock, there are substitutes. Phone sex, vibrators, your own fingers. They're not perfect but they'll do.

And I miss cuddling. Though to be honest, in such a warm

place as this, and with enough pillows in the bed, the only difference between sleeping alone and sleeping with someone else is the lack of snoring.

What I can't get over is kissing. There is no substitute. I wake early and lie in bed, replaying kisses I've had, kisses I should have had. The plump, full feel of a warm mouth against mine; a probing, curious tongue. You can go out and find random sex, sure, but what if you just want a kiss? A more difficult request by far.

I remember the first. The first real one, not a peck in the schoolyard. I was twelve, he was fifteen and J's neighbour. As a treat our parents took us to Alton Towers. It was the first time I'd ever met this boy. He was tall and dark and had a gorgeous deep voice, and I spent all day trying to figure out ways to be next to him, including going on the most disorientating rides. That night in his mum's car we kissed and the other kids watched. In fact, I don't think there was a single kiss we shared alone.

'Say,' I said to J, 'I don't suppose you know what happened to that friend of yours, that fellow Geoff.'

'Wow, it's been about fifteen years since I heard that name,' J said. 'What made you think of him?'

vendredi, le 8 avril

'Yeah, this town is small beans. Thing is, right, I'm in the army so there's nothing I find shocking.'

'Really,' I said. This was the worst sort: people who could not be blown off through lack of conversation. He'd already told me how long he'd been living here, about some girl he was having sex with but who doesn't return his calls now, and extended an invitation to his house, bought with retirement payoff from the paras – with detailed directions of its location – in case there was 'something good on, sport or whatever'. Undoubtedly he had a backlog of stories and was prepared to tell them all. I looked around for the rest of the group he'd come in with, but they were nowhere to be seen. Tomás popped out from the kitchen and half waved. I nodded and smiled.

'Friend of yours?' the man asked.

'Neighbour.' He waited to see if I would expand on that description. I didn't.

'Anyway,' he said, 'I've seen it all, me. There's nothing you could say that I haven't been through. Go on and ask. Kosovo, whatever. Drugs. Criminal underworld, like. Been there, done that, like they say, ha ha ha.' I looked at his round, hard stomach, the downward-pointing moustache. I felt a pang of guilt for hating the fellow, no doubt he was not overwhelmed with female attention. He probably thought he was doing well with me.

'Is that so,' I said. I suddenly missed N very much; he would have put this man in his place and made it look easy. Oh, N, what would you do? 'How about I prove you wrong and then you fuck right off?'

The obscenity startled him, but then it always does. People don't expect words like that out of the mouth of someone who looks like me. He regained composure instantly. 'Go ahead, try me.'

I don't like one-upmanship; it smacks of competition and that is so not my bag, baby. On the other hand, it was time to roll in the heavy artillery. I waved him closer, so only he could hear what I was about to say. He grinned the grin of the Cheshire Cat, already prepared to say that anything I'd done had been done by him, first, and better.

'I once shat on a man's chest. For money.'

I stood up and left.

dimanche, le 10 avril

Email from the Boy is sparse, and his nightly phone calls are a bit stilted – he thinks J is eavesdropping. He's right, but it's not out of malice. It's a small house and the walls are thin. Last night I had to listen to J reaming another girl, so I think subjecting my cousin to a few pallid phone conversations is hardly squirm-making.

I suggest more email and find a few erotic stories on the Web to send to the Boy. Maybe email isn't working, because I haven't heard back.

OK, email is definitely working. Maybe he hasn't had time to read them yet. Or he is trying to find something good to reciprocate with.

He has read them. Hasn't said anything. Scratch the stories.

mercredi, le 13 avril

I ride to the beach so often I'm sure the bicycle knows the way by now: to the end of our road, turn right, turn left, down the hill, over the little bridge, turn right and on to the end. Straddling a rusted blue Schwinn, iPod plugged into my ears, the Stone Roses singing that they wanna be adored, I feel like a teenager.

Earlier this week I noticed a tan line forming in the middle of my thigh, from wearing shorts, but I can't bring myself to go about in only a bikini. I notice plenty of female tourists without the same reluctance.

Once on the beach I like to get as far away from others as possible, turn my music up, or just listen to the surf. The sand is infested with bodies. I'm not here for the bars, the bungee or the Spongebob Squarepants slide. It only costs pennies at the end of the pier to see a world that hasn't changed even with the ravages of tourism. Sad-eyed fishermen willing the Gulf to show them their fortunes. Reptilian birds fighting over heads and guts.

On a wooden bench, I suppose I fall asleep. When I wake and look down at the grey-green water – was that a shark at the bottom, or just a ripple of sand? – I see them. Twelve velvet red, long-stemmed roses bobbing on the surface. I don't know who threw them out there or why. But for the minute I sit watching, while they slide a crooked course to the crowded shore, they could have been for me.

jeudi, le 14 avril

Another important difference between me, Susie and all the other girls of the Boy's harem: I don't want marriage and children.

Maybe, as I get older, the notion that I will never marry or reproduce will be supplemented with '. . . unless I find the right person'. But if I'm meant to feel maternal instincts, shouldn't they have kicked in by now? J and I recently visited neighbours and their newborn. I was relieved to get out without anyone asking whether I'd like to hold the baby. Because there is no way to say no politely.

You may be thinking I'll change my mind. Or that I'm a selfish modern woman, corrupted by idleness, too self-absorbed to care for anything above herself. You may be right.

But, you see, I was a wanted child. My parents planned for me, longed for me. They survived disappointments and heartbreaks to have me. Whatever became of their relationship later, I grew up knowing I was special, wanted. I'd never wish to bring someone into the world less sure of it than that.

So the Boy and I were discussing this stunted maternal drive the other day. I get silly over things like lizards, and sometimes – if they don't poo – kittens, but very rarely react to human children. 'You're just a broody thing,' I accused him.

'No, don't be silly, I don't want children soon,' he said. 'I don't think I could take the thought of going without sex for that long, not just yet.'

Er, no sex while pregnant? Cripes, some women will try anything to get out of it. The only reason I can see to cut back your sexual practices when starting a family is the fear that your children might walk in on you, and then you'd have to sit them down for a chat and explain the facts of life, perhaps a bit earlier than you had expected. Such as what a 'pony-girl' is. And what Mummy uses 'butt-plugs' for.

'Actually, I think it's pretty safe,' I said. 'And anyway there are always alternatives to vaginal sex.' The third-trimester anal, for instance. 'It's the time right after birth that's probably sex-free.'

I backtracked quickly. 'Of course, I don't want to even think about it yet, either,' I said. 'Not quite ready to accept peeing involuntarily when I laugh yet.' He seemed to find this very funny.

dimanche, le 17 avril

Finally, the Boy's figured out how to chat online and now he's on all the time. Only talking to me, I hope. There are a lot of silences in our online conversations, and he comes back and types things like: 'Sorry, I was talking to my [long pause] brother.'

Great. Four nanoseconds after discovering chat, and he's getting friendly with online hussies. The chat program lets you send pictures as well, so I take some photos to whet his appetite. But it's difficult to take sexy snaps of yourself. For one thing, your arm is always sticking out at an odd angle. For another, getting dolled up for a camera with no one behind it reeks of sadness. Like those photos men online take of themselves. I do a set of me posing in transparent black lingerie, which I bought specially, having left most of the tools of my former trade behind. I think it turns out pretty well, and send one as a taster.

\<**TheBoy**\> I have to see more of those pictures

\<**belle_online**\> You like?

\<**TheBoy**\> You know I do

\<**belle_online**\> not until I see you first

\<**TheBoy**\> how's this?

\<**belle_online**\> Yikes! Slow down, I think I saw a flash of pink there.

\<**TheBoy**\> your turn

\<**belle_online**\> Here you are ☺

\<**TheBoy**\> no sign of pink there

\<**belle_online**\> No, but I think the hand down the pants is suggestive, don't you?

\<**TheBoy**\> not as suggestive as this

\<**belle_online**\> you're clearly getting over that sunburn, anyway

\<**belle_online**\> how about this then?

\<**TheBoy**\> o

\<**belle_online**\> r u okay?

\<**TheBoy**\> are your breasts bigger than they used to be?

\<**belle_online**\> I don't know, maybe a little. Time of month and so on.

\<**TheBoy**\> I think that's the sexiest thing I've ever seen, I just came a little

\<**belle_online**\> prove it

\<**TheBoy**\> will that do?

\<**belle_online**\> yes, so you did

\<**belle_online**\> sorry I have to go

\<**TheBoy**\> wait a minute, I'm one picture ahead of you.

\<**belle_online**\> r u sure?

\<**belle_online**\> No, you're right

\<**belle_online**\> next time I'll find something good for

you. For now you'll have to make do.
<TheBoy> I'm wearing these pixels out, soon please!

mercredi, le 20 avril

Brief phone call to Mum. By her choice, not mine – whoever this new man is, he's keeping her busy. Before she rings off, though, she offers the extremely disturbing advice that I should put off getting married as long as possible.

Er, did she even notice which daughter she was talking to? I've been staunchly anti-marriage since about the age of eighteen. Months.

Marriage is a fantastic institution for one and a half people to enter into. I would marry if only the right person came along, really I would. But all the men on my list of ideal husband material (as opposed to just fanciable) are imaginary, or dead, or gay, or some combination of these.

- Ian Curtis (dead)
- Morrissey (gay)
- Judge Dredd (imaginary)
- Johnny Cash (dead)
- Joe Orton (gay and dead)
- Gromit (as in Wallace and) (imaginary)
- D. Boon (dead and gay)
- Humbert Humbert (imaginary and dead)
- Inigo Montoya (imaginary)
- J.T. Leroy (imaginary and gay)
- Quentin Crisp (gay and dead)
- Virginia Woolf's Orlando (imaginary)
- Waylon Smithers (gay and imaginary)

So you see the problem.

Belle's Guide to Your Holidays, part 4: Romance

There is nothing more romantic than an affair while on holiday, right? Wrong. Just because Audrey Hepburn made twitterpating through Rome on the back of a Vespa the last word in feminine aspiration doesn't mean that a surprise foreign engagement will or even should happen to you.

One thing is for certain: the moment your sandal-clad feet emerge from the hotel you'll be fighting the men off with a shitty stick. Why? Is it because they genuinely prefer our pallid European flabbiness to the local options? Look around you – the local girls are dressed for the runway and cute to boot. You, in your Topshop T and cheap sarong are not an irresistible goddess. You're on holiday, and all girls on holiday are easy.

You're probably eyeing some Latin hottie right now, thinking that if it all works out maybe he'll come visit you in Bedford or you could meet again next summer. Meanwhile he's eyeing you thinking that, if it all works out, he'll never see you again.

It is neither of the actors in this one-act drama I pity . . . Your heart and ego, however bruised, will heal from the inevitable end of this romance. No, it's the doe-eyed innocent in Accounts Receivable who's been lusting after you over pints every Thursday for the last six years. If only he knew that all it took to win your heart, or at least temporary access to your pants, was cheap seafood, a dodgy beard and tan and an accent out of *'Allo 'Allo!*

Not to worry, I won't let him in on the secret. What, and ruin my own summer romances?

So we charge ahead, regardless of the consequences, because foreign men are as famed for their bedroom skills as we British women are for sampling them. It's a nice story, and makes good cultural PR, but it's not true. You don't go to a buffet expecting Michelin-starred cuisine. Josef Stalin (himself possessed of a deep tan, luxurious moustache and mellifluous voice) once said that quantity has a quality all its own. In that sense the men you will meet on holiday are true and dedicated card-carrying members of the Party.

However, I know nothing I can write will stop women letting some D-list lothario have his wicked (and disappointingly brief) way with them on holiday. The best I can do is advise rigorous condom use with zero exceptions.

samedi, le 23 avril

J rules again. For one thing, he's spending less time with the Screamer. Not that I didn't like her, but if I'm going to be up all night I want a slice of the action. And incest is not my style.

For another, he's noticed that I've not been out much since the Boy left, and has taken me to see Tomás at work – I've already had everything on the menu, but it really is all very good, and it's lovely to see friendly faces.

'You're full of shit.'

'No, I promise you – listen carefully.'

'Hmm . . .' I squint and concentrate more on the music. 'Fuck me, you're right! Mexican music does sound like polka!'

'See?'

Tomás's brother brings our meals, and comes round again to collect our plates – it's slow in the restaurant tonight so he's given most staff the night off. He waves off any payment and sits down with us afterwards.

J kicks me under the table. I give him daggers. What, are we fifteen?

'I think our gentleman companion here fancies you,' J says in his most exaggerated English, hoping Francisco won't work out what he's saying.

Evidently he doesn't, because he talks on. Now he and J are

comparing tattoos – J has one of a screaming skull emitting smaller, flaming skulls from its eyes, which he swears he does not remember getting, though I reckon from the size and complexity of it, it must have taken some six hours to have done. Francisco pulls aside the shoulder of his shirt to show a delicate fairy etched there. I can smell his skin.

'Does she have a name?' I ask, my finger lightly tracing the wings.

'Raquel,' he says.

'That's lovely.'

'The same as my daughter,' he says.

Oh.

dimanche, le 24 avril

The Boy keeps saying how happy he's been since coming here and he can't wait to visit again. Also that it's been over a week and I'm still one picture behind. I send him a photo he took on our holiday. My top was a little tighter than I remember and I look very busty indeed.

    <TheBoy>WHORE!
    <belle_online>Pardon me?
    <TheBoy>I spelled that wrong, didn't I?
    <belle_online>As far as I know there is only one
      spelling.
    <TheBoy>I meant the noise you do when someone
      looks great.
    <belle_online>Did you mean PHWOAR?
    <TheBoy>Yes, that's it.

But the conversation never really recovers. Maybe he wasn't exaggerating about his spelling after all.

mardi, le 26 avril

The heart is a lonely and extremely self-sabotaging hunter. We've gone back to the phone since the misspelling episode. But with less editorial power over what he communicates to me I notice that the Boy has contracted a bad case of mentionitis. At least four times in the last two days he's made reference to 'someone I know who works in the medical field' and 'a doctor friend of mine'. And I go back on my promise to stay off the diary, and have a peek – he's spending time with Dr Blowjob again, Georgia. So this is how much the holiday meant to him. Fuck all. I suddenly regret sending the sexy photos.

mercredi, le 27 avril

It's late. I'm cycling down the beach. The stars are more numerous here than at home – even with the streetlights I see entire constellations that you would never pick out in London. And I could never tire of the smell of the sea, or the sound of palm fronds in the wind.

When I pass the restaurant, I see Tomás outside and stop. Francisco is there, straddling a giant Harley-Davidson. Tomás must have left his car, because he's climbing on to ride pillion. 'Nice bike,' I say, unsure whether there are different words for pushbike and motorcycle.

There probably are, because they both laugh. 'So is yours,' Francisco says.

'I didn't know you like those,' I say, choosing to avoid the noun in question.

'The restaurant is a second wife,' Francisco says. 'I call this my girlfriend.'

'It's gorgeous.'

'You should come for a ride,' he says, looking me in the

eyes. He's a good-looking man, and damn but does he know it. I think I soaked myself on the spot.

'Maybe,' I said, mounting my rather less high-tech model. 'Race you home?'

They laughed again, and I waved the two brothers off into the clear, warm night.

jeudi, le 28 avril

The Boy rings as per usual. We're just chatting, when I ask if he has any plans for the weekend. He says he's going to a music gig.

That's nice, I say. Who is it? He mentions one of my favourite bands. Wow, now I'm jealous, I say. Who are you going with?

'Uh, uh, uh,' Oh god, the stammer. I know he's about to tell me a lie. 'Mates from work.'

'Really? Who?'

'Um, Andy and C-c-c-c-c-hris had an extra ticket, so, uh, I'm b-b-b-b-uying the drinks.'

I grit my teeth and let it drop. But as soon as he's off the phone I check his email. Two new: one confirmation email for payment for the tickets from the venue, and one from Georgie.

Really looking forward to it! she wrote. *I'm up for anything, just as long as it isn't death metal!* Yeah, I'll bet you're fucking up for anything.

vendredi, le 29 avril

So he's asked her out to a gig. I shouldn't be so upset, nor particularly surprised, except he's taking her to see one of my favourite acts.

229

Okay, I'm really upset because of her *death metal* comment. How lame exactly is this girl? On a scale of zero to Leo Sayer I'd say about point eight Leo Sayer. People that limp shouldn't be let into concerts. This is the sort of woman who turns up her wee nose at the masculinity of rock because it's all a bit sweaty. Maybe I'm a complete raving fangirl, but someone whose knowledge of music extends as far as her (no doubt fetching) eyelashes should be banned from gigs for life.

As long as it's not death metal? Heaven forfend something might be jarring or challenging. Or loud. I bet on closer questioning she would also reject 'gangsta rap' and 'angry female singers'. It's the musical equivalent of 'I love books, as long as they're not hard' or 'I love movies, as long as they're not subtitled.' It's people like her who keep Dido in royalties and James Blunt on Radio One. It's not just death metal they hate, it's anything that can't be played low in the background at a dinner party.

I know life isn't fair, but still. Elliott Smith stabs himself for no good reason, yet this person is still on ambulatory? John Peel falls dead on a Peruvian mountain, but she's kitten-heeling her way into rockpits to chain-smoke and talk over the music with other dimwits? I moshed at a Wedding Present gig in three-inch heels back when girls like her were Blu-tacking pictures of Take That to the bedroom walls. Where's the justice? Where's my machete?

If only it really was a death metal gig. But I suspect even Varg from Burzum's church-burning antics would fail to impress this chumpette. With luck someone will spill beer on her and she'll be too mortally offended to bother the musical fraternity ever again.

My only consolation is that a rival so pathetically vanilla probably carries that quality through all aspects of her life. Straight suck and fuck, and a roast chicken every Sunday. A cottage on the Isle of Wight (if it's not too dear). Which is on consideration exactly what the Boy wants from a woman – in spite of his protestations otherwise. I've been thrown over for a sniveling, pasty nonentity too many times to believe men actually want anything else.

Wasn't it Jerry Hall who said that men need a whore in the bedroom and a maid in the kitchen? It's not true. The kitchen part is correct. But they seem to keep their whores elsewhere. I suddenly want to find and kick this girl very, very hard. Repeatedly. And I want Will Oldham to write a song about it.

samedi, le 30 avril

An email from Georgie, sent from her work: *Cheers for last night! I think I have tinnitus. We'll have to do that again sometime but maybe something a little more mainstream?* She blathers on a bit longer, but it isn't anything you couldn't get from a random Victoria Coren generator.

My stomach lurches and gurgles. I have to stop doing this. I make a promise not to read his diaries and email again.

Dear Belle

Dear Belle,

I have been sexually active now for five years, and have never been able to achieve orgasm 'by the hand' of any of my lovers – but it seems to work perfectly when I'm alone. Am I shy, stubborn, or simply a hard cookie to crumble?

Dear Onan,

Let me get this clear. Fucking, tick. Coming, tick. You're just not doing both together. This is a problem? As Woody Allen said, at least masturbation is sex with someone you love. Perhaps you're putting yourself under undue pressure to perform. Think of the poor souls who are unable to achieve orgasm at all. If it does trouble you, I would recommend letting your lover stimulate you in other ways while you bring yourself off, or go for a completely hands-off session in which your partner simply enjoys the show. In time you may gain enough experience and trust with someone for this to change, but five years is just the beginning of your sexual lifetime. Be patient.

Dear Belle,

Bob Geldof, Bono, or Tony Blair. Which would you do, by choice?

Dear Charidee Case,

Sir Bob, if only for the chance of presenting him with offspring not quite so ludicrously named.

Dear Belle,

I am a youngish lady who has suddenly decided that I have had enough of endless 'proper' relationships with men – you know the stuff, laundry, making tea, making love occasionally and unwillingly. Over the past ten years, I have compulsively gone out with someone and done my best to build every flirtation into marriage potential. I realised that this wasn't making me happy, so I declared I wasn't going to do it any more. And all that's happened is that I have started sleeping with lots of my friends, boys and girls, all in a lovely non-committal way. I am very happy, so much so it is troubling me. What should I do?

Dear Merry Widow,

Nothing, nothing at all. Enjoy yourself. You've done the time in Sexual Purgatory, and it sounds as if all your good karma is visiting you at once. Just be certain to play safe, and if you take pictures, make sure your face isn't in any of them.

Mai

dimanche, le 1 mai

There are facts and there is the truth, and they do not necessarily converge. I was keenly reminded of this after yet another phone call with the Boy.

Usually I'm cool with that. Without interpretation, we wouldn't have art, culture, and *Newsnight*. It's a dichotomy I can live with. Especially if it keeps Jeremy Paxman in work.

But sometimes the gulf between information and knowledge is less enriching. The Boy has a little problem with the truth. But only when it involves him. So I was grumbling about fidelity again today – so what? Just last week he was taking another girl out on the town. And then today, in email, she called him sexy and made it clear that, if they aren't sleeping together yet, it's not far off.

He can't admit to guilt directly, but does snipe back with, 'Someone with your background really should watch where she pitches stones.'

Being female and Jewish, I'm down with the concept of guilt. There is no past faux pas too small for me to chew over daily. If someone points out my faults, not only will I instantly acknowledge them, but I will flagellate myself with the knowledge for at least a decade. I slept with men for money; this does not sit easily on my soul.

The Boy takes full advantage. If I lose my rag over anything he's done, he has only to say, 'Well, considering what you were like last year' to send me off into a miasma of guilt and apologies. He recalls each misdeed with an effortless ease that Google would envy. I can't say I haven't deserved it. When I hang up, I'm angry. He still hasn't owned up to taking Georgia to the gig, and it's a slap in the face as hard as finding out that he called both me and Susie 'kitty'. Damn it, I'm the one he should be going to gigs with. I'm the one who likes music. She's just simpering arm candy.

The problem is that men lie. Worse: they lie, and think they're not.

When the Boy and I first got together, he swore to the moon and back he'd never had a one-night stand. That by bedding him in the first week of our acquaintance, I was as close as he'd ever come. This wasn't something I needed (or particularly wanted) to hear. It was information he offered freely.

Never let it be said that my powers of investigation – or rather, the internet's – are below par: I track down Georgie's number and phone her in the UK.

As soon as she answers I know it's a mistake. How many women found my agency's number on their phone, rang up the manager and bawled her out instead of their cheating husbands? How many rang me? How many independent call girls have I known who had to change their work numbers to get away from the harassment they received – not from men, but from other women?

She sounds haughty, the way I would have sounded if one of them had rung me. 'You said you're his girlfriend?'

'Yes.'

'How long have you known each other?' I give her an answer which, in Hollywood circles, would be equivalent to something like three reincarnations with the same mate. 'I've never heard of you.'

'I'm not surprised.'

'He and I only slept together once, ages ago,' she said. Not that I believed her. But so much for his one-night-stand claim. Anyway, like I said, I read her email. What part of *You are very sexy, and if I wasn't so tired I'd take you up on that offer right now!* isn't two people who are having sex? I ask when the one-night stand happened. She claims not to remember.

I put the phone down: shite. I know women, I know there is no such thing as sisterhood, I know a woman who's after a cheating man will believe anything except the truth, and I know she's going to ring him and pass on exactly what happened.

When he rings back a few hours later, he is angry. 'What do you think you're doing?' he yells. 'What sort of a bunny boiler are you?'

The phrase stops me dead. Bunny boiler? Sorry, but what? He thought, and then deployed, the term 'bunny boiler'? He actually dared invoke *Fatal Attraction*, a mysogynistic cliché so cheesy it makes Camembert blush?

And *I'm* the bunny boiler? He's the one who was once removed from my house by the police. He's the one who stalked N after we split up. He's the one who went through my rubbish. He's the one who read my diary first. Who tells me he will love me for ever, then turns round and fucks some glorified nurse on the side. We have three words for that where I come from, and they are 'pot', 'kettle' and 'black'.

But believing your own lies is the male prerogative. If he says it, it must be true. The time I caught him in bed with the stick insect girl, I bet that's the very phrase he used to palm her off, make her believe he wasn't a complete shit: bunny boiler. If ever a man said it to me, I bet I would believe it, too. Well, fuck it. Fuck men and their stupid games. From now on I'm believing the women.

I confronted him about his one-night-stand lie. 'Well, that really didn't count,' he said.

'How does that not count? How is that not a one-night stand?' I am familiar with slippery man-truth. I came of age in the Clinton era of oral sex not being 'real'. I have no doubt my married ex-clients did not classify what they did as sleeping around.

'If you know someone for a while first, it isn't really a one-night stand.'

I growled. 'So either she's correct, and you slept together once and had a one-night stand, which means you lied to me then,' I said, 'or you did not have a one-night stand, in fact slept with her more than once, and you're lying to me now.' I licked my lips. 'And what's more, you're courting while I – your actual girlfriend – am away.'

'I'm in this situation because you put me there,' he said. 'I can't tell my friends about us, because they'd think I was an idiot for having you back.'

'So you go around telling women you're single. And that is my fault, because you're not man enough to stand up for me.'

'I've never lied to you,' he said, smug as you like. QED. He's the hero for permitting me to date him. I'm the hussy who doesn't deserve the truth. Clearly.

My father always said never trust a man who claims not to lie.

'What's your fucking excuse?' I scream. 'If you want to play around, fine, but don't keep giving me your faithful man shit and then ring up and call me a bunny boiler. I have you bang to fucking rights and you know it.' He threatens to hang up. I do it first.

lundi, le 2 mai

I leave the phone off. No one rings anyway. Tomás comes by in the afternoon for language study. He's picked up a second job at a hotel, so it looks as if our meetings will become even more irregular.

He fumbles, smiling, in his bag and brings out a pineapple. '*Ananas*,' he says, and shows me the bruise on its side. It must be a reject from the restaurant. I wonder how much of his food he comes by this way. With a pocket knife he fillets the fruit expertly and offers me a slice. We pore over vocabulary lists together, munching the pineapple. He eats the woody core; I don't.

We quit early. Now I have enough Spanish for conversations, I ask him how his work is going, how his brother is.

'Some days are better than others,' Tomás says. Then, apropos of nothing, 'You are very beautiful.'

I don't know what he means by that, what is implied if you say something like that in Spanish. Is he . . . does he fancy me? Or is it just a statement? 'I think you are nice,' I say. 'But I have a boyfriend,' and for no reason I start to cry. How different would life be if relationships were as simple as that? The man thinks you are beautiful. You think he is nice. You fall in love, have babies and grow old together.

'*Estás preocupada por algo?*' Tomás asks. Are you worried about anything? His thick-fingered hand rests lightly on my shoulder.

I shake my head.

'So why are you sad?'

'My boyfriend . . . My boyfriend is . . .' *Mi novio es . . .* I gesture for the dictionary to look up the word. Tomás passes it to me, finding the right word takes a few minutes. *My boyfriend is a liar? My boyfriend is a cheat? My boyfriend is a pretentious shite?* 'My boyfriend is a big idiot.'

'It happens to everyone,' Tomás says. '*Debes tratar de resolverlo.*' You should try to resolve it.

mardi, le 3 mai

I click through to the pictures from the Boy's website. A Sunday walk in the country and lunch at a pub he took me to once, years ago, when he still cared about trying to impress me. Lambs, a stone cottage, a national park. Peacocks and a walled garden. And her.

So this is Georgie, eh? Nothing I couldn't have predicted. Short legs, round face. Sunglasses holding her brownish hair back in a way that looks natural on her sort and ludicrous on everyone else. Wearing one of the Boy's rugby shirts. It billows round her like a cape.

Did I really need to see that? See that it was just as I expected, just a parade of stereotypes?

You meet them everywhere, from the enclosures at Ascot to dining-ins at the officers' mess. The mouse-haired posh girls, heavy bosoms sagging in bias-cut satin dresses, each one hanging on the arm of a fit, godlike man who in a true meritocracy would not be plighting his troth to good old Wellsey, the dim, horsey daughter of a merchant banker.

There's nothing someone like me can do to compete. I was at school with several metric tonnes of them and learned the lesson well: no matter how I dress, what I do, it will always be obvious. Hunkering down into academic achievement was all I had to counter with, not that such things mattered to them. These girls wear their expensive lifestyle the way it should be worn: carelessly. I can't do that. I put shoe trees in my pumps and am on a first-name basis with the dry cleaner. I'm a try-hard. Nothing in my life has ever been careless.

But what they don't know – what they don't know – is that I may look tame but I am really feral.

That's why we become the mistresses. The call girls. Men pay for their perfectly groomed bit of fluff on an hourly basis then go home to a lady who cuts her nails with her teeth. And I would rather be bought for the cost of three hundred an hour, keeping my spare time my own, than for a token heirloom ring.

So why is he doing it this way? Keeping me in the dark and playing away with her? I'm a man's woman. Someone who can down gin by the half-pint and shoot a decent frame of snooker. The sort of girl you have an affair with, not the sort you marry. By all rights he should be sliding a ring onto the finger of someone like her and sliding into the ring piece of someone like me. Not the other way round.

I fucking hate him.

Except, and this is the jam in the works . . . I still love him. It's not just wounded pride that makes it hurt. It's the rich, aching desire of wishing he was here. I know I could do better, find a real man, find my equal. That isn't the point. It's him I want.

jeudi, le 5 mai

'Don't do it,' J says, watching me dial. 'When you come to your senses, you'll never want that man again.'

'The heart has its reasons, right?' I say. I haven't eaten in days and can think of nothing else. Tomás came around with three new horror films and I told him I had a cold. I can't hold out any longer, I want to hear the Boy's voice. The phone is ringing the other end, the short, staccato English ring. Brrrrrp-brrrrrp. Brrrrrp-brrrrrp.

J grabs the phone and hangs up before it connects. 'Fucking hell! You're my cousin, and I love you, but you're crackers.'

I love him,' I say.

'That's not love. That's addiction. I know. I was the same way, only with drugs.'

The phone rings. It can only be the Boy, calling back. J shakes his head. 'Then you have to do for me what your family did for you,' I say. 'Let me make my own mistakes.' It's a low blow, but it is the truth, and he knows it.

'Fine,' he says. 'But if that stupid fucker comes back here, he's not staying with me.'

samedi, le 7 mai

Twice a day. That's how often, twice a day. We phone each other, but we're both still angry and distant. We don't have anything to say. Sometimes he draws enough energy to start a tirade at me, and when he does I put the phone down and quietly walk off. Sometimes I can be gone for ten minutes and when I come back he's still going at it.

'You ruined my life, did I ever tell you that? I've lost every opportunity I ever had because . . .'

I walk off again. Because when he's finished, he'll say he loves me, say he hopes I stay safe. I don't say anything back. I remember what J told me, before I came here, those months ago: *You don't have to make a decision.* Eventually the Boy will yell himself out and then we'll see where we are.

mardi, le 10 mai

'Darling, I'm on my way,' a voice said down the not-particularly-clear line.

'Pardon?'

'I'm on my way! I'll be staying virtually a hundred yards from your door from next week.'

'That's lovely. Who are you?'

'L, you silly goose,' she said.

'Omigod! Sorry, the connection is terrible,' I said, sitting up in bed. The fact that it was also half four didn't help.

'No worries, darling. I'll e you the details. Get back to bed before I wake you up properly.'

jeudi, le 12 mai

Tomás knocks on the door early – there's a staff-only party at his brother's restaurant tonight; J can't make it but I can.

Not knowing what to expect, I dress for anything: sleeve-less, low-cut red silk top over a push-up bra, tight black skirt that flares slightly at the knee and fits like a dream, high, high heels. I thought I might have overdressed for the occasion, but the Latinos, they know how to do nights out. If anything I've pitched it a bit too subtle. Tomás is happy to see me, and so is his brother, and so are the half-dozen or so Serbs who have also come to the shindig.

'I thought this was a private party?' I whisper to Tomás, who shrugs. They obviously just turned up with fat wallets, and hey, what can you do?

Francisco hasn't laid on much food apart from olives and nibbles, but the alcohol flows freely. He's even brought in a DJ and after a few margaritas the place is swinging. It's a real mix – some modern Latin stuff, some mariachi music, chart hits and oldies. I barrage the DJ with requests. He plays one of my favourites, '*Besa me Mucho*', but doesn't seem to know anything about Half Man Half Biscuit. Ah well. One of the Serbs is a cartoonist who sand-sketches everyone there – I'm appalled to see he's included my laugh lines. One of the others in his group is a round-faced divorcee, and the two teenagers I initially took to be his hired companions are in fact his daughters. Oops. He keeps buying me tequila, anyway.

And I dance with anyone who asks. Tomás, his brother, the Serbian girls. One of the waiters, a rather fey snake-hipped thing, challenges me to a walk-off.

Oh no 'she' fucking didn't.

'Is he joking?' I ask Tomás. I was running for the train in four-inch heels before this kid even knew how to put one foot in front of the other. And anyway, I thought walk-offs ended sometime circa the last century (and that I was the undisputed world champion). Still, the lithe waiter insists.

The main floor of the restaurant is already clear, the tables pushed up against the walls. Everyone stops what they're doing to watch. The DJ humours us – at Francisco's request – with a little Prince. The challenger is first. He's sharp. He's sleek. He's good, he's very good. But he's just a man after all. And there are no prizes for second place.

Let me explain: if, when a lady decides to abandon a life of leisure for working the seedier side of the street, if she doesn't already know how to walk, she will learn fast or die trying. Because sex work is all about the moves. How to make an entrance. And how – as is so often required – not to. They say Naomi Campbell moves like a thoroughbred? I'd have her at the first hedge.

I motion to the DJ to cut the music. I don't need props.

I point to my challenger and stalk off to the opposite corner. Turn, pose, walk back. A slight bounce of the cleavage and a wink. Keep it simple; no distractions. Lead from the hips. Breathe confidence, *be* confidence. Connect with your inner reservoir of *fuck-you*.

He knows I've nailed it. The kid gives a mock I'm-not-worthy bow. I smile, kiss his cheek, and let the Serbian divorcee buy one last round.

'Amazing,' he hisses wetly in my ear. 'Kid's play,' I say. 'At least this time I didn't have to take my knickers off halfway through.' He gives me a look but doesn't ask.

Tomás says he's staying over at Francisco's; it's walking distance. I ring a taxi and go home to bed. But I am too wound up to sleep. I writhe on the bed drunkenly, feeling my naked body, wondering what life would be like as a Serbian trophy wife.

vendredi, le 13 mai

It's never easy to know when to let something go. Not simply relationships – though, obviously, I include relationships – but also personality quirks, ways of being. One gets so used to telling people 'I am this' and 'I do that' that not being this, or not doing that, leaves a feeling not unlike a tiny cork bobbing on a very big sea. What are you, beyond the collection of the things you've done, said and thought?

Happily, much comfort is to be found in the Good Book – by which I mean, of course, the inspired writings of Douglas Adams. I find J has all the volumes and start reading them again. It's terribly uplifting in its way – you really can get by after your tiny home planet's destruction. Knowing that we are a very small deal makes it all so much easier to let go, stick your thumb out and hope for a passing alien to take pity on us.

lundi, le 16 mai

J and I go round to Tomás's house. Tomás has just bought a new car, and perhaps I've been here for too long now but it's sweet. Low-riding '70s model with pale leather upholstery and the Virgen de Guadalupe on the bonnet. When I return home there are three missed calls from the UK. It was four in the morning his time before he gave up ringing me. I feel like a total jerk. Then I remember about Georgie and feel like a less-than-total jerk.

mercredi, le 18 mai

Things are desperate in the love department. I'm not normally the sort of person who resents the prerogative of young marrieds to kiss and giggle in public, but, for goodness' sake, why do they always have to be doing it on the beach next to me? I not-so-casually kick a little sand in the happy couple's direction every time I get up but they Don't Even Notice.

dimanche, le 22 mai

Do I know what today is? J asks. I don't. Go ahead, have a guess. I know it's not his birthday. Some obscure local holiday? No. Full moon? No, J says, it's a year since. A year since what? A year since I went clean. Why didn't you say? I'll take you out. No, J says. I'll take you out. A year since I realised I almost lost my family. Where to? Where else? J asks. Tomás and Francisco's, of course.

Francisco has brought his Harley to work today. It gleams darkly outside the restaurant like a giant insect, poised to leap. 'Hell of a motor,' J says. 'Ever ridden one of those?' I say no. J says I should give it a go. Then pats his pocket. 'Fucksticks, I forgot my wallet.'

'I'm sure they won't be too bothered.'

'No, I'll just pop home and get it. I'll be back for you in a few.'

He gets up from the table, has a word with Francisco, then leaves in his car. When Francisco comes over to the table I realise: J has paid the bill, he's not coming back to fetch me, he's told Francisco to give me a lift home.

Francisco's mouth is screwed down. 'This is difficult,' he says under his breath. 'My brother is here.'

'I'm sorry,' I say, hoping he knows it was J's idea, not mine. I could walk home, I think. It's not far. But then the bars and restaurants will all be letting out about now, and the narrow streets will be full of drunken British thugs, and I will at the very least feel uncomfortable. 'You don't have to, I'll walk,' I offer.

Francisco waves his hand dismissively. 'Wait outside,' he says. 'I'll be ten minutes.'

The motorbike speeds away from the restaurant and my hands are tight round Francisco's waist. We take the long route, the way along the beach. The long curve of yellow streetlamps is reflected on the calm water. My hair whips wildly around my face and his, and he urges the motorcycle faster, faster than I think must be safe.

We stop in front of my house. 'I like you,' Francisco says, unzipping his leather jacket.

I don't know how to reply. I don't know what weight the words carry in Spanish, what my response may or may not imply. 'I like you, too,' I say.

And then suddenly he pushes me against the wall, making my elbows raw, and he is kissing me. He grinds his hips into mine and pushes me off the ground with the force. His tongue is quick and certain, and mine replies in kind. Then, just as quickly, it's over. We stand a few feet apart.

'*Tiene una esposa*,' I say. It's not a question, it's a statement: you have a wife.

He looks at me, holds his hands out at his sides and shrugs. It's a classically male gesture, a so what? Implying that it doesn't matter to him and it shouldn't matter to me. I am being disingenuous, I know this, but he doesn't. He doesn't know about my past, the number of husbands I've had, the number of fathers.

And I know that, for all the outward show, the Catholic piety of people here goes about as deep as my Jewishness does. An identification, a way of life – not a system of belief. I wouldn't be the first girl he's had on the side. My refusal would give him no more than a moment's pause. Anglo girls are ten a penny.

I say goodnight and enter the house. The lights are off, but I know J is there, know he heard everything.

lundi, le 23 mai

'Cardinal rule,' L says, turning over to tan her front. Her skin is fair and freckly, but she's managing well thus far. 'Don't bring up the wife and child unless he does first.'

'You sound like you've been involved with married men before,' I say.

L harrumphs but doesn't answer. She's staying at a rented *cabaña* – alas, she notes, devoid of *cabaña* boy. 'The long and short of it is this: if a man wants to be single, he'll be single. If he wants to cheat, he'll cheat. No sense throwing his lies back in his face.'

'Noted,' I say, rubbing more suncream into my shoulders. I don't see the point, as the light wind blows sand into the sticky cream, meaning that every time I rub more on I take some skin off with it. Surely this negates any positive, skin-protecting effect the cream must have? On the other hand, perhaps it's exfoliating. 'So how are you enjoying your time out?'

L laughs. 'My entire life's a time out,' she says. 'The actress who never acted, the lawyer who has yet to practise law.'

'It's a hell of a way to live.'

'It's a tough life, but someone has to do it,' she says.

mardi, le 24 mai

J was out with a different girl. I saw her briefly before they left: short, dyed blond hair, the slightly hassled look of a single mother. I cycled down the beach, oblivious of the crowds and noise around me. Before I knew it I was at Francisco's restaurant, so I went in.

Tomás didn't seem to be around. I chose a small corner table and started writing in a notebook. Francisco came over and offered a menu, but having had everything on it three times over, I told him to bring me whatever he thought I would like and a carafe of wine. He smiled: this pleased him. I saw the restaurant was very busy for midweek but he waited on my table himself.

After the first glass of wine I went to the toilet. When I was washing my hands the door rattled. '*Es ocupado*,' I said back.

'*No, es Francisco*,' he hissed from the other side. I let him in.

Without even locking the door he pushed me against the sink and started kissing me. One hand pulled me up onto the edge of the sink and the other fiddled with my left nipple through my shirt. He was definitely someone who had moves and knew what to do with them, I decided.

'Saturday night,' he said. It was a command, not a question, but to be honest I like a man who says – not asks – what to do. 'I'll see you after work.'

He left the toilet and I waited a minute before emerging. It was all I could do not to fall over on the way back to the table. He brought out my courses as if nothing had happened, I settled the bill and walked home. What to do with this? I wondered. A married man. But I'll bet he's great in bed. And no good reason to deny myself . . .

The Boy rang shortly after I returned. Idly I wondered what – or who – was keeping him up so late.

'You seem to have a far more active social life by yourself than you ever do with me,' he said.

If that's what he thinks, good. 'That's because you never took me anywhere and never introduced me to your friends,' I said.

He went quiet. It was, after all, the truth: introducing me to more people than strictly necessary would have put a serious damper on his extracurricular activities.

'I'd better be off to bed, then,' he said.

'Enjoy it.'

''Bye.'

mercredi, le 25 mai

'Let me see if I understand,' J says. He's taken me out for ice cream and a tan. No, really – it turns out his favourite place to go is a combination tanning salon and ice cream parlour. Genius. Whatever will they think of next? 'He says he wants to marry you, but has he ever actually asked you to marry him?'

'Not as such, no.'

'And he let you leave the country and come here,' J says, swirling his spoon around in the remains of a knickerbocker glory. 'But if he'd given up the other girls and asked you to stay in England, you would have done?'

'That's about the size of it, yes.'

'So what do you have to feel guilty about?'

'Everything I did wrong.'

'Everybody makes mistakes,' J says. 'You make the best decision you can at the time. Sometimes it's wrong. So what?'

I look in the bottom of my empty bowl. I all but licked it clean. I fucking love ice cream, could eat it in place of almost everything else in the world.

'No ring, no contract,' J says and punches me on the shoulder. 'Come on, stop shitting on yourself. You're much better than that. And what's a kiss? Nothing worth feeling this bad about.'

I smile and let him pay.

jeudi, le 26 mai

Belle's Guide to Your Holidays, part 5: Chemists

If there is one place in the world specifically designed for humiliation, it is the chemist abroad.

First the fact that the only items on open display seem to be tampons, breast pumps and douches, making one feel as a female more soiled and wretched than even two thousand years of Catholic catechism could do.

Being in the market for neither feminine hygiene nor lactation aids, one is left to approach the chemist himself at the service counter, which is invariably a) not in a quiet corner of the shop, b) thronged with old men, and c) staffed by people who do not understand your feeble attempts at their language, much less a single word of yours. Rest assured that when you finally manage to locate the Spanish (or Greek, or Italian) for laxative (or condom, or pessary) it will happen at a point when the entire village is making its customary weekly pilgrimage to the shop and everyone has fallen silent the moment you blurt out the fatal word.

That will also be the point at which, if indeed it is a box of condoms you are attempting to purchase, you discover that the chemist is the father of your intended amour. How much more fortunate are those who travel knowing none of the local language at all, so they are excused by simply pointing to the appropriate word in a phrase book!

Having procured the desired item, you find the usual methods of payment are useless here. If they accept cards, yours will not be on the list. If they accept cash, you will be fortunate enough to have wandered into the single remaining establishment on the continent that did not change over to euros. In fact, they work on the barter system here, and if it's Tuesday it must be the day when only chickens are legal tender in Belgium.

In grocers and markets worldwide, if items are not priced it usually means that you are expected to negotiate the cost. At a foreign chemist items are unpriced for exactly the opposite reason. It's their way or the highway. What are you going to do, comparison shop? A packet of six laxative pills costs in the region of £7.50, with the breakdown as follows: £2 tourist tax, £1.50 local heritage preservation tariff, £1.75 protection money to the local police, 35p because it's an odd-numbered year and the remaining 90p for rounding up to the nearest pound. The remaining £1.10 is the actual value of the item, and you will learn this two days later when, for lack of any other printed material, you read the packet insert while squeezing out the first (and as it happens, only) diamond-hard poo of the entire fortnight of your holiday.

vendredi, le 27 mai

Pre-cheating preparation checklist:

- Condoms, procured. Although on closer inspection of the bag from the shop I notice the same surname as Francisco and Tomás's. Ah, crumbs, it was probably his father.
- Clothing, chosen. Tight jeans, cool short-sleeved black silk blouse, fetching jewellery. Nice knickers. Nicer bra.

- Hairy bits, shaved. I am not yet ready to put my fluffy bits into the hands of one of the waxing technicians at J's tanning-and-ice-cream place.
- Good hair day, as planned for as possible. Skipped washing today and hoping for favourable weather conditions tomorrow. It is a fickle beast.
- Conscience, suppressed. This largely achieved through listening to lots of music at full volume, the better to drown out any doubts.

samedi, le 28 mai

It doesn't happen. I'm primed and ready and it doesn't happen, and not because I don't want it to. I really, really do. But dressed and made up, sitting nervously on the end of my bed, waiting until what I think might be closing time on a busy weekend night, it gives me a lot of time to think.

I shouldn't be doing this, think of his family.

Since when have you ever worried about a man's family?

Okay, think of the Boy.

Yeah, think of the Boy – there's one reason why you shouldn't say no.

Finally I ring the restaurant. Tomás answers, surprised and happy to hear my voice. I hesitate and ask for his brother and he goes silent. I lose my bottle. I ask again for Francisco. It takes a moment, and he comes to the phone, sounding tired but sexy.

'I'm sorry, I can't see you tonight,' I say. No explanation. Not just because I don't know the Spanish for it. But also because I don't think he would particularly want, or need, my excuses.

'Yes, I see,' he says. 'It's very busy here, I must get back to work. Good night.'

'Good night.' And that's it, I've blown my one chance with

him, I know. The unopened packet of condoms sits on the end of my bed, next to my handbag.

lundi, le 30 mai

The Boy rings. We're still at arm's length. I make roundabout apologies, not placing blame on anyone: *I'm sorry you're still angry. I'm sorry that what I did upset you.* I usually hate half-hearted apologies, the kind of thing a politician would say to look good without actually admitting guilt. I shouldn't even be talking to him, but I want this relationship to last, and know from experience that forgiveness trumps anger every time. Ninety per cent of me is unconvinced that I'm the one who should be on bended knee. But the remaining, louder, 10 per cent really wants a cuddle. And sex.

Unlike him, I am not convinced that a secret summer romance would cheer me. So I email him a few new photos. The beach, the fruit stand, the house. And one photo of myself post-beach, naked, in the bathroom mirror. Suddenly we're on speaking terms again. Such is the power of tan lines.

mardi, le 31 mai

Someone knocks at the door. I go to answer; it's Tomás. 'You don't have to knock,' I smile. 'Come in, please.'

He stands on the step looking at me. His face is blank, I think perhaps he's angry. 'I hope you will not continue seeing my brother,' Tomás says, formally.

I sigh. Of course. Surely he's stood by and watched Francisco fooling around before. Possibly not with a neighbour, but still . . .

'I'm not interested in your brother,' I say. 'He is married and has children.'

Tomás nods soberly. 'He has.'

'Please don't stop talking to me because of this,' I say. '*Tú eres mi amigo.*'

He smiles. 'You are my friend, too,' he says, in English. I smile and invite him in.

Dear Belle

Dear Belle,

After an eight-hour romance, I woke in my bed to find that my new lover was gone . . . and he left a fiver by the bedside. Have I joined the ranks of your profession?

Dear Pocket Change,

Only if you agreed on the fee beforehand, in which case perhaps you should reconsider your rates?

Dear Belle,

I have recently had to admit to myself I am in love with my flatmate. He is a gay man, I am a straight woman. Every time I try to get close to him, he takes it as a further affirmation of our friendship. Something in me believes no one is totally straight or totally gay. (Indeed, sometimes I feel like a gay man inside.) Should I persist or is this a lost cause?

Dear Fag Hag,

The sooner you give this up the better. Telling yourself that 'no one is truly straight or gay' may be statistically true, but is a huge insult to the significant number of people who *are* truly straight or gay, not to mention a dangerous fantasy about as attached to reality as 'She says no, but she means yes' and 'Someday my prince will come.' Even if he can be swayed, what makes you think you're the gal he'd go straight for?

Dear Belle,

What is the right thing to do, as a client, when one discovers, after pulling one's member out, that the condom has broken and you have left your happy juice inside your service provider?

Dear Accident Prone,

As in any other relationship, the correct thing to do would be to inform the young lady immediately. If you have reason to suspect that you may be carrying any diseases – because, after all, you're visiting whores, something I reckon you do rather often, am I right? – it's best to tell her that as well, and offer a way she can contact you should anything unusual come up. Because a condom breaking puts both parties at risk, remember.

Juin

mercredi, le 1 juin

I won't go so far as to say that there are two types of men in the world – although I snidely suggest that there are, and the categories run roughly along the lines of, say, men who cheat and men who lie about their cheating – but there are, it cannot be gainsaid, definite types.

One in particular I've always had a weakness for is creepy-hot. You know, men who are undeniably sex on legs, but just might also practise devil worship on the side. In a sexy way of course.

Admiration of these specimens is in no way to be confused with the delusions of those hopeless women who 'marry' mass murderers on death row in Texas. Ladies, please, a word in your ears: convicted felons are not hot. They're just creepy.

Unless we're talking about Ted Bundy, but that's by the by.

Anyway, creepy-hot. There's a lot of it about at the moment. Such as Johnny Knoxville, who looks like he's always carrying a flick knife. 'And Johnny Depp,' L says, motioning to the bartender to bring us two more margaritas, double-quick. 'That man has so much creepy-hot going on he's practically their patron saint.'

jeudi, le 2 juin

L escorted me home and accepted the offer of a cuppa, but I was aware that we were still drunk and loud and I hated coming home drunk in front of J. Not that he ever said

261

anything, but to me it felt about as decorous as reaching into your £800 handbag to pay for a *Big Issue*. L excused herself while the brew was still hot, in any case.

I couldn't stop thinking about the Boy and had to stop myself ringing him. Maybe the dynamics of love are too complex for me to work out, and the simple fact of his imperfections – and my own – is not sufficient to make it not worth preserving; maybe the point of love is that you are loved not in spite of your imperfections but because of them. Otherwise romance would occur only among the ten-times-charcoal-filtered beauties of television and film, and in spite of the limitless evidence from celebrity gossip mags that their editors believe it should, I cannot believe that. I thought about whisky, which takes its flavour from a barrel that has already been used once (and sometimes twice). A clunky metaphor, but apt – after all, I was pissed. I detected some-where in the abstracted rumblings of my digestive tract the body's rejection of any mental exertion while tiddly on rum and coconut milk, and ran for the loo.

dimanche, le 5 juin

I suppose Georgie must have tired of toying with my boyfriend, because today alone he's rung three times. It's annoying that men are so transparent, but I can't say it's not nice. And when I went on the computer for a chat he was there. My only complaint is that he seems more keen to exchange social pleasantries than to talk about sex. Does this mean he's forgotten? What if I go back and he's gone off me altogether?

At least there are small victories. Such as the life-saving facial product L recommended for sun-battered skin. I replace my carnal urges with the compulsion to exfoliate. Not least because the treatment comes with a vibrating wand you're meant to apply the cream with.

lundi, le 6 juin

Some juxtapositions are too awkward to be explained away, like an orange in a dead politician's mouth.

Suddenly deciding to join the gym right after Christmas, for instance: it's an indefensible combination. Coming out with a plan for alternative fuel days after OPEC starts to collude on oil prices: no one's fooled.

The Boy inviting me to a wedding on the day I return home as soon as he finds out when I'm due to fly: absolutely transparent. It irks me to be second choice; but then, having worked as a call girl, I should be used to it.

mardi, le 7 juin

One out of every four women would like to sleep with Robbie Williams, apparently. And L is one of them.

Ladies, do you realise what this means? It means that far from being career-and-family-juggling, I Don't Know How She Does It, multitasking and thoroughly modern Millies, we are in fact hopelessly feminine and utterly predictable about it, to boot. We fancy a bit of rough. We all want to be the one who turns a bad boy good.

'It's just that he seems so . . . isolated,' L says in her defence.

Oh, it's a poor reflection on the cultural inheritance of the late twentieth century to find out that deep down we're collectively gagging for the chance to be exactly like our foremothers, whose mates were no more adult than the children they raised. That the thought of a smouldering look from someone who, near as I can reckon, most resembles a selectively shaved gorilla sends the ladies into such paroxysms of knicker-dampening is utterly depressing. Is this what the suffragettes would have wanted for us? Is this the future that Ms Steinem *et al.* secured for us?

263

'I mean, I feel like we're connected, somehow. I know how he feels,' she says.

Just the other day, in fact, L and I were jawing over coffee, wondering aloud how on earth men managed to put trousers on, much less assume responsibility for most modern governments. There must surely be enough combined spirit and wit in women to move civilisation forward in a positive way. Without secretly pining for sweaty builders and pop stars who want to be them.

'I've been thinking about sending him a letter,' L says, 'To say, hey, I'm not after you for your money, I have plenty. I just think I could be someone who cares.'

Worst of all, it has made me despise Robbie simply for existing. When J puts one of his CDs on, I make for elsewhere. If when flicking channels my eyes rest on one of his histrionic video performances, I turn the television off and head for the safe, warm embrace of the BBC World Service. It is just not possible to bear a world in which so many women fancy this man.

'I think you should go for it,' I say. 'After all, what's the worst that could happen?'

A particular pity because he looks like he could be such a nice lad, once I got my hands on him.

mercredi, le 8 juin

I dial the familiar number, but my hand is shaking a little . . . It's awkward making contact after so long. I feel a little excited and a lot guilty.

The familiar voice answers. 'Hello, gorgeous,' N says.

'How did you know it was me?'

'No number came up. Who else could it be?'

'An Indian call centre?' N laughs. 'I'm sorry I haven't been better about contacting you. I am a bit of a shit.'

'No worries. I'll beat you about the face and neck later.

And you know that's not an idle threat. So when are you coming home? I miss the hell out of you.'

God, I miss him, too. 'Soon,' I say. 'Next month.'

'Can't wait to get my hands on you,' N growled.

'What about the girlfriend?'

'What about her? She dumped me right after St Valentine's Day.'

'Nooooooo.'

'Yes,' he says. 'If I'd known, I would have been rid of her before Christmas and spent the time with you instead.'

'You're too sweet.'

'All part of the service, ma'am.'

jeudi, le 9 juin

I went back to the Boy's blog. Glutton for punishment, I suppose. But I also wanted to know whether there was anything I'd missed, either good or bad.

He hadn't updated it in a couple of weeks. I rolled my eyes. He'd never been very good at sticking with things. I scrolled back through the archives, looking again and again at the evidence of his affair with Susie, at the lies he'd told everyone, including himself: the ways he'd hated me and wanted to hurt me.

Except, it didn't look quite like that this time. Yes, he'd fooled around; and every one of those girls, he'd compared against me. Yes, he was angry; and over and over he'd written how he'd wished things were different, that I had been different, that we were together.

He didn't rabbit on about making a life with Susie, he didn't indulge in maudlin recollections of previous good times with the others. It was me he thought of when he was alone; me he said he wanted a future with.

And hidden in a long entry I'd only skimmed before: 'Now I know that she needed me most when she first moved to

London and was struggling to find a job, and I wasn't there.'
(Because he'd started seeing Susie on the side and was still
chasing Sierra Hohum . . .) I'd started working as a call girl
because I'd had difficulty finding a job that paid reasonable
money. He didn't openly wonder whether I might not have
chosen sex work if he'd been around more. But it was
interesting to see he'd considered this.

I was upset, but not in a bad way. I decided to quit while I was
ahead and make a real effort to stop reading his blog for good.

vendredi, le 10 juin

'Best travel sex tips,' I said.

L was sipping something giant and frothy, with several bits
of fruit impaled on a stick floating in it. She put down her
drink. 'Never fuck another tourist.'

I nodded; good advice. 'Never fuck a local. Oh, and bring
your own condoms.'

'Voice of experience?'

'I was a girl guide. Be prepared, and so forth.'

L smiled. 'Never do abroad anything you wouldn't touch at
home. Bungee, raw fish, etc.'

'Never do abroad anyone you wouldn't touch at home.
Bungee operators, etc.'

'Ha!' L tapped her teeth with the arm of her glasses. 'Come
early and come often.'

I smiled. It was getting harder to best her. 'Fuck the police.
No, seriously, fuck the police.'

L nodded and her lips pulled at the straw in her drink. We
were quiet for ages. 'My best tip, passed from generation to
generation of women in my family,' she said. 'Learn how to
say, "If you don't stop touching me there I'll call the police"
in as many languages as possible.'

'How many can you say it in?' I asked.

'At least eight.'

samedi, le 11 juin

I can't get sex off my mind – correction, I can get sex off my mind, but the replacement activities (sitting on the beach, walking with J) are not sufficiently distracting to keep me from thinking about it for long.

The funny thing about being starved of sex is that you remember things you might otherwise have forgotten: a particular night, or a lover whose name has long since slipped your mind. I've spent more than a few hours recalling:

- The man at uni who had dated all the girls in our circle of friends but me. We finally did it, the night after graduation. Anal. We never spoke again until five years later when he emailed me out of the blue (he's married now).
- The man who loved asphyxiating me, and since I didn't know any better, I didn't refuse him. Until, that is, the time I became unconscious, and remained so for several minutes, according to him. I don't remember it. But I never let anyone throttle me again.
- The time I had sex in a hotel room (not with a client), and the man used the clips of a trouser hanger to pull on my nipples – quite clever improvisation, that; it comes with a built-in handle, and we took it away when we'd finished – while I masturbated to orgasm. Afterwards, we watched Eurotrashy soft porn on the television.

dimanche, le 12 juin

I'm wearing a retinol-enriched mask; J has a lavender eye compress over his face. 'The sound of ceiling fans on all night,' he says.

'Low-riders blasting bass at 1 a.m.,' I say.

'Five-pound cocktails,' J says.

'No, they have those at home, too,' I say. 'Pork in everything, even the vegetables.'

'People asking you where you're from on a daily basis.'

'Sleeping alone.'

'You don't have to sleep alone, you know,' J says. 'That's your choice.'

'Whatever. Radioactive green soda.'

'Squid in cans.'

'Hey, I thought that was a good thing.' J takes the compress off and looks at me. I laugh. 'Just kidding.'

'Ants in the house.'

'You're right, I wouldn't miss that, either.'

lundi, le 13 juin

As the wedding the Boy has invited me to is with some of his rather posh friends and literally the day I arrive back, something to wear is obviously an issue. L came round to brainstorm on the options:

- Summer dress and espadrilles
  Pros: easy to get here
  Cons: look it

- Trouser suit
  Pros: easy to wear after a long flight
  Cons: L says 'ewwwww'

- Nice silk blouse and skirt
  Pros: casual
  Cons: too casual

- Jeans and a T
  Pros: it's what Julie Burchill would do
  Cons: 'I appreciate the fact that you spent two hundred

quid on jeans so your arse would look fractionally more like Cameron Diaz's, but really, no.'

- Travel to a big city here and buy something
  Pros: good exchange rate, will probably get a deal
  Cons: I don't really go in for the *Dynasty* look.

- Let the Boy pick up something of mine from A4's and hope for the best
  Pros: out of my hands
  Cons: he'll probably pick the big red meringue I wore to a school disco in 1992.

- Borrow something off L
  Pros: far nicer than anything I can afford
  Cons: will have to wait for her to come back to the UK, or post to her here. 'Hey, what am I going to do with this kind of dress here? I don't even know why the hell I brought it.'

mardi, le 14 juin

Tomás has given me a phone card, and though it means having to find a public telephone, I use it to ring Daddy.

'Hello, honey, how are you?' he asks. I tell him I'm planning to come home next month. 'That's great news,' he says. 'There's someone I'd very much like you to meet.'

Good thing he can't see my face, because it just turned in on itself. We exchange pleasantries, and he's about to ring off, when I can't resist asking.

'Daddy, did you and Mum ever really love each other?'

He pauses. 'I loved your mother very much,' he says softly. 'Still do.'

'You two are always so vague when you talk about each other, and now you're both seeing other people and . . . I don't know, I don't want to come home to two new families.'

269

'Honey, it's hard being alone,' he says. Oh yes? I think. Tell me a-fucking-bout it.

'Do you even remember how you felt when you met? How can you just walk away after all you two have been through?'

'Oh, sweetie, there are so many things you don't understand.'

'Really?' I say. 'Well, I'm almost thirty. Don't you think it's time I did?'

He sighs. I can hear in his voice, far more clearly than ever before, a note of defeat that was never there when my parents were together. I wonder who this woman is; she's probably young, and knowing how soft-hearted my father is, she's probably a mess. Probably using him for money and free babysitting. He deserves so much better. 'Things between me and your mother have always been complicated, right from the start,' he says.

'But you met as kids. You've known each other for ever. What's difficult about that?'

'Yes, we did,' he says. 'And then I didn't see her for years, until me and her brother were at university together and she came to visit. She was still at school then.'

I knew my parents had married early, when they were both still students. 'Well, what could possibly have been difficult when you were both so young?' Thinking about the wringer I'd been through in the last few years, with relationships, with my work, with not being able to be honest to my family – the very people I loved most in the world.

'I never told you this, honey, and your mother would probably prefer you not know, but she was pregnant when she came to visit. Her brother couldn't take her to have a termination, so I went with her instead. That was it. We were together after that.'

Oh.

'Listen, sweetie, I have to go, I'm going out,' Daddy said. 'I'll ring you at home soon.'

And that was it, he was gone.

I walked home slowly via the T-shaped *bodega*, where I

bought a chocolate milk. Why did they never tell me? I thought we knew everything about each other. Scratch that – almost everything. Honesty was always held to be so important at home.

And yet . . . I could imagine the strain on a young couple. He loves her, she's pregnant by someone else, someone who won't even do what is needful, and he has to take care of the mess left afterwards. The mess another man has put her into. Over time, they might get over it. Or they might bury it, it might fester and poison everything. I know that I don't want to know exactly why they split; knowing this is enough.

I turn round and go back to the phone, ring the Boy, and tell him I love him.

mercredi, le 15 juin

The Boy rang late. He was in a mood. I hate it when he does that; if he doesn't want to talk to me, why bother calling? I asked him what was wrong.

He sighed. 'Oh, nothing really. Just reading some things I wrote last year, and . . .'

His diary. I hadn't checked it in ages, he'd stopped writing in it about the time I'd phoned and confronted Georgie about his two-timing.

'Really?' I said, neutrally. Was he trying to catch me out? I had even now never admitted to finding his blog, only to reading his email.

'Do you really care about me?' he asked in his little-boy voice. 'Really, really?'

'Oh, you silly,' I said. 'What have you written that's made you so upset?'

I decided not to let on. Best left in the past.

'Old chunterings from when we didn't really get along.' Well, that would be about 90 per cent of the time we've been together, I thought.

'Maybe you should just erase that and let it be, whatever it is,' I said.

He thought about it. 'Maybe I should.'

jeudi, le 16 juin

Tomorrow I will be dining in high style with two girls I was at school with, L and Miriam, who is staying with L for the week. In an interesting, if unlikely, turn of events, we have ended up in the same place at the same time with similar taste in food. I am reliably informed of, and suitably excited about, a 'dessert room' (for yes, this girl has an insatiable sweet tooth) and promises of much swank. It should be an enjoyable evening.

It's been so very long since I have had female friends – round about the time we three were at shcool, in fact – that the etiquette of feminine gift-buying is beyond my ken. On the other hand, we have a lot of the same tastes, so how hard can it be? Though perhaps a shared love of boxing matches and *Star Trek* spin-offs isn't quite enough to go on. I know lingerie is out, books are too predictable (in another odd coincidence we are all reading *Jonathan Strange & Mister Norell* at the moment, and it is good), and jewellery smacks of trying too hard.

So it's out to the shops for me. Life is rough sometimes.

Today I had a tub of little sweets from M & S in the post! Courtesy of the Boy, who is patiently (I hope; unlikely) awaiting my return. It was like a whiff of Englishness came through the door. They were slightly melted into a chocolate-and-coconut slurry, but gorgeous.

I wonder if the girls would be interested in a half-eaten clutch of biscuits?

L's hired a car – not so much a car, really, as a fortress on wheels – and she and Miriam come to collect me. 'Pardon the smell; my neighbour's dog was exercising his inner Keith Richards and I spent the afternoon scrubbing doggy vom off the backseat.' It's a good hour's drive to the restaurant. It's silly, but I'm relieved that at least I dressed appropriately: silk blouse, pencil skirt. Not that these two would hold any sartorial misstep against me. They knew me in glasses.

I've not been to the city since arriving here, apart from going to and from the airport. It's much more modern than I expect, with lots of new buildings going up, plenty of large pastel flats, built in a vaguely Spanish style. L nods; says this is the good part of the city. I wouldn't want to see some of the rest.

The restaurant is indeed swank. A driver whisks the car away and we enter. L, who studied languages before acting and law, confirms our reservations in flawless Spanish. I leave it to her to order, then produce their gifts (a silk scarf and *A Room of One's Own* for L; a silver necklace and Seneca for Miriam). L and I split a bottle of wine – Miriam is driving us back – then another, and are tiddly before the food even arrives.

'Would you look at these women,' L says, slightly louder than I think strictly necessary. 'Nipped and tucked to within an inch of their lives.'

'You reckon?' I say. The women do indeed look almost airbrushed. There are plenty of pretty girls in London, but almost none who look like that.

'Look at her thighs,' L hisses as one walks by on the arm of a man three times her age. 'She's never done a day's workout in her life. That's not meat on her bones. That's veal.' Miriam and I laugh into our drinks.

'Do you think they're working girls?' I ask carefully. L and Miriam most emphatically do not know what I used to do.

'God, no,' L says, hand to bosom. 'They wouldn't dare lower themselves so. More importantly, I don't think the concept of any hourly work, even sex, would agree with them. But I bet in five years' time' – and she nods at another veal hanging off another septuagenarian – 'she'll be what we like to call a professional widow.'

'Works for some,' Miriam smirks into her steak.

When the plates are whisked away L asks the silver-haired gent looking after our dining room whether we could see the wine cellar. Now, that's chutzpah, I think. And he gives us a tour himself before we are shepherded into the dessert room.

L and Miriam share a chocolate-three-ways something or other, but my mind isn't on sweets. It is on home. I have a glass of their most expensive port instead.

samedi, le 18 juin

Tried to reach A1 again; still no answer. Gave in and rang the Boy instead. The pickings at home must be slim for him because he's gone all needy.

'You never say you love me,' he whined.

'If you say it too much, it loses all meaning,' I said.

'You never loved me as much as you loved him,' he said, and I know whom he meant, the one before him.

'That's not true,' I said. What I had fallen in love with was an image, a cipher; the man I had wanted to spend the rest of my life with never existed. It was true that I went on missing that work of fiction for ages. Still do at times. But I would never have him back, because the person I fell in love with never existed.

'It is,' the Boy said. 'He broke your heart.'

'Why, is that something you aspire to?' I said. Men are so odd. The other one, I should have seen it coming. He kept quiet when he should have spoken, said things I recognised only in retrospect for the idiocies they were.

Once, when visiting up North, that man and I were meeting my friends. Naturally curious, A2 asked where he was from. He wasn't sharp enough to spot the trap being laid, so when he replied with 'London-ish', someone else asked where exactly. He said St Albans. My friend laughed derisively; he was from Luton. Neither of them was from London at all. My lover had been caught out in a lie that was conceited and weak. My friends' opinion of my judgment slipped precariously after that, but I attributed the fault to myself, not him. I was under a spell.

But I know no matter what happens, I could hate the Boy and would still love him because I know he is real. I know his faults and want him just the same. He knows mine and wouldn't walk away just because I'm not perfect, unlike that other man, whose first argument with me was also the last. I know the Boy could ride out the gales as well as the glass.

I repeated the question. The Boy hesitated. 'No, I want us to live together. I want to love you when you're fat and old.'

'That's why you're with me and he's not,' I said, softly. I hoped he read the implicit love in my voice. I can't bring myself to say the word often. It should mean more than a drunken text. I hoped someday he'd understand that.

dimanche, le 19 juin

Spotted A4 online.

> <belle_online> how goes it, hot stuff?
> <luvly_jubly> not too bad
> <belle_online> have you heard from A1 lately?
> <luvly_jubly> not particularly
> <belle_online> I sent him an email last week. It sounds odd, it's just he's usually so prompt about writing back
> <luvly_jubly> I can ring him if you like
> <belle_online> would you? Thank you

<luvly_jubly> no answer
<belle_online> what, you rang just now?
<luvly_jubly> yep
<belle_online> bum. Did you leave a message?
<luvly_jubly> it didn't go to answerphone
<belle_online> That's odd. No wife?
<luvly_jubly> No
<belle_online> hmm
<luvly_jubly> will send him an email
<belle_online> let me know if you hear back
<luvly_jubly> will do
<belle_online> ta

lundi, le 20 juin

J and his new woman (there's always a new woman, I've decided; no point even learning their names) drove me to the beach. There was a thunderstorm approaching, and as we watched the sky grew darker with bolts of lightning coming closer and closer to shore.

It struck me, the power of what was headed toward us. Talking about it on the way home, we agreed that there is something rather humbling about not being in control – we were talking about the weather, obviously, but meant other things. Feeling a blast of sand and salt on the face as black clouds rolled towards us was frightening and exhilarating. Staying in the thick of something greater than individual humans was (nearly literally) electrifying.

I thought about the past few years, relationships and all that other maudlin rubbish. Change, power, blah blah blah – yes, I'm aware of sounding like a Keane song here – but it really was incredible.

That said, we did drive away as quickly as possible.

Just heard from A1. His father, who'd been hovering at the edge of death for years, has passed. I didn't know what to say. Who does? Can I do anything? Apart from bring your father back to life, I mean?

A1's father was legendary. He was a big guy, big laugh, strong Eastern European features that belied his anglicised name. He was a Jew, kiddo, but not a reedy, neurotic Woody Allen type. The elder A1 wheeled, dealed and chewed scenery with the best of them. He gave me a lift from one end of the country to the other once, and here I was, a frightened teenager who was sleeping with his too-old-for-me son, and you wouldn't have known it. Mr A1 chattered and joked the entire way down and gave my mother the eye when we arrived at our destination. He was a class act, a long-lost member of the Rat Pack.

A1 wasn't raised particularly Jewish – or, in fact, at all. The family joke was that his dad was a Jew, and his mother from some strange Christian cult, so when they married they compromised and went C of E.

Mr A1 had a talent for inappropriate jokes, most of which I found the opportunity to recycle years later when I was entertaining men on an hourly basis. He had known the charms of call girls, too – one of his favourite anecdotes concerned a prostitute.

It was when he was in the army, and he and some friends threw their spare money together to get a girl for an hour. There wasn't enough time for every lad to have a few minutes with her on his own, so they took her into a men's toilet and watched as each in turn did the deed.

When it came Mr A1's turn, he just wanted oral relief. She went down in front of his friends and provided it. Then, with his come still in her mouth she said – and here he would imitate her voice, her mouth full of his seed, a sort of half-gurgle – 'For another pound I'll swallow it.'

'It's yours now, love,' Mr A1 said. 'Do whatever you like.'

If I was ever meant to have a father-in-law, surely this was the man. When A1 and I split I was sad, not just for the end of that relationship, but for losing his family. They saw me here and there, of course; but it wasn't the same. It's never the same. You become ancient history to each other, a story to tell the new wife, an anecdote. Like the one-pound-more whore. You hear the old boy laugh somewhere across a room and it feels like you're still part of that inner circle – but you're not.

In the last few years, Mr A1's voice and his laugh were stolen from him. The two-pack-a-day habit he picked up in the war and put down some twenty years later had caught up with him, and eventually the emphysema was so bad he had to be on oxygen all the time. At his son's wedding we all but carried him around. You could see the look on his face and what it meant, touched though he was to see his son paired off. It was a look that said, I was vital once, I used to be the life of the party, now people just pity the old man.

I phoned up A4, emailed a few people, and generally felt unable to do anything more meaningful. Left a message for the Boy saying what was going on. He rang me a few minutes later.

'Sorry, I'm a bit shaken,' I said. 'Thanks for ringing back.'

'What's going on?' he said. 'Did you actually know this guy?'

Did I bloody know him!

mercredi, le 22 juin

This, in case I ever have to tell my children or grandchildren, is how it happened. I'm cruising around on a bicycle, long skirt tucked between my knees, huge sunglasses, enjoying the sunshine. A man waves at me. He's wearing white linen trousers and a blue T-shirt, he's cute, I wave back. He tilts his head and I stop to talk. What's the worst that can happen? He mentions maybe lunch? I know a place. We have a lot in common – we're from the same area, have similar experiences, laugh at the same things. Soon we're finishing each other's sentences.

He looks at his hands, sad. 'What's wrong?' I ask. 'I wish I could go with this,' he says. But he has a girlfriend, she's coming to visit next month. I have a boyfriend.

His name is David, I'm meant to be leaving in about a fortnight, and I am so fucked.

jeudi, le 23 juin

<belle_online> ugh
<luvly_jubly> What's wrong?
<belle_online> sloopid slow connection, looking for a flat
<luvly_jubly> Oh okay
<belle_online> Don't suppose you know anywhere going?
<luvly_jubly> actually
<luvly_jubly> I'm moving back north
<belle_online> Noooooo!
<belle_online> what about work?
<luvly_jubly> this is for work
<luvly_jubly> A2's starting a northern office in Macclesfield
<belle_online> you know what they say about macc
<luvly_jubly> what's that?
<belle_online> they don't
<luvly_jubly> Anyway
<belle_online> anyway?
<luvly_jubly> you can move in to my place
<belle_online> you're joking!

<luvly_jubly> all your things are here already anyway, would save my back
<belle_online> true
<luvly_jubly> and you already have a key
<belle_online> true
<luvly_jubly> and it would save you having to stay somewhere looking for a place
<belle_online> enough already, you've convinced me! You will probably live to regret this
<luvly_jubly> probably

vendredi, le 24 juin

'I'm a mess, I'm an idiot when it comes to men,' I say to L. 'I used to have a clue, you know? I used to be cool. Now I'm like some stupid chick-lit woman, and I've no idea why.'

'What on earth makes you say a thing like that?' she said.

'Well, why am I with my boyfriend when we so clearly drive each other mad, and not in a good way? Why do I meet a great guy just when the timing couldn't be worse? How did I manage to lose a great guy like A4? Will I ever do anything right?'

L reapplied lotion to her thighs. A tightly swimsuited young man brought our drinks over on a tray, and she smiled at him winningly. 'Don't be silly,' she said. 'You do what you have to do.'

'The question is, do I really have to do this? Act like a completely stupid girl just because I don't want to be alone?' I readjusted my bikini top, checking to see whether the strap marks were in awkward places.

L sipped the icy concoction. Her lips always look so lush; when I asked her secret, whether cosmetic procedure or clever make-up application, she replied, 'Genetics, baby. Read 'em and weep.' I spent something like the weekly income of a local on a tube of her preferred lipstick, anyway.

'It's not stupid,' she finally said. 'You've glimpsed the future, and while it's nice to be running around with a cute little body like yours now, someday you'll have to choose between your face and your ass, and whether you are willing to compromise when it comes to relationships or prefer to become the intensely lonely fossil who, on finishing the eighth double Scotch of the evening, blankly stares into the middle distance, considering the irrevocable march towards death.'

Yikes. 'Sounds like you've thought about that a lot,' I said weakly.

'Also a part of my genetic inheritance,' she shrugged. 'It's what made me a good law student. And will guarantee that I reach the age of sixty with a houseful of furs and antiques rather than children.'

samedi, le 25 juin

The Boy rings to say that, because of family obligations, he won't be able to ring me over the weekend. This has the ring of untruth but I bite my tongue. Fuck it, let what happens happen. Things could all be different in a week, anyway.

dimanche, le 26 juin

David and I go to his house. He has local beer in the fridge and lets me choose the music. It's a nice house, I say; is he renting? No. Owns. He's moved here permanently, to start a business. His girlfriend didn't join him. He got the dog.

The dog is called Fritz, and hasn't taken his eyes off me since I came in. I scratch his belly and pet his ears.

'I can tell you're a sensual person,' David says.

'How's that?'

'By the way you touch his ears.' Fritz suddenly licks my face. 'Don't do that Fritz, I haven't even kissed her yet!'

I don't fall for someone often, and feel like fate is mocking me. He's funny. Smart. Has his own business. And is, of course, not quite single. His on-again, off-again partner, who lives as far from here as mine does, is visiting after I go. He says he's sure they'll break up then, but at least he's straight with me. It makes him feel guilty, he owns up to her existence. It's a bittersweet flirtation. In a parallel universe we're probably carrying on a scorching love affair without even a pang of guilt. But in this one, we're both Jewish.

'What do you want to do?' I ask.

'You know what I want to do.'

'I don't. You haven't even kissed me yet.'

'I'd like to take you on the floor and spend the next three hours fucking.'

What is it about relationships that makes shared misery feel so much like intimacy? I think, rather despising myself for doing so, about what makes a good crew on a yacht: good sails in charmed conditions, bad ones in wind against tide, and, quite simply, time on the water. Miles under your bow make a dilapidated cruiser more attractive than a box-fresh trimaran sleeping six.

I look at David and decide that he is thinking something similar (though perhaps with fewer awkward boat analogies). And that we are both weighing up the investment of time and effort on our respective craft, and how fully fitted the spec for the new model looks.

'Really?' I say.

'Really,' he says.

My breath is heavy and uneven. 'Oh.'

Before we part I step towards him – a move which, in other circumstances, would signal the big romantic clinch; in this case neither of us can bring ourselves to cross that line. I can smell him, feel the warmth of his skin. But we don't even kiss. I stay up all night wondering what the Boy's up to and thinking what an idiot I am.

lundi, le 27 juin

I find out why my boyfriend is incommunicado. It's all in the online photo album, isn't it? I so despise indiscretion.

He is at home seeing his family, all right. Seeing his family – and taking along his ex-girlfriend Jo, who has been nursing a crush on him ever since they split. It's a blow. I'm hardly blameless, what with going off and falling for someone else, but still . . .

mardi, le 28 juin

'So you read her email and saw the photos,' L said. 'What's this one like?'

'I shudder to recollect. Plain and dumpy.' And weirdly convinced, as so many large girls are, that head-to-toe black is a slimming look – not when you're standing against a pale background, it's not. And you're almost always standing against a pale background.

'You reckon he's shtupping her?'

'No,' I say. 'It's the lie more than anything. If she's just a friend, sure he can spend time with just a friend. I spend loads of time with other men. I don't know why he feels he has to hide it, I don't hide my male friends from him.'

L came out of the dressing room, wearing a pink bikini. 'I know, I know, doesn't go with the hair. But if I was a blonde, right? I'm so buying this.'

'Truly stunning piece of logic. You should have had all currency instruments confiscated on entering the country.' Keeping up with L is costing me, too – nothing wildly extravagant, mind, just the endless rounds of drinks, shopping, and so on. But I can't claim I don't enjoy it.

L retreated behind the faux-bamboo door to change into

street clothes. 'Has it occurred to you that he's worried about your male friends? That he finds them threatening?'

'But that's the point – I make them obvious, so he knows they're not a threat.'

L peered over the door, sunglasses holding back her hair. 'You know what I think? You should forget about the lad here and the one at home and marry that one you're always talking about.'

'Which one is that?'

'You know, the one with the flat.' Oh. A4. 'You guys are so still in love and you know it.'

'What? It's been six years,' I said. 'Anyway, if he wants to be together, it's up to him. He's the one who dumped me.'

L came out of the changing room, unsuitable bikini in hand, and thrust a credit card at the woman behind the counter. 'What does that mean?'

'You know, he split with me. So it's up to him to declare his intentions. I'm not going to go begging.'

'What the hell kind of a rule is that?'

'Standard operating procedure, surely?'

L gave me a look. 'Never heard such nonsense in my life,' she said.

mercredi, le 29 juin

Man to Woman: your handy cut-out-and-keep translation:

I've never cheated on a girlfriend. I've never had sex with two women in the same day, at least not without showering first. Probably.

My phone doesn't get very good reception here. I'm going to turn off my phone when I'm at her house, in case you ring.

I think of you all the time. I think of you when I'm sending you a text.

Where have you been all night? Don't you dare do any of the things I do!

You're the only woman I've ever really loved. I tell this to all the girls.

I'm not a liar. I am a liar.

I have a vague feeling I wasn't always so ambivalent about men, but it's difficult to remember.

jeudi, le 30 juin

Visited David and went for a walk. Fritz came. Fritz is a boy dog and has a rakish one-ear-up, one-ear-down look. Fritz gets all the ladies.

But in spite of Fritz's dog's-dog, low-maintenance appearance, this pup has needs that mark him out as a little more metrosexual than you might expect. Such as scratching requirements. This is a dog that will push its bum into your face and demand to be scratched there, often, because it's the one place he can't reach.

So we're meandering around a lake, it's a balmy afternoon, the sort you think summer was expressly made for. Ducks and a few honking geese, other people and other dogs, children playing in the fields. Fritz is let off the leash for a few minutes, runs as far from us as he can, then begins a little dance: three circles clockwise, three anti-clockwise, have a poo and kick the grass over it. It's a level of fussiness about his toilet that is, frankly, unbecoming in a male.

We hook the lead back on and round the pond. A child comes up to us, a boy, maybe twelve. His hair is long and he's wearing a T-shirt that reads '*Ha Ha Ha*'. 'Can I pet the dog?' he asks.

'Sure.'

And the kid, he goes straight for the spot. The bum spot. Fritz is digging it in the extreme. 'You love that, don't you?' he asks the dog. 'My dog loves that, too.'

As we go on our way, the kid yells after us, 'Don't do it too much, though, or he'll start to *demaaaand* it!' Which, of course, Fritz already does. 'He'll start coming up to you and sticking his bum in your face!' And the kid sticks out his own bottom, and wags it.

Dear Belle

Dear Belle,

I am a little torn. I have a new boyfriend who seemed great but has now started saying 'Please' when asking for a shag and putting on a little-boy look. This is not the first time I have had one of these types. Have you any training tips?

Dear Mary Poppins,

Personally I like a man with a lot of fight in him, and changing someone's nappies is not my idea of a good time. (Fans who kink that way: rest assured, there are still plenty of working girls who will be happy to do this for you. I simply am not one of them.) Provided such behaviour is not a deal-breaking turn-off for you, I don't see the harm in indulging him. Just so you remember to impose limits if (and when) he reaches your bearability threshold.

Breaking a manchild of such habits is probably a fruitless exercise, so you must ask yourself whether it is a path you'd at least consider going down. If all else fails, promise him he can have whatever he likes so long as he finishes his peas.

Dear Belle,

I have a new boyfriend and everything appears to be going well, but I have just discovered that his ex-girlfriend is the spitting image of me. Should I assume this is just one of those things and persevere with our promising relationship, or will it all end with me jumping off a church roof cf *Vertigo*?

Dear Twin Town,

By 'spitting image', do you mean you look like a distorted rubber mask of her? Or do you mean that she and you share a few general characteristics? Just as women have ideals and preferences in their romantic partners, so do men, and unfortunately their ticksheet for the perfect woman is sometimes – by which I mean always – a touch more superficial than ours. Men can be picky about such things as height, weight, and hair colour (hmm, starting to sound like your average client here). So you have blonde highlights, just like her, possibly dress similarly, and are within a order of magnitude of her weight. Unless he demands that you get her tattoos in the same places and takes you to her parents' for Christmas dinner, I wouldn't worry.

Dear Belle,
   Last week when I was sleeping with my girlfriend she fell asleep while I was on the job. Now she's says it's nothing, she was just very, very tired. I don't believe her. How can I make sure she stays awake?

Dear Night Shift,
   Start fucking her earlier, or be faster about it.

Juillet

vendredi, le 1 juillet

I'm abnormal, I know it. I don't love *Dirty Dancing*.

It was buried deep at the bottom of J's video collection. What the hell? I thought. Maybe the passing of fifteen-odd years has lent this film some magic that I, as a world-weary preadolescent, missed.

The girls at school were besotted with Johnny and driven to raptures by his dance numbers with Baby. I am probably horrified by the condition of being human on a daily basis, but this stood out as one of the highlights of the wretchedness that was school. When it comes to sentimental education I'll have de Sade over Swayze any day.

Did teenagers really bring themselves to first orgasm thinking about Johnny's manly mullet? I can't remember what I first masturbated to – correction, yes I can remember, and it was a cartoon, and I'll thank you never to mention it again – but it certainly wasn't pap like *Dirty Dancing*. Unfortunately I was of the generation old enough to know who Duran Duran were, but too young to get backstage and jump on them. All the young gods of the eighties had long gone by the time I felt a stirring in my knickers. It was a long, long time until Take That wooed the girls of this nation with their homoerotic routines and tanning-bed charm. We were hard up for first-time fantasy material. I can sympathise.

But perhaps I'd been wrong and judged the film too harshly. Adulthood has a way of showing your childhood attitudes and fears to be unfounded. So I settled in with a brew and the phone on silent.

Enm . . . is this film for real? Did anyone really think those capris looked good? Is this why men of a certain age still unbutton their shirts to the waist?

No. No. And again, no. That's two hours of my life I'll never have back.

samedi, le 2 juillet

If there is anyone who pays most dearly as a result of globalised media, it is women. Once upon a time we could count on men to be men: either slimy and disposable or lumpish and loyal. Now, with the shelves of every bookshop in the land heaving under the weight of female empowerment tomes, there arises a new – and far more dangerous – type in the male species.

This abomination is the man who tells you exactly what you want to hear, and possibly even means it. Having attuned my ear over a decade-plus of dating to the sweet nothings of lying charmers, I find my gut response to such talk is immediate distrust. Anyone who says he wants to spend the rest of his life with me must, by definition, be a cheater who is about to break my heart. And the only man a girl can really rely on is her daddy.

It's an alarming trend which does nothing whatsoever to preserve either masculine or feminine mystique. If I had wanted an equitable relationship, I would have arranged to be born a penguin.

dimanche, le 3 juillet

Somewhere in the nether regions of my brain lie the remnants of school biology lessons. The difference between water-soluble and fat-soluble vitamins, how you need to replace one every day but the other is held in your body's fat stores until needed.

Is there such a thing as fat-soluble sunshine? Because if I'm to go home soon, I need to start gathering it up in preparation.

mardi, le 5 juillet

It's that time of year again, isn't it? Somewhere between early spring (the wedding season) and late summer (the everyone copping off on holiday season). The exes-writing-letters season.

My previous amours are divided into two camps, those who stay friends, and those who disappear. Every year around this time a few of the disappeared make themselves known again with the casual 'Oh, I just thought I'd drop you a note' email. It's not my policy to respond, though it is interesting to see who sends them.

So far I have heard from the Asian fellow who was raised on a farm, the odd quiet guy with the cool tattoo, and the long drink of water one of my university housemates wrote short stories about.

The surprise this year? All the exes are writing to let me know they're married. Do they expect gifts or something?

On a hunch I go and check the Boy's email. Yep, the fever has struck him, too: two sent letters.

To Susie he writes a bunch of sappy crap:

Hello, a bit out of the blue I suppose. If ever you are sitting round yours on a sunny day or warm evening with nothing to do, please call me, lass. I would love to take you out to a country pub on the moors and treat you just once. Or even just to the cinema?! I do know that you have completely moved on, but I would really like to very much. We spent most of our time together hundreds of miles apart, and now ironically we are not together but only 500 metres apart! It's all very frustrating but beautifully ironic. Sigh. Take care, lass, and thank you for all the happy memories.

Actually, it was thousands of miles apart, not hundreds, but then he's never been especially good at maths. And to the stick insect Lena, who I caught him in bed with the first time we were dating, some really quite unbelievable statements:

I know I really ruined my chances with you and I want you to know that your man is very lucky. You are by far one of the sexiest, cleverest and all-round stunning girls I have ever met, lass. If you ever change your mind, I live in hope.

Now, maybe I live on a deluded island of self-belief here, but I own a mirror. I've seen this girl. I've met her. I know that I'm prettier, smarter and certainly a better all-rounder than she is. If that's what he finds valuable, if that's what he thinks stunning, why do I bother?

mercredi, le 6 juillet

So far no replies to the Boy's two desperation letters. Good. I pray they don't write back, but I don't hold out hope.

When I was young and my mother was in one of her moods (of which there were three: premenstrual tension, post-menstrual tension, and present menstrual tension), she said to me that women often hope that an old flame may be revived – but men know there is nothing so dead as dead love.

I beg to differ. Men, in my experience, are the worst of the worst for drunk dialling. Many even go the step further to the probably sober, entirely premeditated desperate email-out-of-the-blue. I'm very sorry, but what part of not having seen me naked in the last decade did you not understand? One-off hook-ups are one thing – everyone has a moment of weakness – but the concept of bleating your desperation out into the ether, year on year, in hope of a pity fuck, is horrific. For one thing, if there is no friendship to speak of, how can you possibly expect benefits?

And yet it seems – if the women's magazines are to be believed – other women are willing to open their beds to these rakes long past what I would consider an appropriate expiry date. Something, I believe, about a repeat affair meaning not having to increase the total of men one has slept with. Puh-leese. As if a lady would reveal the real number, anyway.

Through the miracle of the internet men have come to expect that behind every park bench is a lady awaiting a shag. That every phone call is a gate to a date. That one has only to put together the most rudimentary, smiley-studded text before the mount of Venus is attained.

So you let him into your house and your bed. And then the next morning you go all Bridget Jones on him and start obsessing about whether the wedding should be in May or June. What are we left with? The realisation that the wags are correct: there really aren't many women in this world who can take sex as lightly as a man can. Perhaps my mother was right after all.

Fellow girls: please stop giving it away. You can not handle the consequences, and more to the point, you're putting the working girls out of business. Exercise your feminist right to say no.

jeudi, le 7 juillet

Tomás came over first thing and woke me up. That was how I found out about the attacks in London. We woke J and his girlfriend, put the television on the news and sat for hours, stunned. The news here is less protective, shows more blood, more screaming; throws more suspicion and rumours around than the news at home would dare do. Tomás made strong coffee and hot milk. I thought about ringing home but knew there was no chance of the lines being free.

After several hours, names of the victims started to come through. The first name I saw made my heart stop. It was my mother's.

It wasn't her, it couldn't be, I knew that. J squeezed my shoulder – we didn't say it out loud so the others wouldn't worry, but I knew we were thinking the same thing. Mum isn't dead. She is at home hundreds of miles away, watching the news, just as I am; or she is out with her new boyfriend, or trying to ring relatives elsewhere in the country; maybe talking to my father, I don't know. I knew she was nowhere near London today but seeing her name shook me, just the same.

I have never felt so far from home in my entire life.

vendredi, le 8 juillet

It wasn't Mum; she's fine. But I'm still shaken. I want to hide; I don't want to fly home, I don't want to be standing at the airport, on the Tube platform, eyeing everyone else and wondering, just as they all will be, Who's armed here? Who might be carrying a bomb? If it was a month earlier, maybe I wouldn't go back. But my ticket is booked. I've rung the airline just to be certain, surely everyone is trying to fly home today. My seat is booked, my reservation will be honoured. There's little I can do.

The night before I am due to leave, David comes along to say goodbye. In thirty-six hours' time I will be in the arms of my boyfriend and he will be in the arms of his girlfriend. Meanwhile, everything back in London seems complete chaos. It's difficult to make any conversation that doesn't revolve around those subjects. So we talk about sex. The things we like, don't like, and would do if there wasn't this damned business about being committed to other people. I'm almost painfully turned on.

'You're very cute, you know that?'

Take me, please, here, now. On the suitcases. 'Thank you. So are you.'

'Your eyes are gorgeous.'

Yes, and they'd like to see a bit more of you. 'Thank you. So are yours.'

'And your eyelashes.'

Have I ever wanted to touch someone this badly in my life? 'Yours, too.' Apparently there's a phenomenon known colloquially as terror sex, where people after a traumatic event on the scale of what just happened in London have extraordinary sex. Something about the urge to seek an attachment. I know it exists. Two weeks after the World Trade Center was attacked I met A2 in the US and had what I still remember as my biggest orgasm ever.

'Out of curiosity, do you have any condoms?'

If I could orgasm without being touched – an unlikely occurrence, but let us say for the sake of argument it was a possible outcome – it would have happened just then. 'Yes,' I say. 'I should take them back and demand a refund. I don't know what sort of spell the chemist put on these, but I haven't had sex since buying them.'

'That is a waste.' I don't ask if he means a waste of me or of the prophylactics.

But we can't do it. We don't. Neither of us is brave enough to move from the realm of the desired to the realm of the definite, where we may be disappointed, or never see each other again, or never want to be parted. I see him in his underwear, he sees me out of my bra ('How did such a small girl get such boobies?' he says, and we both laugh), and painful though it is, we stop. We are good. Our reward will be in heaven, except I don't believe in heaven. There is no reward.

samedi, le 9 juillet

'Don't you fucking cry,' J says, crushing me to his shoulder. Over my head I hear him sniffling. He holds me at arm's length, looks at my face. 'You're gonna be okay, right?'

'Yes,' I say. Tomás hands me an envelope. He's made a card, drawn a picture of our houses next to each other. Inside, in Spanish, a wish for safe travel and luck; a photocopy of something by Mother Teresa he's always had taped to the top of his bathroom mirror. That's when I really start bawling.

'I'll call, I promise.' J puts a finger to my lips. 'Shut up,' he says. 'You live your life, we'll live ours, everything will be fine. I'll see you,' he says, as if I'm going round the corner, not thousands of miles away.

L picks me up in an unfeasibly large people carrier. 'This ride, darling, is ever so pimped,' she says and laughs. The room is packed up, two suitcases, two boxes. A lamp and a throw that I give to her. There's enough time to hit a café for breakfast and I tell her all about David. She shrugs. 'Hard breaks, kid,' she says. 'Rejection kills, but disappointment only maims. You'll get through.'

'What if I'm making a mistake, though, going back?' I don't have to get on that plane. I don't have to leave here, now or ever. We could live in a little beach shack, raise children, grow old brown and happy together, and never have to wear winter coats again.

She looks at me with her patented special-kid look, as if I'm a particularly dense twelve-year-old in need of a smack round the head. 'What if we're all making mistakes? What if staying would be a mistake? You think anyone else gets a preview of the rest of their lives? You make a choice and you fucking go with it because otherwise nothing would get done.' She finishes her coffee. 'Just let me know how it all works out, sweetie.'

'Okay.'

'And whatever you do, don't for fuck's sake ring him from the airport. Either of them.'

'Okay.' I'm lying; we both know it.

At the terminal she flags down a man to help with the luggage. He doesn't seem interested. In fact, no one does. We drag the boxes along the ground, panting theatrically the whole way. She waits in the queue with me and gives me a hug when the check-in is complete. 'Look after yourself, honey.'

'You too,' I say. But I know she'll have less trouble than I will.

dimanche, le 10 juillet

The Boy is standing just the other side of the arrivals barrier, between crowds of families and drivers holding signs with names on. He looks different from the person I remember – tired, maybe, a bit dumpy and unshaven.

Then again, it is six in the morning and I hardly look catwalk-ready. There's an odd, faraway look in his eyes, as if I don't quite match his memory, either.

He drives us to Wiltshire, where he's booked a room at an adorable B&B for the night. We fall straight into bed, with the alarm set for four hours' time; when it rings we rise, shower, have a quick fuck, then dress for the wedding. I'm wearing a peacock silk halter dress, the loaner from L, with gold sandals; he looks nice in his dinner jacket, if still a touch tired.

I touch his chin. 'Now now, let's have a good time.'

And the wedding is, in its way. There is much drinking of Pimm's and walking around gardens and making conversation with aged aunties. After the meal, we dance to 'God Only Knows' and I realise it's the first time we've ever danced slow together. There's a dark-haired man who's been making eyes at me the entire time, but I ignore him. Only . . . ?

Do I recognise him?

From *work?*

Ah, shite. Everyone always talked about what to do if something like this happened – I think Angel always secretly hoped it would – but I never honestly thought I'd run into an ex-client outside the confines of a hotel room.

The bride has thoughtfully booked a club in town for the younger guests after the formal affair breaks up. We go along in a taxi, and I am sitting across from the man who's been watching me all night, trying to remember who the hell he is. Was it one of my last appointments, the one who gave me his business card, the nice one who reminded me of the ex who haunts me? Ah yes, that's it. Now what was his name again, and do I let on? If so, how?

At the club the Boy is in his element – he's been drinking all day and needs little excuse to dance like a loon. He picks the bride up by her hips, parading her around the room on his shoulders; then he attacks the groom and does the same to him. Everyone laughs at his antics, and for once I don't mind. They all know he's here with me and I'm sort of proud.

The Boy lurches off to the toilet and his place is quickly taken by a tall Asian man who is far more sober than I am and also a clearly superior dancer. 'You should go find someone worthy of your moves,' I joke.

'Oh, but I have,' he says, and swoops down to make a move.

A hand comes out of nowhere and bats him away – it's the other man, the one who's been looking at me. With an arm protectively round my waist, he guides me away and we start to dance. 'I'd be careful if I were you,' he says. 'You're being watched by more than a few people here.'

'Not in a bad way, I hope.'

'Not at all.'

I'm drunk enough to cut to the chase. 'Your name wouldn't happen to be Malcolm, would it?' I say, and smile in a friendly way.

'Jonty.'

Ah, I was wrong about spotting an ex-client, then. It happens. 'Oh, okay. I just thought maybe we recognised each other. My mistake, then.'

'Would it be a good thing if I was this . . . Malcolm?'

'Probably a bit of yes and a bit of no. Slightly more yes than no, if I was here on my own.'

'Then that really is a pity.'

The Boy had come back from the toilet and was watching us dance, arms folded in that particular way I despise. Jonty handed me over, but not before leaning close to my ear and saying, 'I would recognise you anywhere.'

And that was that, until we left. The Boy ran off to lift various members of the wedding party off the ground, leaving me to flag down a taxi to take us back to the B&B. Jonty came up behind me and, hands on my hips, turned me round and planted a not-so-innocent kiss on me. Not over the line, but just under it. 'So what are you doing with him?' he asked, indicating my man. 'He's such a Boy Scout.'

Maybe so, relatively speaking. 'I like Boy Scouts,' I said. Saves me from myself sometimes.

mardi, le 12 juillet

Things you should never do on your first day of work.

1 Wear fishnets. Particularly if you're the only woman in the office. But my only other pair of stockings, which I'd worn to the wedding, had a ladder and there was no time for a side trip on the way to the office.
2 Spend the entire day on the phone, giving your boyfriend directions to the new house so he can start moving in.
3 Squeal and kiss your boss on seeing him. 'Ohmigod! Giles! It's been too long!' Wait five minutes, at least. Especially if he has potential clients with him, meeting 'the core team'.
4 When the person overseeing your introduction to the new computing system asks if you have any questions, do not make it 'Where's the nearest place to buy chocolate?'
5 Have argument on phone in front of entire office with said boyfriend, who is clearly feeble of mind if he does not understand left, then left, then through two mini-roundabouts, then right and it's on the right.
6 Have a hangover, though to be honest I'm not certain, given all of the above, that anyone particularly noticed. Apart from Giles, who just left a bottle of water and two Nurofen on the corner of my desk.

mercredi, le 13 juillet

I couldn't help it, I had to look. Even though I'd promised myself I wouldn't. *Be careful*, a voice in the back of my head warned. *That way madness lies. What's done is done, let the past stay where it belongs.*

But in the end I was unable to resist. The internet is too seductive. It's too easy to keep tabs on other people.

The site was just like I remembered. I clicked through the

pages until I found what I was looking for. I narrowed my eyes. *Fucking typical*, I thought. *I should have known. After all these months nothing's changed.*

My profile was still up on the agency website.

I looked closer . . . Those weren't my photos! I read the description again, the summary I had sweated over my first week with the agency, working and reworking the words, hoping not to sound too amateurish, too desperate. *Friendly and petite Northerner, enjoys long conversations and longer nights in* . . . That was definitely the profile I'd written. And that was certainly my working name – and as far as I knew, there wasn't another escort in the city with the same name (I'd called myself after Mum's favourite childhood cat). But those photos were definitely not me.

Someone else was playing me now, had taken on my persona. I had to smile and shake my head. What else had I expected? Maybe one or two old clients got confused, ordered up someone they thought was me . . . but the business has a short memory. I'm sure they've all but forgotten me now.

Later, I was clearing space in the back room – it's terribly damp, and the Boy is frightened that all the work in his portfolios might go mouldy – when I knocked over a box of his things.

By 'knocked over', of course, I mean 'went snooping through' and by 'his things', obviously, I mean 'old letters and cards'.

Right on the top was a card; I didn't recognise the handwriting. I opened it. It was from the wife of a friend of his: thanking him and Susie for attending their wedding.

It hit me like a body blow. I remembered that night; I was still living in London then. How he'd rung me, drunk, and asked why all of his friends were marrying, and why weren't we? So he'd been there with Susie all along.

'It doesn't matter now,' I said aloud to the empty room, carefully replacing the box.

But I don't know who I was trying to convince.

jeudi, le 14 juillet

'It was as if everyone thought I'd really died. The phone wouldn't stop ringing,' Mum said. 'People I hadn't heard from in years. It was like seeing my own funeral.'

The sound of her voice comforted me. 'I knew it wasn't you – it's not that uncommon a name – but you never know.' I didn't go on and on, it seemed selfish, but it shook me. Not just the bombings – seeing footage from the investigations of the bombers themselves, the images of narrow terraced houses up North, the sort I knew so well.

'Honey, when was the last time I was in London?' she laughed. 'At any rate, it gave me a good opportunity to tell everyone the news.'

'What news is that?'

She lowered her voice conspiratorially. 'He *proposed*.'

'Oh, Mum, he didn't! Have you told Daddy?'

'I'm not going to go through with it; don't worry. I've been there before, it's not fair to have a second go. Especially when you girls are still on the shelf! But you should see the ring – it's *gorgeous*.'

I sighed. The more things stay the same, the more they change.

vendredi, le 15 juillet

The Boy came home in a rubbish mood and I can't say I was feeling up for fun and games, either. I hadn't had any lunch and was halfway through an apple when he arrived. He suggested we take a walk and I reluctantly agreed. That was when he started talking about trust, and long-term plans, and wondering what he was going to do with the rest of his life.

I sort of lost it. 'Excuse me for wondering why you weren't trying harder to figure this out when you were screwing Georgie over the summer,' I grumbled.

'Why do I suspect whenever we talk, you're going to bring up things like that?' he said acidly.

'Oh, you and your double standard can fuck right off,' I shouted. 'Every time you look at me I can almost hear you thinking, Why am I with a whore? Why didn't I end up with Susie or Jo or whoever?' He crossed his arms, something that always sets me off – it's usually the first sign that he's about to start telling me what a terrible person I am, how he tolerates me, and so on. And I wasn't in the mood. So I stopped yelling and started crying.

I felt a right twat for crying. He walked away quickly, and when his back was turned I looked down at my hand. The apple.

Well, fuck that, I thought. Fuck that every time I lose my temper it means he doesn't have to apologise.

Fuck the lies. The playing at being an adult. No one who wears short pants into his thirties should be telling me how to run my life.

Fuck the shifting ground, constantly trying to live up to a changing standard of what he wants from me and when. What was it L said? That I was the best he would do? She was right. It was time for me to stop crying and start being the one in charge.

I chucked the apple at a wall. It exploded with a satisfying smack.

The Boy arrived home early, but I had come home earlier and was already cooking. He went straight in to watch telly and we didn't exchange a word. I served up the meal and we ate in silence.

'House rules,' I said as we finished eating. 'I'm doing all the cooking, so you're doing all the washing up.'

'Okay.'

'No more leaving the house to make your phone calls.'

'Yes.'

'I don't care how many days your job keeps you away, you're paying half the rent and bills. And I'm not having your name on the lease.'

'Okay.'

'And you're to ring me from work every day. And if I get even the faintest whiff of funny business, you know you're out on your arse, right?'

'I know.'

I waited while he cleared the table. It was easier than I had thought. Was there something else I should demand? I wondered. Was he still playing away, hoping to get off with someone else on the side? Would I come home one day to catch him having sex with someone else again – but this time in my bed?

He came past my chair and kissed the top of my head. 'I hate when you go all quiet,' he said softly. 'It's worse than you yelling.'

There are no guarantees. Faith is based on belief, not evidence. And only faith keeps people together. I didn't have to make a decision now.

Later, curled up in bed, his face in my hair, me pretending to be asleep, he whispered, 'I hope someday you'll know I never lied,' but that could pass without comment, I decided.

dimanche, le 17 juillet

'Daddy, I have to go, someone's at the door,' I said. 'Yes, yes, love you, too, byeeee.' I opened the door to a woman about my own age. 'Hello. I don't think we've met yet. I'm Christine, your downstairs neighbour,' she said.

I smiled and shook her hand. 'I think we have met, actually, but only for a moment. My best friend used to live here.'

'Ah!' she said. 'I thought you looked familiar.'

'You too.'

'I hate to come over and start complaining, but . . .' She looked down at my shoes. 'This is a little embarrassing. In fact, I'm glad it's you who answered the door.'

'Really? Why?'

'I hate to ask, but, um, could you ask your boyfriend to be a little more quiet when . . . you know . . .'

'He's quite a big fellow, he does make a lot of noise walking around,' I agreed. 'I'll ask him to take off his shoes in the house.'

'Oh, no, it's not that,' Christine said. 'It's, you know . . .'

'No, I'm sorry?'

'Late at night. Could you ask him to be . . . a little more quiet . . . I mean, our bedroom is just below yours and when you two are, you know . . .'

'Say no more,' I laughed. 'He is a bit of a screamer, isn't he?'

lundi, le 18 juillet

I do love a beer. Source of amusement and – if the books are to be believed – one of the six beverages to change the world. Proof, as they say, that God loves us and wants us to be happy.

But if you can't judge a book by its cover, by what can you? Its beer, naturally. I'm not talking about books here. I'm talking about men.

There are exceptions to every rule, but the shakedown is as follows in the pub setting.

Staropramen drinker: likely to spend most of the evening texting some other girl.

Stella drinker: likely to spend most of the evening pretending to text some other girl.

Budweiser drinker: likely to spend most of the evening showing you porn on his camera phone in a bid to impress you. Has never had a text from a girl.

Real Ale drinker, bearded: someone's divorced Uncle Tim.

Real Ale drinker, semibearded (facial topiary): secretly despises the taste, feels he 'ought' to drink it.

Real Ale drinker, unbearded: socially inept computing student.

Guinness drinker, Irish: will break your heart.

Guinness drinker, non-Irish: nursing broken heart.

Guinness drinker, American: lost in Hertfordshire.

London Pride drinker: not from London.

Trappist brew drinker, under 50: fussy type with an excess of both spare time and self-regard.

Trappist brew drinker, over 50: monk.

Cider drinker, teenager: made an impulse decision when he couldn't spot the alcopops.

Cider drinker, adult: from Norfolk.

Friends, I have an admission to make. I am seeing a cider drinker who is neither underage nor East Anglian. We are, I believe, in uncharted territory.

I went round to the estate agent's with the banker's draft for the deposit so I could officially take over A4's lease. The Boy picked me up afterwards, it was near his work. 'Ugh, that was the biggest amount of money I hope to part with for a while,' I said. 'But at least it's all over with.'

'Poor you,' he said, rubbing my hair in the exact way I hate. 'You're short of pennies?'

I patted his hand and removed it to my thigh. 'Not short, as such. Just have to watch my outgoings for the rest of the year. The holiday was a little more expensive than I'd planned.'

'Really? How much was it?'

Ooh, I should have seen that one coming. Probably going to go straight to his diary and call me an extravagant cow or something. 'About eight thousand,' I said, knocking a few grand off the total. I'd had plenty to spare, but there are always a few things you don't anticipate. Such as keeping him on the phone hours at a time for the sake of trying to keep him away from Susie and Georgie.

He frowned and we drove on in silence. Of course, to one of his posh totties, eight thousand would be lipstick money. But us underclass, we're not allowed to spend. Hm, didn't someone write a song like that once?

'What's wrong now?' I said.

'I'm just being silly,' he said. 'But that's half the cost of a wedding. You could have spent that money marrying me, and we could be living together in your new little house.'

I almost laughed. Was he kidding? He hopped into someone else's bed literally an hour after I left Britain and spent the summer getting blowjobs from junior doctors. Was he really still entertaining the notion that a) I believed anything he said and b) I would marry someone who acted like that?

'Well, I don't mean to be blunt, but if you'd wanted to marry me you would have asked.'

'But I do want to marry you, I tell you that all the time.'

'Funnily enough, you only ever say it when we're arguing. Now let's drop the subject.' To my credit, I said all this at a normal volume. To his credit he did not mention it again.

mercredi, le 20 juillet

'Looking good,' Giles said as I came into the building.

'Careful, you, or people will start to think we're up to something.'

'A man can live in hope,' he said. 'Listen, we need you to meet the Japanese clients this afternoon – is it enough warning? I'm afraid you're the only person we have capable of explaining the conversion algorithms adequately.'

Some days I don't wonder what would have happened if I'd stayed a call girl.

jeudi, le 21 juillet

He licked my tan lines, hardly faded since returning. 'What right do you have,' he murmured, 'to be firmer and sexier than any teenager?'

I wrapped a towel round myself and led him down the back steps into the garden. 'Against the far wall,' I whispered. 'The neighbours are out.'

He spread the towel gently on the ground instead. 'Quickly,' I hissed. 'Before the insects find you.' But he didn't listen, slowly running his tongue until everywhere that had been covered by a bikini last month was soaking wet.

vendredi, le 22 juillet

Met N for a meal at our favourite Italian, just the two of us. I'm aware that a certain amount of friendship maintenance needs to be undertaken, even if it is a case (I suspect) of too little, too late.

N's looking good: leaner and more tanned than when we last saw each other. He tells me about his recent women: a German postgraduate who loves pain, the lady we had the threesome with. And he's made friends with the man running his local sex shop, who is now passing on to N all the videos he can't hire out legally.

'You really do have the most amazing luck,' I say. It's ages since I've seen any quality porn, and N promises to pass some on, particularly one involving a heavy rope bondage session and a spiked glove. He swears up and down the woman looks like an older version of me.

I've been a bad friend and I know it: ignoring him for months, taking him for granted. I know in my heart of hearts that regardless of how the Boy feels about him, he'll always be my friend, and no man should ever change that.

'No worries,' N said in his light way. 'I'm here for you, no matter what. You know that.'

I do, but I wonder why my friends are still my friends sometimes, when I've been so callous to them.

samedi, le 23 juillet

One of the things we've always enjoyed doing together is exercise, so yesterday, in lieu of a Friday night DVD or going out for a meal, I suggest we go for a run in Richmond Park.

The Boy and I are about equal in speed: he's bigger, I'm more efficient. Soon we fall into step with each other, the way we did years ago. But my mind is in other places. On his ex, dumpy Jo, the girl he took home the week before I came back. I can see her pursed pout on the yacht, the broad smiles of her in the family garden. I know she would give up her boyfriend to be with him. In fact, I'm having a knock-down, drag-out argument with her right now, conducted in my head: 'Get near him again, bitch, and I'll break his heart so hard and so fast that he can rub his sad little erection against your giant arse all you want but he'll never feel like a man again.'

Holy moly, did I really just think that? The vitriol of it surprises even me, and I stop running. The Boy notices I've dropped off and turns back. 'You okay?' he pants.

I nod, bend over and pretend it was an old knee injury playing up. I straighten and look into his eyes. On every identity document he has, they're down as brown, but I know the truth. His eyes are dark green with flecks of blue. They're beautiful. He's the loveliest man I've ever been with.

'I just wanted to say, I'm really sorry for everything that happened last year.'

He's surprised. 'What brought that on?'

'Nothing in particular. Come on, I'll race you this lap!'

dimanche, le 24 juillet

My life as a call girl revolved round the phone. If I didn't answer a call straight away, the work might have gone to someone else, which meant that for almost a year I was umbilically attached to the mobile. In the toilets, at dinner, half asleep, visiting family: apart from when I was on a call, there were few times I wouldn't answer.

Now all that has changed. Especially after having been away so long without a mobile, or even reliable landlines. I can go days without checking voice mail, and it's an incredible luxury. The phone goes dead and it's not a life-or-death problem. It's sitting on my desk more often than about my person, and sometimes I'll even be near it and can't be bothered to answer.

Fate has a funny way of making you see yourself as others see you, because there's hardly a minute when my boyfriend isn't on his phone. Worse still, he has one of these sexy little camera/email/does-everything-but-your-washing-up models. We've been sailing in a gale and he's on the phone. He's forever texting at the dinner table. Now I see how unbearably annoying it must have been for my friends.

I'm obsessed with schemes for getting rid of the thing. It wouldn't do to chuck it away, since I suspect it has a greater place in his heart than I have (this particular one having been a gift to him from the fat ex, Jo). When it's raining, I keep hoping it will turn up waterlogged. If he's washing up and takes a call, I fantasise about giving him a bump from behind and plop! it drops straight into the sink.

Of course, it may be the romantic associations of his phone that make me despise it so. That, and the fact that he'd rather be doing household chores and talking to other people than spending time with me.

But what better way to guarantee I will never have to do the laundry again than by not-so-accidentally leaving his phone in a trouser pocket? The idea has possibilities. I'll have to think on it.

lundi, le 25 juillet

<luvly_jubly>How are you getting on in the new place?
<belle_online>beautifully, thank you. It's so familiar to me from your living here that it's hardly felt strange at all.
<luvly_jubly>Pleased to hear it.
<belle_online>how are things oop north?
<luvly_jubly>Bit of up, bit of down. Found a really good cheese shop not far from where I'm staying.

<belle_online>ace

<luvly_jubly>neighbours haven't been a problem have they?

<belle_online>downstairs? no, hardly see them, why?

<luvly_jubly>the noise hasn't disturbed you?

<belle_online>what noise?

<luvly_jubly>She's a bit of a screamer . . . they used to be at it all the time

<belle_online>hm

<belle_online>can't say I've noticed

mardi, le 26 juillet

Maybe it's a reaction to not being slathered daily in sunscreen, but my skin is going horribly dry. Luckily I have laid in a pantry-full of supplies from abroad. In particular one product from the US, which comes in a dispenser not unlike a stick deodorant, and smells of lemons. It's gratifyingly smoothing and as close to a miracle in a jar as I can find. Probably made with the blood of young virgins or something.

After a shower I was rubbing it on. The Boy came through and looked a bit puzzled until he realised I was not, in fact, applying Mum to the backs of my hands. I asked if he would mind rubbing it in.

Once upon a time in our relationship, he took every request for a massage of any sort as an invitation to sex. A sort of tit-for-tat thing: I'll rub your back if I get to slip into you from behind right afterwards. And while I appreciate that all sexual relationships have an element of give and take, that was a little too commodified for me. A little too much like being a call girl, only with rubs instead of money.

So I explained how I felt, and now I can ask him to rub me down without expecting sex immediately after. Though I think he still tots up the number of massages and extracts payment for them in sexual favours later. I'd actually rather give oral

314

sex than have to lavish a reciprocal backrub on him – my hands are half the size of his and his back is twice as broad as mine so proportionally speaking I end up having to do four times as much work. He's not good with maths but he sort of understands. What he doesn't seem to realise, though, is that I'm winning all round: sex *and* massage. He's just having sex.

'I love this cream, it's so thick and clingy,' I said.

'Hey! That's my job,' he said, putting on an exaggerated pout.

'What, being thick and clingy?' I asked. 'Do you really want me to describe you that way?'

'Well, no, but you probably would.'

'It smells very strong, doesn't it,' I said of the cream.

'Yes,' he said.

'Thick, clingy and strong-smelling.'

'Just like me?' We laughed, me because it was true, and he because he knew that's what I was thinking.

mercredi, le 27 juillet

We went to one of the Boy's work dos, as a couple, together. I played it down but was secretly thrilled. He kept looking over at me uneasily whenever we were parted – I wasn't saying something I shouldn't, was I? But he had nothing to worry about. For one thing, I was caught in conversation with one of the most boring women in the world.

M was a tall girl and heavy, dressed in flat London black with flat London hair, and was telling me she despised the concept of the one-night stand.

This, I realised, was the flip side to fifteen-year-old tramps giving blowjobs at bus shelters and twenty-somethings with their booty-call fucks. The thirty-something single city woman who has convinced herself that only true love is worth waiting for.

I don't understand. M and thousands of women like her

deciding that not only do they prefer time alone to a bad relationship – fine decision, yes – but that if there's no relationship at all, there's no sex. So the teenagers are banging mindlessly, surely unable to glean much benefit from the act apart from having something to do between CBeebies and *X Factor*, while the very women who are not only cresting their sexual peaks but also have the discretional income and storage space for a host of boytoys and their accessories choose instead to spend their time in the company of BBC Three and a vibrator.

I mean, what gives? Sex does not equal relationship. If the man is sexy, but not the one, no one said you have to give him your keys (or, come to think of it, your number). I was stunned that a woman would so happily suppress her needs. I'd love to dine at a Michelin three-star establishment every night, sure, but in the meantime I still have to eat. And if the restaurant isn't so hot, honey, I don't go back. Simple as.

And London is a lonely place. Sometimes human contact for its own sake is nice. One day during my first six months in London, I decided to not talk to anyone for twenty-four hours, to see if it could be done. It could. And it was depressingly easy, as well.

I gritted my teeth. The Boy smiled at me uneasily from across the room, I gave him the raised eyebrow of Everything's Fine. 'And if Mr Right just happened to walk through the door tonight . . . ?'

'That's different,' she said. 'Not that I'd take him home on the first night, either.' Obviously. Because you'd rather the love of your life thought you frigid than you thought yourself a slut. Because your approach to the sexual double-standard is to accept that men can have stringless fun but you must martyr yourself on every loser attractive enough to dampen your knickers.

We're our own worst enemies.

Crossword clues are an enigma of the order of football results, lonely-hearts listings and the shipping forecast: either you understand them or you don't. I don't, and it worries me.

Not because it makes me feel stupid not to know how to do them – if I were cleverer, I might feel stupid, but ignorance is indeed bliss – but because it seems that not a year passes without some new scientific study proving how such games improve one's odds of avoiding dementia in old age. As this is something that is not uncommon in my family, naturally I'm concerned.

Never does a study come out saying what constant novel-reading does for one's grey matter as the years pass. Probably obliterates all the neurons, with my luck.

Anyway, it was with some relief that sudoku was welcomed into my house, because it's something I can do that will hopefully decrease the chances of mistaking a set of keys for my family in the decades to come. Also, I've tried introducing the Boy to it, on the scientifically unproven but hopeful theorem that engaging his mind more in his spare time might keep him from being so easily impressed by girls even dimmer than myself.

Unfortunately, he's what my mother would call a 'toe-tapper', someone with so much nervous energy that you're lucky if he keeps focused on a non-physical activity for more than three nanoseconds. On the plus side, this means we can resort to sex in lieu of conversation; on the minus side, the same.

We were in the bath reading magazines this afternoon (mine from an outdated Sunday paper; his a comic), and it occurred to me that it was probably the longest we'd been sat in the same place in weeks, if you don't count the bed (and to be fair when in bed it's rarely sitting that's taking place). I thought it might be a good time to introduce him to sudoku.

'It's like this, you see. You can have the numbers one to nine on a single line . . .'

'Nnn hnn,' he mumbled, putting down his reading material.

'Then you have them in a square, and in a column.'

'Yes,' he said, absently pawing me. I could feel him getting excited.

'Would you mind taking your hand out of my crotch?'

'Okay,' he said, resting his hands on my breasts.

I put the paper aside and wriggled up onto his lap, but it was no use. By the time we'd finished, the floor – and the puzzle along with it – was soaked. So much for sudoku. Perhaps it is time someone conducted research into the mind-preserving properties of heavy petting.

vendredi, le 29 juillet

Some intimate acts are too intimate for me. Toilet habits, for one.

The Boy has no concept of doors like normal people have. He either pounds around slamming them (not out of anger; he just does) or leaves them open at the most inappropriate moments. Such as when using the toilet.

This morning I woke to the sound of his feet leaving the bed and hitting the floor (boom) then his going towards the toilet (boom boom boom boom) then throwing the seat up (thank goodness for small mercies! he remembered! boom) and, finally, sweet release. I can't bear the sound and put the pillow over my head.

Having a man in the house means thinking about the toilet more than I consider strictly good for me. Such as when cleaning: how do they manage to get urine on the bottom of the seat? And when friends are over: surely, dear God, he will remember not to leave the toilet door open?

It's not that I'm squeamish about waste products. People

have weed on me, I've defecated on a client. But that's the point – those are acts so privileged, so intimate, and if lucky so well paid you wouldn't dream of doing them on a daily basis without a standing contract with a supplier of industrial cleansers. If the Boy ever wanted to void himself on me, in the act of love, that would be fine. For some reason, having to listen to it at other times freaks me out.

You know, he has never expressed interest in watersports. For a man who seems to take such pride in his steaming emissions, I find it odd.

He lumbers back to the bed. 'Do you *have* to do that?' I hiss from under the duvet. He thinks it's funny.

After four years I can only just bear the thought of him using the toilet in my presence. If I'm in the shower. If the curtain is pulled. If the noise of the water is so loud I don't hear anything.

But if we're going to live together, I'm going to have the door fitted with a spring hinge. Man-tinkle hitting the porcelain is not an appropriate alternative to an alarm clock.

samedi, le 30 juillet

Unmarried couples living together. A modern perversion and leading cause of the sky-high divorce trend, if the right-leaning papers are to be believed. I can sympathise. There is nothing so unnatural to the human state of being as being tied to one person in domestic cohabitation indefinitely. Looking at one naked body for the rest of your life, it simply isn't right.

Which is why I had such a thrill when a package came through the door today – unmarked, brown paper wrapping.

Glorious porn. Bouncing tits, shining cocks, come by the bucketful. If I can't arrange a threesome yet, at least a girl can window-shop.

The Boy woke up in a mood. He rolled out of bed early, monopolised the toilet for half an hour. I could hear him tearing through all my bags in the cupboard – what the hell? If he came across that box of condoms, I could only imagine what he'd think. At least it had never been opened. He pounded downstairs without so much as a 'Good morning.' Goodness knows why. He left with no explanation and no clue as to where he was going, or when he'd be home.

My stomach turned over. Oh, we weren't going to start down this route again, were we? Fucking hell. I know these things take time, but I had hoped at least that most of the past was firmly where it belonged – behind us – and we could begin to be together, like a real boyfriend and girlfriend.

I toyed with my phone. The number had been programmed into it for ages, of course; it was always there as a back-up. In case everything went tits-up and I really needed some collateral.

I brought the contact list up and cycled through the numbers – there it was, under S. Susie. I dialled the number.

My heart was beating fast and hard, the blood rising up my neck. The phone on the other end rang and rang. No answer. Finally it went to answerphone. I hung up, no message. It was then I heard the front door slam.

'Thank God for that,' I heard the Boy say in the hallway. I quickly locked the screen on my phone and shoved it under a sofa cushion.

'Are you okay, dear?' I could hear the high, false note in my voice.

'I don't know whether it was something I ate,' he said, coming through to the sitting room. 'But I've had the runs something terrible all morning.'

'Oh, honey,' I sighed. 'Why didn't you say?'

'It's a little bit embarrassing. Besides, I went though the cupboard in the bathroom and couldn't find anything for it.'

'Is everything okay now?'

He shook a small paper bag from the corner chemist. 'Just in the nick of time,' he said.

I couldn't have agreed more.

dimanche, le 31 juillet (later)

The phone rang. I clocked the number: Susie. My heart started beating violently. Let it go to voicemail or answer? I answered the phone.

A sharp Southern voice, a bit of a lisp. 'Hiya, this is Susie. Did you ring?'

'Pardon?' I was taken aback for a moment; did she know who it was she'd called?

'I had a call from this number this morning. This is Susie. Were you trying to reach me?' Not a hint of the haughty, playing-at-posh woman that Georgie had been. Just some girl. I looked around – no sign of the Boy. Must be upstairs reading, thank goodness.

I hesitated. After all this time, I could finally settle a score, make her know that I was the real girlfriend, had been all along. Then I remembered all the trouble phoning Georgie had caused. And even if Susie didn't hang up on me and straight away dial the Boy, who would no doubt tell her a pack of lies, what right did I have? I knew they were over. Maybe she even had good memories of him. Maybe the thought of him still made her happy. She wouldn't tell me anything I didn't already know. A few more details, but whom would that help?

'It was a misdial. I wrote down a wrong number. Sorry about that.'

'Oh, okay,' she said. She sounded so young.

'Well, bye, then,' I said. And hung up.